DataCAD

FOR THE ARCHITECT

Computer Graphics Technology and Management Series

Series Consulting Editor: Carl Machover
Edited by: David M. Gauthier

AutoCAD: Methods and Macros

by Jeff Guenther, Ed Ocoboc,
and Anne Wayman

VersaCAD Tutorial: A Practical Approach to Computer-Aided Design

by Carol Buehrens

DataCAD for the Architect

by Carol Buehrens

AutoCAD Programming

by Dennis N. Jump

DataCAD

FOR THE ARCHITECT

Carol Buehrens

COMPUTER
GRAPHICS
TECHNOLOGY
AND
MANAGEMENT
SERIES

TAB Professional and Reference Books

Division of TAB BOOKS
Blue Ridge Summit, PA

Technical Adviser: Kevin Neubert

FIRST EDITION
FOURTH PRINTING

© 1989 by **TAB Professional and Reference Books,** an imprint of TAB BOOKS.
TAB BOOKS is a division of McGraw-Hill, Inc.
The TAB Professional and Reference Books logo, consisting of the letters ''TPR'' within a large ''T,'' is a registered trademark of TAB BOOKS.

Library of Congress Cataloging-in-Publication Data

Buehrens, Carol.
    DataCAD for the architect / by Carol Buehrens.
        p.   cm.
    Includes index.
    ISBN 0-8306-9175-8   ISBN 0-8306-9375-0 (pbk.)
    1. DataCAD (Computer program) 2. Architectural design—Data processing. 3. Architectural drawing—Data processing. I. Title.
NA2728.B84   1988
720′.28′40285—dc 19   88-24913
                                                    CIP

TAB BOOKS offers software for sale. For information and a catalog, please contact
TAB Software Department, Blue Ridge Summit, PA 172945-0850.

Questions regarding the content of this book should be addressed to:

Reader Inquiry Branch
TAB BOOKS
Blue Ridge Summit, PA 17294-0850

Contents

Acknowledgments

The author wishes to thank Mictrotecture for their support during the development of this book, and on continued support on the daily use of DataCAD. Special thanks to Alan Long and Clay Rogers who were always available for questions and returned many phone calls.

To our many users and students of DataCAD, who are architects or work in the architectural field, thank you for your comments and suggestions. The author would also like to thank the architects who took time out of their busy schedules to review this book.

Thanks to Brad Durham, who helped establish project criteria and provided valuable assistance.

Thanks to Brenda McManigle, who showed confidence in me and in the courses I develop.

Special thanks to Karl Buehrens, my husband, for the encouragement given throughout this project. And to Adam and Lora Buehrens, who gave mommy plenty of hugs and kisses to keep her going.

About the Author

Carol Buehrens is a CADD Course Designer/Training Specialist for THE CADD LEARNING CENTER, a division of CR/CADD, one of the largest CADD systems dealers in the United States. She designs courseware and professional texts for a wide variety of engineers from both the architectural and mechanical industries.

With 15 years of design and manufacturing experience, Carol has devoted 12 years to computer aided design and drafting training and design technology.

Carol began her interest in this highly specialized area as a general machinist, from which she entered into the design drafting field. In 1975, she became directly involved in CADD/CAM.

Since then, she has created CADD training programs for McDonnell Douglas Automation Company, Northrop Corporation—Advanced Systems, Bechtel Corporation, GE/Calma Corporation, Calcomp, and CR/CADD. She has also authored books through these corporations for 10 different mainframe, minicomputer, and microcomputer CADD software programs, including the *VersaCAD Tutorial—A Practical Approach to Computer-Aided Design*, published by TAB BOOKS Inc.

Kevin Neubert, technical advisor, is a subject matter expert in the field of Architecture and CADD. He has 11 years of architectural experience, with 5 years of using CADD to develop architectural drawings.

DataCAD

FOR THE ARCHITECT

Overview

DataCAD for the Architects is a tutorial book designed for use with the DataCAD computer-aided drafting and design software package. This book contains easy-to-follow, fully illustrated instructions that take the reader from the beginning to the advanced level of using DataCAD to create architectural projects.

This overview is designed to help you understand how this book is formatted, and what you can expect to learn from it.

THE DATACAD SOFTWARE PROGRAM

DataCAD is a micro-computer based software program that helps you draw with increased efficiency and precision. It allows you to use the computer as a design and drafting tool.

Like any new tool, you will be required to learn new concepts and skills in order to use it. Once you understand the basic concepts used in computer drafting, using DataCAD will become easier. Then, with practice, you will become a proficient and expert user of the DataCAD program!

DATACAD RELEASE VERSION 3.6

This book is designed to be used with the DataCAD release version called 3.6, scheduled to be released to the general user group in August 1988.

IF YOU HAVE AN EARLIER OR LATER RELEASE OF DATACAD

You can still use this book if you have a different release version than 3.6! You will notice, however, slight changes in the menu options or particular procedure followed in the operation of the menu options.

THE "DATACAD FOR ARCHITECTS" BOOK

DataCAD for the Architect is designed as a self-teaching guide to using the DataCAD software program. You can follow the steps and work through the projects independently, or with the aid of a classroom instructor.

This book is also designed as a continued reference, and contains a special section called The DataCAD Operations Guide, which contains easy steps to follow for daily use of DataCAD.

Beginning Assumptions

This book assumes that you have little or no experience drawing with DataCAD. You may or may not be an experienced computer user. This does not matter. Drawing with DataCAD does not require you to be a computer expert.

If you have already used DataCAD a little, then you will be happy to find that this book can answer the many questions you may have. If you have been using DataCAD for an extended period of time, you will find the second section of the book most helpful— The DataCAD Operations Guide.

Another assumption is that you have the DataCAD program loaded on your computer, and have it configured to work with your hardware. This is accomplished by following the procedures outlined in your *DataCAD User's Manual*, or in a special INSTALLATION insert which was supplied with your program.

How This Book Is Organized

This book is divided into 14 lessons. These lessons take you from the beginning concepts of DataCAD, to more advanced uses and operations. The lessons are systematic, meaning that they tend to build on each other, and are presented from easy to harder skills sequentially.

Lesson 1. **Beginning DataCAD** – Introduces DataCAD and the basic concepts for CAD drawing. You will start the DataCAD program, create a drawing file, use the mouse input device to draw lines, look at menus, erase, and file the drawing.

Lesson 2. **Initial Drawing Set-Up** – You will create two drawing set-ups. The first will be ¼″ = 1′ scale drawings, which will be used for creating floor plans. The second will be for 1″ = 20′ scale drawings, which will be used for site layouts.

Lesson 3. **Basic Drafting Techniques** – Guides you through using basic drawing capabilities for creating walls, doors, and windows.

Lesson 4. **Windowing** – You will use the different window techniques for controlling the view window of your drawing.

Lesson 5. **Adding Symbols** – You will retrieve, add, and rotate symbols as you place them into your drawing. DataCAD comes with a variety of developed symbols that you can use.

Lesson 6. **Adding Dimension and Text** – Your projects need to be dimensioned, and this lesson shows you how.

Lesson 7. **Viewing Your Drawing In 3-D** – Your house is created, and now you want to see what it really looks like in 3-D. You will look at your drawing in perspective and from a bird's-eye view. You will also remove the hidden lines so that your walls look "solid."

Lesson 8. Plotting Your Drawing – Now you will learn how to send your drawing to the plotter, and get a finished product!

Lesson 9. Creating Site Plans – Most of the site information for your layout is provided by the civil engineer—but are his calculations correct? You will learn to use the formulas that are given to you to draw the initial site plan.

Lesson 10. Creating 3-Dimensional Lines – You have been creating your drawing in the orthographic view. Now you can view your drawing in 3-D and create lines that are 3-dimensional.

Lesson 11. Copying Techniques – What is the easiest way to create a drawing that has repeated items in it? This lesson shows you how to do this and more. You will also learn how to modify the items you copied.

Lesson 12. Detail Drawings – You will create your own detail, learn how to cross-hatch, reduce the size of items, find out how to measure lines, and other more advanced techniques that DataCAD provides.

Lesson 13. Creating Templates and Symbols – Make your own symbols, organized in templates, for your DataCAD drawings. You can also extract reports from your symbols. This lesson provides you with the skills necessary to use and modify these reports.

Lesson 14. Creating Your Default Drawings – Design Default Drawings for your own office or classroom use. All of the steps you need are included here, with explanations provided for the customization of these Defaults to your own standards.

Hands-On Learning

It is hard to learn a skill by reading about it. Reading helps us achieve a knowledge about a subject, but skills are learned by doing. This is called "hands-on learning."

To make it easier for you to acquire your new DataCAD drawing skills, this book is designed to help you "do" by putting your "hands on" the DataCAD system. You will be guided through performing actual skills with easy-to-read instructions.

Classroom Environment

Because the book is divided into concept "lessons," the book is readily fitted into the classroom curriculum. If you have bought this book as part of your CAD drafting course, you will find it easy to use and reference as course text.

Step-by-Step Tutorials

Step-by-step tutorials help you perform DataCAD operations, providing you with easy to read instructions. Each step is numbered and an abundance of illustrations are included.

"Self-Paced" Design

We all learn at different speeds. We tend to want to decide for ourselves the amount of time we want to spend on a subject or on learning a new skill. All age groups, in fact, acquire new information at speeds comfortable to them as individuals.

This book was designed with this type of learning strategy in mind. It allows you to advance at your own speed. You can look back at certain lessons for reference to go over a skill on which you want to spend more time.

How to Use This Book

Each lesson contains 4 basic elements:

1. Learning objectives.
2. Concept explanation.
3. Project and tutorial.
4. Exercise with multiple choice questions.

What You Should Do

- You should read the objectives at the beginning of each lesson, describing what you will be doing.
- Then, you should read the concept explanation.
- It is very helpful if you briefly review the tutorial you will be following, so that there are no surprises.
- You should then sit down at the computer and follow the step-by-step instructions provided you. (Make notes, if you want to, right in your book.)
- Reference the DataCAD Operations Guide, which is in the back section of the book, when instructed to do so. Later, this guide will be your reference tool for on-the-job usage.
- After you have completed the tutorial, check your project to make sure it is correct. If it is not correct, go over the steps again. Be sure to carefully read the instructions and illustrations.
- Complete the exercise found at the end of each lesson. If you do not remember the answer, look back at the tutorial or explanation in order to find it. You may also want to look at the DataCAD menus.
- A very good idea is to also look in the *DataCAD User's Manual* in order to find more information about the options you are using.

Throughout this book you will be given instructions that are new to you. It is important to understand the format in which the tutorials will be presented.

Numbering Scheme

Your instructions will appear following a "step" number (e.g., Step 1, Step 2). This signifies that:

1) **There is an action you should perform.**
   (e.g., **Step 1** – Pick the LineType option.)
2) **An action has occurred.**
   (e.g., **Step 2** – The menu in Fig. 3-10 is displayed.)

If the number is followed by a parenthesis (e.g., 1), 2), 3)), then important information is being conveyed to you which you should read. (Such as above.)

Instruction Terms

Certain terms will be used that indicate what you are being instructed to do. Basically, these are:

1) **Press** – you should press the key found on the keyboard.
2) **Pick** – you should pick an item on the drawing with the mouse button 1 or pick an option from a menu. Again, you would use mouse button 1.
3) **Object Snap** – you should put the cursor by an item, and press mouse button 2. This action will "grab on" to the item.
4) **Type in** – you should type in a value from the keyboard. When necessary, the value should be followed by pressing the **[Enter]** key.

Drawing Projects

Most lessons include drawing projects that have been designed to help you practice the particular skills being taught.

If you choose to create your own drawing projects, remember to be careful in selecting projects that fit the criteria for the lesson. Many drawings can be found in architectural drafting books that work quite well for practice.

Exercises

Each lesson is followed by a multiple choice exercise. These exercises allow you to recall the operations you learned during the lesson. The answers for these exercises are found in Appendix C.

Lesson 1:
Beginning DataCAD

WHAT YOU WILL BE DOING:

YOU will be learning about the components of your computer system, and a little on how the DataCAD system is structured. You will start DataCAD and use simple techniques to draw lines. You will use the Mouse input device to pick menu options, line start and end points, change from the main menus, and to Quit an operation.

OBJECTIVES:

Your lesson objectives are, then, to:

- Learn the basics of DataCAD.
- Start DataCAD.
- Use the mouse input device.
- Draw lines.
- Set the Object Snap options.
- Object snap onto lines.
- Erase lines by entity, area, and polygon fence.

Remember to reference the section called *The DataCAD Operations Guide* when instructed. This section is your "quick" guide to DataCAD operations.

INTRODUCTION TO YOUR COMPUTER SYSTEM

Although different types of computers are not exactly the same, your DataCAD computer system is typically made up of 5 major pieces. They are:

1. Display Screen
2. Processor
3. Disk Drives
4. Keyboard
5. Mouse

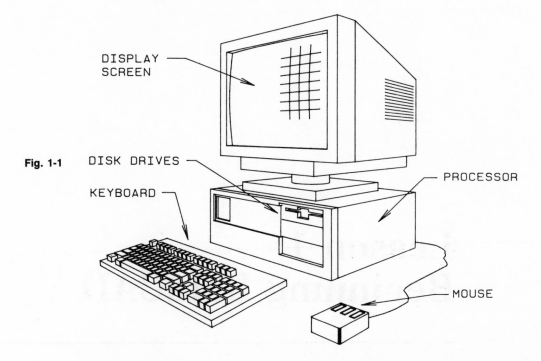

Fig. 1-1

The first thing you may notice about your computer is the many special keys on the keyboard. Many of these keys, which are not found on the everyday typewriter, assist you in the operation of DataCAD. Some of these helpful keys are noted below in Fig. 1-2. Your keyboard may look slightly different than this. Locate these keys on your own keyboard.

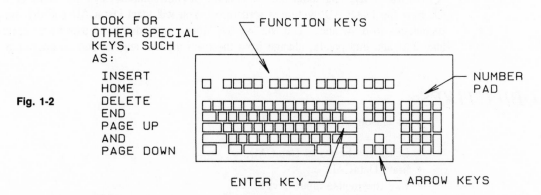

Fig. 1-2

DATACAD DIRECTORY STRUCTURE

Your DataCAD system is organized like you might organize your file cabinets. In fact, every file on your computer can and should be organized in a well planned system, in order for you and your computer to easily find your important files.

You can think of the organization of your computer, then, as a filing cabinet, as shown in Fig. 1-3.

Directories, which help to organize the data in your computer, can be thought of as the individual drawers in the cabinet. This is illustrated in Fig. 1-4.

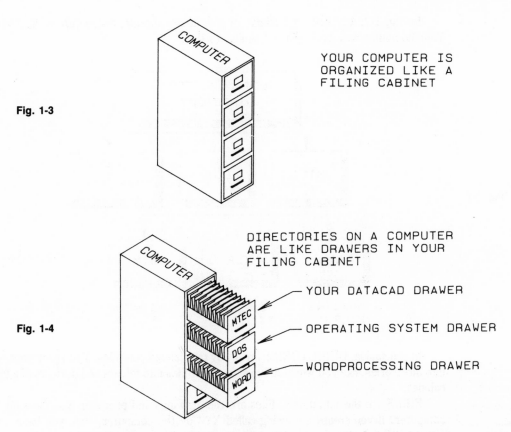

Fig. 1-3

YOUR COMPUTER IS
ORGANIZED LIKE A
FILING CABINET

DIRECTORIES ON A COMPUTER
ARE LIKE DRAWERS IN YOUR
FILING CABINET

Fig. 1-4

——YOUR DATACAD DRAWER

——OPERATING SYSTEM DRAWER

——WORDPROCESSING DRAWER

Each drawer of your file cabinet can contain file folders, as indicated in Fig. 1-5. These folders can also be compared to as sub-directories (or "directories within directories") on your computer.

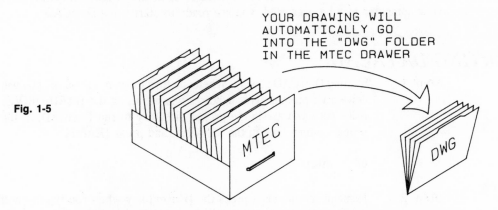

YOUR DRAWING WILL
AUTOMATICALLY GO
INTO THE "DWG" FOLDER
IN THE MTEC DRAWER

Fig. 1-5

The folder can contain your files, just as the sub-directories contain the data files for your drawings (drawing files) and software programs, or even additional directories. (See Fig. 1-6)

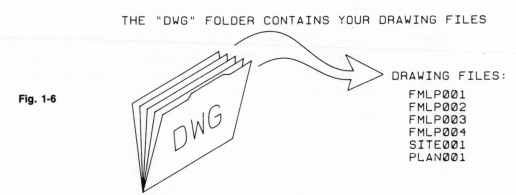

THE "DWG" FOLDER CONTAINS YOUR DRAWING FILES

Fig. 1-6

DRAWING FILES:
FMLP001
FMLP002
FMLP003
FMLP004
SITE001
PLAN001

In Fig. 1-7, a typical organization of a computer directory structure is illustrated. Your computer may be organized similar to this.

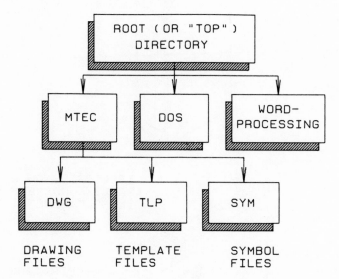

Fig. 1-7

In conclusion, DIRECTORIES are a way to organize your files. You group your files into directories, like you would group your paper files into folders and drawers of a filing cabinet.

FILES are the actual data. Files are the drawings and programs you have on the computer. If you create a drawing called XYZ on the computer, then you have a file called XYZ. It is that simple. All of this is transparent to you, of course, while you are using DataCAD. DataCAD makes your files for you. You don't have to be a computer expert!

Now that you know a little about how the components of your computer, and how your computer may be organized, you are ready to start using DataCAD.

STARTING DATACAD

Step 1 – Starting DataCAD is easy. When you turn on your computer, you will receive a **C:** prompt. This indicates you are using the HARD DRIVE. To make sure you are in the proper directory to run DataCAD, at the **C:** prompt simply type in the following, and press **[Enter]**.

   cd \ mtec

Step 2 – Remember, you must press the **[Enter]** key when you type something in. This signals the computer to read the command you gave it.

Step 3 – Now you can type in and **[Enter]** the following:

   dcad

Step 4 – The next thing that will appear on your screen is the copywrite menu. This is the copywrite agreement that you made with the Microtecture Corporation when purchasing DataCAD. Read this message, then press [Enter] to continue.

   [Enter]

Step 5 – The DataCAD opening screen will be displayed, as indicated in Fig. 1-8. If there are any existing drawings, they will be listed in the left column of the screen.

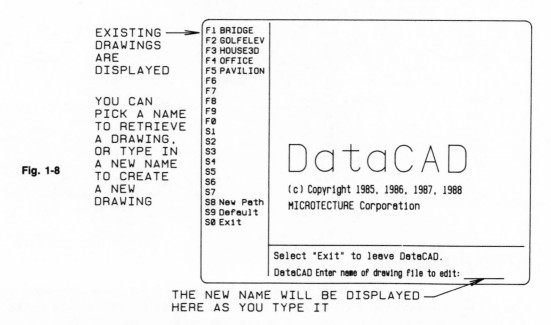

Fig. 1-8

EXISTING → DRAWINGS ARE DISPLAYED

YOU CAN PICK A NAME TO RETRIEVE A DRAWING, OR TYPE IN A NEW NAME TO CREATE A NEW DRAWING

THE NEW NAME WILL BE DISPLAYED — HERE AS YOU TYPE IT

BEGINNING A DRAWING

To begin a new drawing, all you have to do is type in a new drawing name. Drawing names can only be 8 characters long. Because of this, you will want to develop special naming conventions for your drawings. For practice drawings, you can use a simple naming convention.

Step 1 – Type in the name for your new drawing:

fml-prac (Your **F**irst **M**iddle and **L**ast initials, **PRAC**tice)

USER NOTE–Certain characters are illegal in names of files. This includes:

/ ? \
: . ;

The characters that are *legal* include:

A thru Z	0 thru 9	–	@
%	,	$	{ }
#	( )	!	&

THE MAIN MENU SCREEN

Once you begin a drawing, the DataCAD main menu screen will be displayed. There are 4 major areas that make up this screen, as indicated in Fig. 1-9. They are:

- Menu Window – Your menus will always appear in this column.
- Drawing Area – Your drawing is displayed here.
- Status Area – This area informs you of your present settings: The active layer, the present viewing scale, the selection set (on newer releases), and the SWOTHLUD status.
- Message Area – Your coordinate readout, System messages, and user prompt appear here.

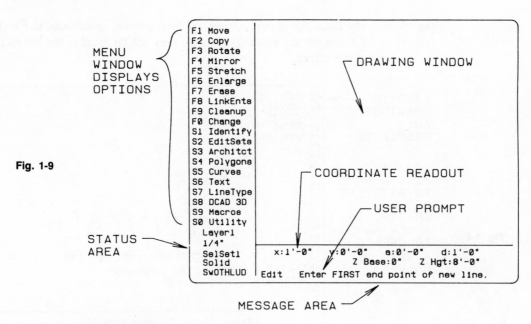

Fig. 1-9

WHAT IS SWOTHLUD?

The word SWOTHLUD, which appears at the lower left corner of the status area, represents the current setting status. Each letter stands for a particular setting. It keeps you informed "at a glance" of what settings you have active.

The letters "SWOTHLUD" stand for:

Snap –   Increment snapping is on.
Walls –   You are creating walls (compared to lines).
Ortho –   Ortho lock is on (angle lock on line or wall creation.)
Text –   Text is displayed on screen (instead of blocks only).
Hatch –   Hatch is displayed on screen.
Line weight –   Thicknesses of lines are displayed.
User linetypes –   Linetypes are displayed (compared to appearing as solid).
Dimensions –   Dimensions are displayed on screen.

When a switch is active (e.g., walls are being drawn), the letter will appear capitalized. If the switch is off (e.g., walls are not being drawn, lines are), the letter will appear in lowercase (e.g., SwOTHLUD). You will see how this works later in this lesson.

THE SCREEN CURSOR

Notice that there is a small + on your screen. This is called a *cursor*. When you move your mouse, the cursor on your screen will move. As you found out earlier, if you move the cursor into the MENU OPTION area, the option closest to the cursor will be highlighted. The cursor is also used to pick items in the drawing area.

DRAWING LINES

Notice that the "W" in the status line (SWOTHLUD) appears in upper or lower-case (SwOTHLUD). As mentioned earlier, this means that you will either be drawing walls (a double set of lines) or single lines. (Other letters may appear in lowercase also.)

You will want the W to be in lowercase for your first drawing lesson. If it is in UP-PERCASE, follow the next step, **Step 1**, to change the status. If your W is in lower-case, skip this step and to to **Step 2**.

IF THE W (in SWOTHLUD) IS UPPERCASE -

Step 1 -   Press the double line key [=] (equal sign). This will turn off the walls mode for now.

[=]

Notice that the user prompt (bottom of screen) is asking you to pick a point to draw a line. To draw lines, all you have to do is point with the cursor and press mouse button **1**. This is called "picking". You can continue drawing lines, always picking the next point with mouse number **1**. To quit drawing the line, you simply press mouse button **3**.
Let's try it!

Step 2 -   Move the cursor to the desired area in the Drawing Window you wish to begin drawing a line.

Step 3 -   Press mouse button **1**.

Step 4 -   Continue making multiple lines, moving the cursor, and using mouse button **1**, as shown in Fig. 1-10.

Step 5 -   To end your line, press mouse button **3**.

Fig. 1-10

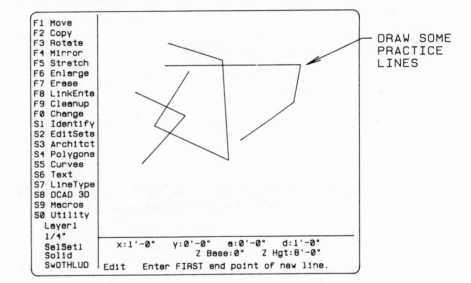

YOUR THREE BUTTON MOUSE

You just used your mouse to pick points on the screen for your lines, and to detach the line. These are only two of the uses for your mouse. The three buttons, and their uses, are described in Fig. 1-11.

The first button, as you found out, it used to "pick". You can pick a location on the screen for a line or wall, or you can pick an option from the menu.

The second button is used to object snap to an existing object, such as a line. Object snap means to "grab onto an object".

The third button is used to "quit" a line, or quit from a menu.

MOUSE BUTTON FUNCTIONS:

1 - PICK ITEMS AND
    MENU OPTIONS

Fig. 1-11

2 - SNAP TO OBJECTS
    CAN ALSO BE USED
    AS [Enter]

3 - QUITS OUT OF MENUS

PICK 1   SNAP 2   QUIT 3

MOUSE

Let's try it!

Step 1 –   Make sure there are a few lines in your drawing area.

Step 2 –   Pick a start point for a line, using mouse button **1**.

Step 3 –   Move the cursor close to an existing line, as shown in Fig. 1-12.

PLACE THE CURSOR
CLOSE TO THE
ENDPOINT OF
A LINE

Fig. 1-12

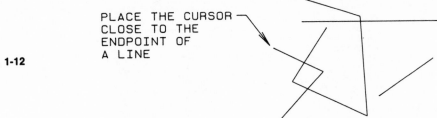

Step 4 –   Press mouse button **2**. The first endpoint of the line will snap unto the endpoint of the existing line, as in Fig. 1-13.

LINE
END-
POINT

NOTICE THE NEW
LINE IS ATTACHED
TO THE END OF
THE LINE YOU
"SNAPPED" TO

Fig. 1-13

NEW LINE

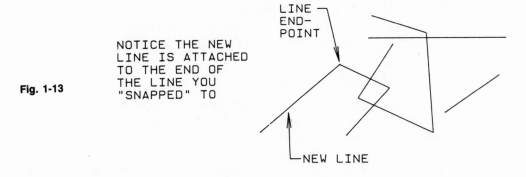

QUICK ERASING

You can quickly erase entities you drew by using the < key. To erase all the lines you drew as a multiple line *during a single series* (without pressing mouse button **3** to detach your line), you would use the **[Shift]** and < keys together. Lines drawn as a single series are called a "group" of lines.

Step 1 –   Press the < key. Did one of your lines disappear?

<

Step 2 - Press the **shift** and < keys together. How many lines disappeared? Remember, a bunch of lines drawn together without detaching (by pressing mouse button **3**) are thought of as one "group". Using the shift and < together will erase the last group you have drawn.

[Shift]<

RESTORING

You can restore the last entity or group you erased!

Step 1 - Press the > key. Whatever you deleted last (group or single entity) will be restored.

>

THE EDIT AND UTILITY MENUS

There are two MAIN menus in DataCAD. They are:

- **EDIT** - menu options that allow you to create or change items, such as walls, windows, doors, etc.

- **UTILITY** - menu options that allow you to define certain settings, defaults for your drawing, and other utility items such as drawing file control

To change between the two main menus, all you have to do is press the mouse button **3**. (Of course, if you are drawing a line, the first time you press mouse button **3** it will detach your line. The second time you press mouse button **3** will switch menus.)

Step 1 - Look at the MESSAGE AREA at the bottom of the screen, as shown in Fig. 1-14. Does it say Edit or Utility?

Fig. 1-14

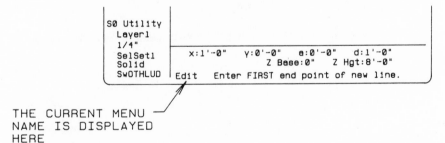

If it says **Edit**, then you are in the EDIT menu. You could switch to the UTILITY menu by pressing mouse button **3**.

Step 2 - Press mouse button **3** until the main menu changes to EDIT. Notice the options that are displayed.

Step 3 - Press button **3** until it changes to UTILITY. This is called "toggling" between menus. Notice the options that are displayed in the UTILITY menu.

OBJECT SNAP

As mentioned before, object snap allows you to grab onto items, such as existing lines. You can grab an item by its endpoints, middle point, center point, etc. Your object snap is currently set to "endpoint". That is why, when you picked close to an item and pressed mouse button **2**, your line grabbed onto the "end" of the existing line.

Suggested "common-use" settings for object snap are:

End point
Mid point
Center
Intersection

The object snap settings are illustrated in Fig. 1-15.

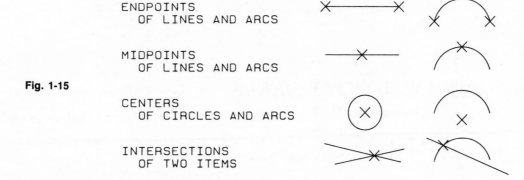

ENDPOINTS
    OF LINES AND ARCS

MIDPOINTS
    OF LINES AND ARCS

Fig. 1-15

CENTERS
    OF CIRCLES AND ARCS

INTERSECTIONS
    OF TWO ITEMS

SETTING YOUR OBJECT SNAP

You can quickly set your object snap to these settings.

Step 1 – Press the mouse button **3** until the UTILITY menu is displayed (Utility appears in the MESSAGE AREA).

Step 2 – Pick the option displayed called **ObjSnap.**

  ObjSnap

Step 3 – The OBJECT SNAP menu is displayed, as in Fig. 1-16.

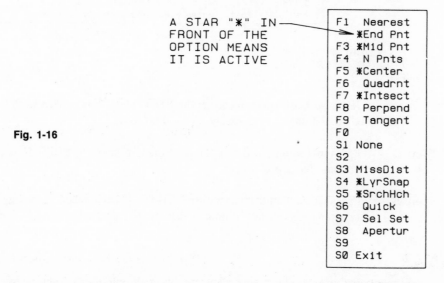

A STAR "*" IN
FRONT OF THE
OPTION MEANS
IT IS ACTIVE

F1 Nearest
F2 *End Pnt
F3 *Mid Pnt
F4 N Pnts
F5 *Center
F6 Quadrnt
F7 *Intsect
F8 Perpend
F9 Tangent
F0
S1 None
S2
S3 MissDist
S4 *LyrSnap
S5 *SrchHch
S6 Quick
S7 Sel Set
S8 Apertur
S9
S0 Exit

Fig. 1-16

Notice that some options may have a star * by them. This means that they have been set already, and they are **ACTIVE**.

Step 4 –   Pick the **Center** option until a * appears by it. Now it is *active*.

*Center

Step 5 –   Pick the rest of the options you wish to have *active*.

*Midpoint
*Intrsect

Step 6 –   If you pick a option by mistake, or wish to turn one off, just pick it again and the * will "toggle" off.

Step 7 –   When you are through, press the mouse button **3** to quit out of the OB-JECT SNAP menu.

Step 8 –   Check to see if you can object snap to the middle of a line, by holding your cursor at the midpoint of a line, and pressing the object snap button, mouse button **2**.

Did it work? If not, check your settings again.

QUICK KEYS

Most of the options you can pick from menus can also be entered quickly by simply typing in a key, or a combination of keys, from the keyboard. These are called *"quick keys"*. You can use quick keys from within other menus, to access the next needed menu fast and easy.

You can use quick keys to enter the OBJECT SNAP menu.

Step 1 –   Press the [Shift] and X keys simultaneously.

[Shift]X

Step 2 –   You will enter the OBJECT SNAP menu! Press mouse button **3** to quit.

USER NOTE–You can switch to the OBJECT SNAP menu, using **[Shift]X**, anytime you are drawing lines or walls, or even from another menu. Once you quit the OBJECT SNAP menu, you will be returned to whatever you were doing or whatever menu you were in last.

ERASING ITEMS BY PICKING

You have already learned how to "quick erase" as you are drawing lines. Since you will be starting a new project, you will want to know how to erase all of the lines at once from your screen.

Step 1 –   Select the **Erase** option from the EDIT menu.

Erase

Step 2 –   You can erase an Entity (single item), a group (all drawn together), or an area (items that can be enclosed by a box).

Pick the Entity option until it is active (*Entity).

Entity

Step 3 –   Pick a line to erase. It will be deleted!

Step 4 –   Pick the **Area** option until it is active (*Area).

Area

Step 5 –   Pick two points indicating a rectangle around the lines you wish to erase, as indicated in Fig. 1-17. Only the items completely enclosed in the box will be erased.

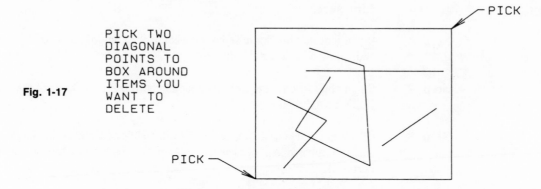

PICK TWO
DIAGONAL
POINTS TO
BOX AROUND
ITEMS YOU
WANT TO
DELETE

Fig. 1-17

Step 6 –   If you made a mistake, pick **Undo**, and all of the items would come back! Try it.

Undo

CREATING A FENCE

You can also draw a "polygon" fence around the items you want to erase. This way, you can stretch the fence around items you don't want erased.

Step 1 –   Pick the **Fence** option until it is active (*Fence).

Fence

Step 2 –   Pick the first point of your fence.

Step 3 –   Pick the second point of your fence.

Step 4 –   Now pick a third point. Notice that a corner of the fence is always attached to your cursor. This is how you would "wrap" the polygon fence around items you want erased. (See Fig. 1-18)

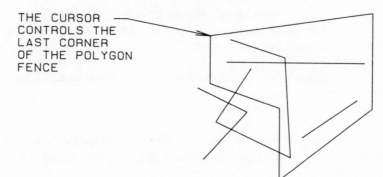

THE CURSOR
CONTROLS THE
LAST CORNER
OF THE POLYGON
FENCE

Fig. 1-18

Step 5 – The **Backup** option allows you to "re-pick" the last corner.

Backup

Step 6 – Press mouse button **3** to execute the erasing of the items you have a fence around.

Step 7 – Continue playing with DataCAD for a few minutes, drawing and erasing lines. Get a good feel for using the mouse, and pointing to objects. When you feel comfortable using the mouse, switching menus, and practicing what you learned during this lesson, continue to the next steps.

EXITING DATACAD

If you are going directly to the next lesson, you will not want to exit DataCAD. However, you may exit DataCAD and continue your lessons later. If you DO want to exit DataCAD, follow these next steps. *To assure that your drawing is permanently saved when you leave DataCAD, make sure that you pick the YES option from the Quit menu.*

Step 1 – Select the **Quit** option from the UTILITY menu.

Quit

Step 2 – Notice you are given three options:

Abort – This means you want to leave DataCAD, *without saving* the current drawing.

Yes – This option allows to leave DataCAD, and *save* the current drawing at the same time.

No – Selecting this option means you do not want to leave DataCAD, and you will be returned back into the program, with your current drawing displayed.

Step 3 – Pick **Yes**, to *save your current drawing to your hard disk* before leaving the DataCAD program. Your drawing will be saved. The next time you enter DataCAD, all you will have to do is pick your drawing from the drawing list!

Yes

DataCAD Exercise 1

Please complete the following exercise by reading each question carefully, then circling the letter that corresponds to the correct answer.

1. The first (left most) button on the mouse is used to:

   a. Pick on the screen.
   b. Object snap or to enter a typed value.
   c. Quit an operation or exit a menu.

2. The second (middle) button on the mouse is used to:

   a. Pick on the screen.
   b. Object snap or to enter a typed value.
   c. Quit an operation or exit a menu.

3. The third (right most) button on the mouse is used to:

   a. Pick on the screen.
   b. Object snap or to enter a typed value.
   c. Quit an operation or exit a menu.

4. Your DataCAD drawing appears in the:

   a. Drawing Window.
   b. Status Area.
   c. Menu Window.

5. The Mouse is called an:

   a. Processing device.
   b. Input device.
   c. Output device.

6. To make the selection of DataCAD options found in the different menus easy, you can use:

   a. The mouse to pick the menu options only. There is no quick way to enter menus.
   b. Either the mouse to pick options as you read them, press the correct function keys, or (preferably) use the "quick" keys, by pressing the correct key(s) on the keyboard.
   c. The mouse or function keys only. It is not recommended that you use the "quick" keys from the keyboard.

7. The letters "SWOTHLUD" displayed on your screen:

   a. Mean nothing to you, and are only displayed for programmers.
   b. Help to let you know what your coordinates are.
   c. Are to help you know what the current status of certain settings are (e.g., if you are drawing "W"alls or lines.)

8. Object snapping means to:

   a. Grab onto an item.
   b. Pick anywhere on the screen.
   c. Snap to a grid dot.

9. To erase the last line you drew, you press the:

   a. / key.
   b. < key.
   c. > key.

10. To restore the last line you erased, you press the:

   a. / key.
   b. < key.
   c. > key.

11. To enter the Erase menu quickly, you press the:

   a. E key.
   b. [Alt] E keys.
   c. < key.

12. To erase many items at one time by indicating a box around them, you use the Erase option, then pick the:

   a. Box option.
   b. Area option.
   c. Group option.

13. To restore all of the items you erased by indicating a box around them, you use the:

   a. Restore option.
   b. [Shift] < keys.
   c. Undo option, *before you leave the Erase menu*, or press the > key.

14. To save your drawing as you leave DataCAD, you select the Quit option, then pick the:

   a. Yes option.
   b. Save option.
   c. Abort option.

Lesson 2:
Initial Drawing Set-Up

DURING this lesson, you will create a basic drawing setup. This set-up will help make it easier to draw your projects during the following lessons. You only need to set up the drawing once. After that, you use the same set-up over and over!

Drawing files that contain set-up information are called *Default Drawings*. During this lesson you will create one type of Default Drawing—a ¼″ scale drawing set-up that you will use to complete your practice floor plans.

Later, you will again create default drawings in the lesson called: *Creating Default Drawings*. This advanced lesson covers what can be included in these drawing files in greater detail, and how to create the many different types you may need for your own drawings.

OBJECTIVES:

Your lesson objectives, then, are to:

- Define the Object Snap settings.
- Create, name, and add color to layers.
- Change the size of your text.
- Create a layout area for your drawing.
- Save your new drawing file to disk.
- Identify the drawing as your default drawing.

DEFAULT DRAWINGS

Default Drawings are simply drawing files that contain pre-set information, that you can use over and over again. Once you create a drawing file with the information you need, you can use it as a default drawing.

It only takes a few minutes to create the settings for a default drawing, and it is one of the first things you will want to do for your own use.

A typical default drawing set-up includes the following:

1. Lay out area
2. Plotting settings, such as Scale and Paper size.
3. Scale Type, Angle Type, and other options found in the Setting menu predetermined.
4. Dimension standards.
5. Text font and size defined.
6. Layers named and colors assigned.
7. Display options set.
8. Grids and Grid Snap defined.
9. Line Type spacing.
10. Object Snap settings.

You will want to develop several Default Drawings for your personal, company, or school use—at least one for each size and type of drawing you create.

HOW A DEFAULT DRAWING IS USED

Once you have created your default drawings, you use them over and over again for all of your drawings.

When you start a new drawing, you first want to identify which default drawing you will be using. The default drawing serves as a basis for your new drawing. Then you simply create your new drawing file, and all of the defaults you set appear! This flow is described in Fig. 2-1.

Fig. 2-1

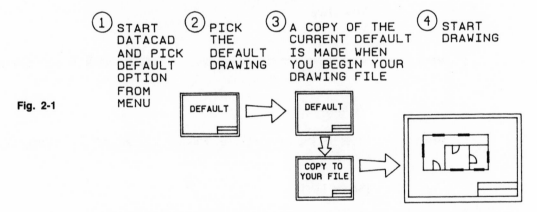

Your first Default Drawing you create during this lesson will be very basic, with only the minimum variables set. The reason for this is simple: with just the minimum settings, you can start drawing immediately. Later, during the lesson called *Creating Default Drawings*, you will learn more details about setting up your default drawings.

THE DEFAULT FILE DIRECTORY

Just like the special drawer in the filing cabinet for the DataCAD software (**MTEC**), there is a special folder in the drawer for your default drawings. This folder is called DEFAULT. (Fig. 2-2)

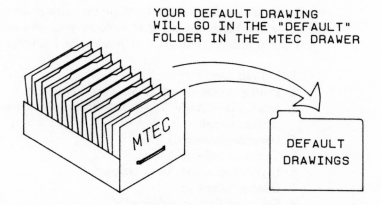

YOUR DEFAULT DRAWING
WILL GO IN THE "DEFAULT"
FOLDER IN THE MTEC DRAWER

Fig. 2-2

MTEC

DEFAULT
DRAWINGS

TURNING OFF ANY CURRENT DEFAULT DRAWING

Just in case someone has already set up a default drawing, or changed the present default settings, it is a good idea to make sure you retrieve the original DataCAD defaults. This is done by turning off any current default drawing.

Step 1 -   *If you are not in the DataCAD program,* start DataCAD, by typing in:

cd ∖ mtec
dcad

If you are presently in the DataCAD program, start a new drawing, by selecting:

File I/O (Utility menu)
New Dwg
Yes

Step 2 -   When the drawing list is displayed (on the left side of the screen) select the **Default** option.

Default

Step 3 -   Press the **[Space bar]** once. This will clear any default that may be assigned.

[Space bar]

Step 4 -   Press **[Enter]**. You will be returned to the Drawing List menu.

[Enter]

CREATING YOUR DEFAULT DIRECTORY

You create your default drawing as you would any DataCAD drawing. However, you have to make sure you create this drawing in the correct directory.

Step 5 -   Select the **New Path** option. This option allows you to tell DataCAD to look in certain directories (or "file drawer and folder") for a drawing. (In (In this case, your Default Drawing.)

New Path

Step 6 -   Type in the pathname for your default drawings. The easiest name for this directory is: **DEFAULT**.

Remember to press the **[Enter]** key after typing the pathname in.

default

Step 7 - If a file folder (directory called "default" does not already exist in the MTEC drawer, you will be given an opportunity to create one, as in Fig. 2-3.

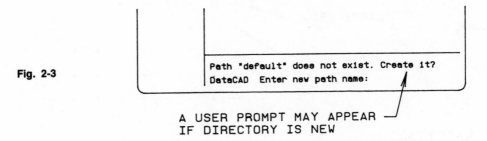

Fig. 2-3

A USER PROMPT MAY APPEAR
IF DIRECTORY IS NEW

Step 8 - If you are given a Yes/No choice to create this directory, select the **Yes** option.

Yes

Step 9 - Now you can create your Default drawing file. Type in the new name for your Default Drawing: 1-4PLAN. This name will represent a drawing set-up for a ¼ plan layout.

1-4plan

*Note - Certain characters are illegal in directory and file names. This includes the /, :, ?, and any blank spaces. The \ character is also illegal in a name, since it delineates between directory names. Also, due to DOS format, the actual name is limited to eight (8) characters.

Step 10 - An empty drawing file will be displayed, which holds the DataCAD original settings. A grid pattern will be displayed on the screen. DataCAD includes this pre-defined grid pattern in their default settings. (See Fig. 2-4)

DATACAD DRAWING GRID

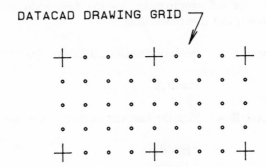

Fig. 2-4

THE GRID SETTINGS

The grid in the DataCAD default drawing is displayed in the following settings:

Large Grid = 16 feet
Small Grid = 4 feet

This grid definition will work well for your first drawing set-up. Later, during the Default Drawings lesson, you will learn to customize your grid settings. (See Fig. 2-5)

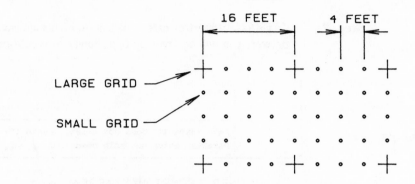

Fig. 2-5

SNAP SETTING

The "snap" definition for your cursor is set to four (4) inches. You can verify this by moving your cursor into the drawing area. You will notice that the cursor jumps to 4" increments. If you look at your coordinate readout, you will see that only 4" coordinates are displayed. (See Fig. 2-6)

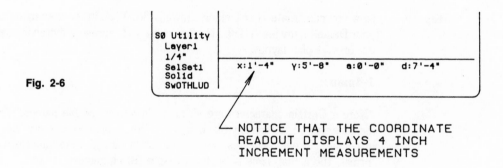

Fig. 2-6

This snap is designed to make it easier to place lines, walls, and other objects.

SETTING THE OBJECT SNAP

You will want to make sure the object snap defaults are set. This way, you will not have to set them each time.

Step 1 –   Press the **[Shift]** and **X** keys. The OBJECT SNAP menu will be displayed.

[Shift]X

Step 2 –   Pick the following options, until they have a "*" in front of them:

*EndPnt
*MidPnt
*Center
*LyrSnap

(The "LyrSnap" option tells the system to search on all layers as you try to object snap onto an item.)

Step 3 –   Press mouse button **3** to quit.

CREATING LAYERS

Each layer you define will hold a certain type of item. Your walls, for instance, will all be on their own layer. Your doors will be on their own layer too. Dimensions also are placed on a special layer. (Fig. 2-7)

Fig. 2-7

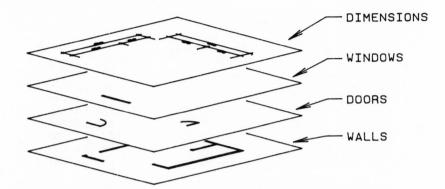

This type of item separation makes it possible to turn off and on the layers that contain the items you wish to view or plot. For example, you can turn off the furniture level and the reflected ceiling plan, in order to display only the floor plan and the electrical plan. (See Fig. 2-8)

Fig. 2-8

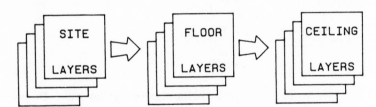

YOU CAN TURN OFF AND ON THE LAYERS
YOU NEED FOR YOUR FINISHED PLANS

Step 1 – Press **L** to enter the Layers menu. This is the quick key to access the LAYERS menu. Or, you can select the **Layers** option from the UTILITY menu.

L

Step 2 – Pick the **ON/OFF** option.

ON/OFF

Step 3 – Notice that there is only 1 layer: **Layer 1**. You will want to add 8 more layers, to make a total of 9 layers.

Step 4 – Press the mouse button **3** once, to quit back to the LAYERS menu.

Step 5 – Pick the **NewLayer** option.

NewLayer

Step 6 – Pick the **8** option, and **[Enter]**.

8

Step 7 – Pick the **Name** option, to name your layers.

Name

Step 8 – Pick **Layer1**, as in Fig. 2-9.

Layer1

Fig. 2-9

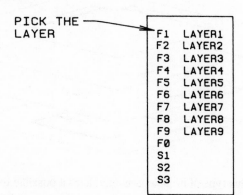

```
PICK THE          F1   LAYER1
LAYER             F2   LAYER2
                  F3   LAYER3
                  F4   LAYER4
                  F5   LAYER5
                  F6   LAYER6
                  F7   LAYER7
                  F8   LAYER8
                  F9   LAYER9
                  F0
                  S1
                  S2
                  S3
```

Step 9 – Type in the new name for this layer: **Walls** and press **[Enter]**.

Walls

Step 10 – Pick **Layer2**.

Layer2

Step 11 – Type in the new name for this layer: **Doors** and press **[Enter]**.

Doors

Step 12 – Continue naming the layers for your default drawing, as indicated below and in Fig. 2-10.

Layer1 = **Walls**
Layer2 = **Doors**
Layer3 = **Windows**
Layer4 = **Cabinet**
Layer5 = **Furn**
Layer6 = **Plumb**
Layer7 = **Dims**
Layer8 = **Notes**
Layer9 = **Border**

Notice - **NEVER** *name two layers alike!*

Fig. 2-10

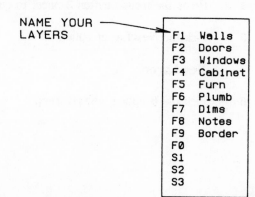

```
NAME YOUR         F1   Walls
LAYERS            F2   Doors
                  F3   Windows
                  F4   Cabinet
                  F5   Furn
                  F6   Plumb
                  F7   Dims
                  F8   Notes
                  F9   Border
                  F0
                  S1
                  S2
                  S3
```

Step 13 – Press mouse button **3** to quit back to the Layer menu.

SETTING THE LAYER COLORS

When you define a color to a layer, items drawn on that layer will appear in that color. Later, you can identify colors to match certain pens in your plotter.

Step 1 – Pick the **Color** option, to give each layer a color.

Color

Step 2 – The color you define will be set for the ACTIVE layer. Notice that the current active layer is **Walls**, and the layer name is displayed in "white", as indicated in Fig. 2-11.

Fig. 2-11

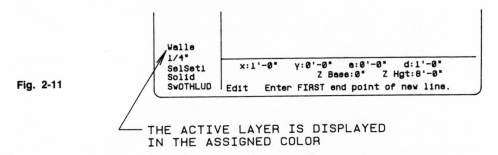

THE ACTIVE LAYER IS DISPLAYED
IN THE ASSIGNED COLOR

Step 3 – You will keep this layer white, in order to see the walls that you draw easily.

Step 4 – Change the active layer to **Doors**, by simply pressing the **[Tab]** key once. If you press the **[Tab]** key again, the active layer will turn to **Windows**, as indicated in Fig. 2-12.

Fig. 2-12

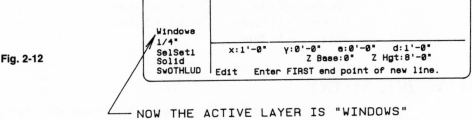

NOW THE ACTIVE LAYER IS "WINDOWS"

Step 5 – Continuing to press the **[Tab]** key will scroll you through the entire layer list. You can go backwards through this list, by holding down the **[Shift]** key, then pressing **[Tab]**.

[Shift] [Tab]

Step 6 – Change the active layer until you are returned to the **Doors** layer (Fig. 2-13)

Fig. 2-13

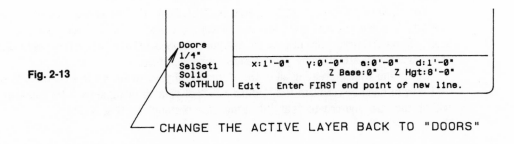

CHANGE THE ACTIVE LAYER BACK TO "DOORS"

Step 7 – Pick the **Green** option.

Green

Step 8 – Press the **[Tab]** key to change the active layer to **Windows**. (Fig. 2-14)

Fig. 2-14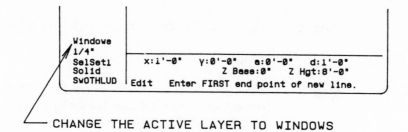

```
Windows
1/4"
SelSet1    x:1'-0"   y:0'-0"   a:0'-0"   d:1'-0"
Solid                      Z Base:0"   Z Hgt:8'-0"
SWOTHLUD  Edit    Enter FIRST end point of new line.
```

CHANGE THE ACTIVE LAYER TO WINDOWS

Step 9 – Pick the **Color** option again.

Color

Step 10 – Pick the **Cyan** option.

Cyan

Step 11 – Now the **Windows** layer name displayed will appear in a cyan color.

Step 12 – Continue setting the colors for your layers, matching the settings listed below:

Walls	= **White**	Plumb	= **Lt Blue**
Doors	= **Green**	Dims	= **Brown**
Windows	= **Cyan**	Notes	= **Brown**
Cabinet	= **Lt Mgta**	Border	= **Yellow**
Furn	= **Lt Blue**		

DRAWING BOUNDARY

As part of your set-up, you will add a rectangle to help indicate your drawing area. When you plot your drawing, then, it will easily fit on a drawing sheet. For this default drawing set-up, you will plan for a D size sheet.

The D size sheet is 24 inches by 36 inches. The actual drawing area is 23 by 32 inches, when you allow for a standard border. You will want your scaled plot to fit inside this area.

Plotted (scaled) size verses actual size

Using DataCAD, you are able to plot your drawing at a different scale than you drew it in.

Your CAD drawings should be drawn in FULL SCALE. This is referred to as "actual size". When you plot your drawing, it will come out at a scaled size (such as ¼" scale). DataCAD makes this easy to do, and you usually only have to plan for these differences when you are creating your default drawing set-up.

Since you will be creating all of the elements of your drawings in FULL SIZE (1" = 1"), you need to calculate the "actual size" of your drawing area. This calculation will be the size you create your "drawing area rectangle". (Fig. 2-15)

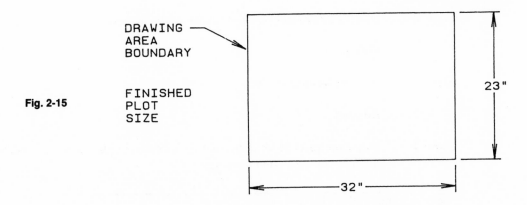

Fig. 2-15

The formula for this calculation is: **sheet size divided by plot scale.** Since you are setting up for a ¼″ scaled plot, the formula is as follows:

23 X 32 :   **23 divided by .25/12 = 1104.0017″ divided by 12 = 92** *feet*
               32 divided by .25/12 = 1536.0024″ divided by 12 = 128 *feet*

The actual size of the drawing area rectangle needs to be 92′ X 128′. (Fig. 2-16)

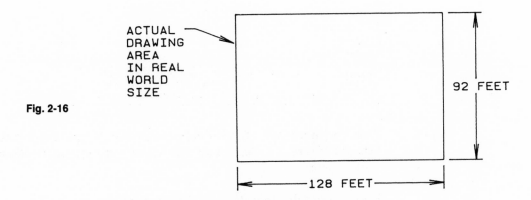

Fig. 2-16

Dimensions for this plot area and additional sizes for several plot scales are included in Appendix B *DataCAD Operations Guide*, Scales and Formulas section.

CREATING A RECTANGLE

You can define a rectangle by its two diagonal points. You will pick the first point with your cursor. Then you will type in the measurement for the second point. This is achieved by using *relative cartesian coordinates.*

Step 1 – Your **Border** layer should be active. This is the layer that is going to hold your rectangle. If it is not displayed as active in the status area, press the **[Tab]** key until it is. (Fig. 2-17)

Fig. 2-17

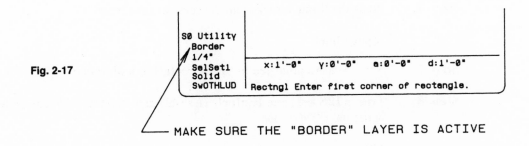

Step 2 – Pick the **Polygons** option from the EDIT menu.

Polygons

Step 3 – Pick the **Rectngl** option.

Rectngl

Step 4 – Pick a grid point on your drawing, as indicated in Fig. 2-18. This will be the first corner of your rectangle.

Fig. 2-18

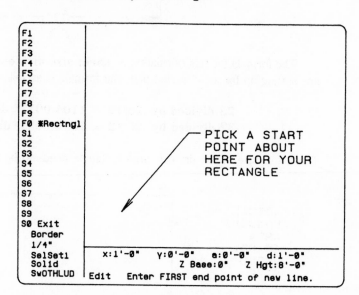

Step 5 – Press the **[Insert]** key. This key allows you to set the type of coordinate input you will use. Coordinate input modes allow you to type in the dimensions of items.

Keep pressing the **[Insert]** key until the user prompt reads: **The input mode is relative cartesian.** This is illustrated in Fig. 2-19.

[Insert]

Fig. 2-19

 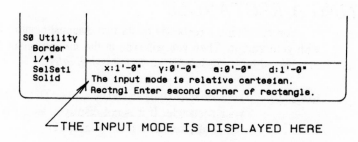

Step 6 – Press the **[Space bar]** to invoke the coordinate mode.

[Space bar]

Step 7 – Notice you are prompted to "**Enter relative x distance.**" (Fig. 2-20)

Step 8 – Type in **128** and press **[Enter]**. This will tell the system: 128 feet in the horizontal (X) direction.

128

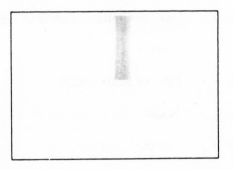

Fig. 2-20

```
 SØ Utility
   Border
   1/4"
   SelSet1     x:1'-Ø"    y:Ø'-Ø"    a:Ø'-Ø"    d:1'-Ø"
   Solid       You may select 1 or more values.
               Rectngl Enter x distance from the origin: ____
```

YOU ARE PROMPTED TO ENTER X DISTANCE ⌐

Step 9 –   Now you are prompted: **Enter relative Y distance**. Type in **92** and press **[Enter]**. This is the distance in the vertical direction.

92

Step 10 –   Now your rectangle is displayed, as in Fig. 2-21.

Fig. 2-21

Step 11 –   If your rectangle appears off the screen (Fig. 2-22), you can easily *resize* your viewing window.

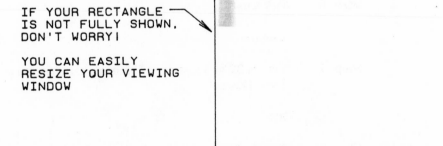

IF YOUR RECTANGLE ⌐
IS NOT FULLY SHOWN,
DON'T WORRY!

YOU CAN EASILY
Fig. 2-22   RESIZE YOUR VIEWING
WINDOW

Step 12 –   Press the **[/]** key (forward slash—also has a ? on it).

/

Step 13 –   Select the **Re-Calc** option. This option recalculates the extents of your viewing window. (Fig. 2-23)

Re-Calc

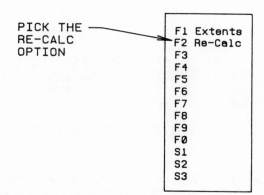

PICK THE
RE-CALC
OPTION

Fig. 2-23

PRE-SETTING THE PLOT SPECIFICATIONS

You will want to set up the plot scale of your drawing.

Step 1 –   Remember to press mouse button **3** to quit to the UTILITY menu.

Step 2 –   Pick the **Plotter** option from the UTILITY menu.

Plotter

Step 3 –   Pick the **Scale** option.

Scale

Step 4 –   Pick the ¼″ option.

¼″

Step 5 –   Pick the **PaperSiz** option.

PaperSiz

Step 6 –   Pick **Custom**.

Custom

Step 7 –   Type in **32** for the width. (This menu assumes you are inputting inches.) Press **[Enter]**

32

Step 8 –   Type in **23** for 23 inches in the height. Remember to press **[Enter]**.

23

Step 9 –   Press the mouse button **3** once, to return to the Plotter menu.

Step 10 –   Pick the **Layout** option, to lay the "plotting area outline" on your rectangle.

Layout

Step 11 –   Notice that a layout box is attached to your cursor, and that you are dragging it around by its centerpoint. (Fig. 2-24)

For a ¼″ scale plot, the text should be set at **6 inches**. The formula for this is:

12 divided by drawing scale X desired text size.

or -

12/.25 = 48
48 X .125 = 6 inches

Step 6 – Pick the **6″** option, type in **0.6** for your text height. The system will read this as 6 inches. Press **[Enter]**.

0.6

Step 7 – Press mouse button **3** once, then pick the **Dim Styl**.

Dim Styl

Step 8 – Pick ***FixdDis** until the star (*) turns OFF. This option fixes the distance between the drawing and the dimension. To allow you to easily adjust this distance and place the dimension with the cursor, you want to turn it off. So, there should be NO STAR by **FixdDis**.

FixdDis

Step 9 – Press mouse button **3** once, then pick the **ArroStyl** option.

ArroStyl

Step 10 – Make the **TicMrks** option active.

*TicMrks

Step 11 – Press mouse button **3** to quit to the EDIT menu.

SETTING THE TEXT SIZE FOR NOTES

You also need to adjust the text size you will be using to add your notes.

Step 1 – Pick the **Text** option, found in the EDIT menu.

Text

Step 2 – Pick the **Size** option.

Size

Step 3 – Change the size of your text to **6** inches again, which will be plotted at ⅛ inch.

0.6

Step 4 – Press mouse button **3** to quit to the UTILITY menu.

SAVING YOUR DEFAULT DRAWING

Now you are ready to save your default drawing.

Step 1 -   Pick the **File I/O** option, found in the UTILITY menu.

  File I/O

Step 2 -   Pick **New Dwg..**

  New Dwg

Step 3 -   Pick **Yes** to save your default drawing.

  Yes

USER REMINDER - *Do NOT pick ABORT, or you will trash the settings you just created!*

Step 4 -   The Default Drawing list is displayed. Notice that your default drawing is added to this list. (Fig. 2-26)

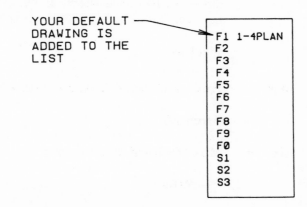

Fig. 2-26

CREATING A 1:20 SCALE SITE DEFAULT DRAWING

Follow the SAME STEPS that you did to create your ¼″ scale drawing, using the following variables:

1. Name of default drawing: **1-20SITE**

2. Add 6 New Layers, to make a total of 7.

3. Name Layers:
    Layer 1 = **PROPLIN**
    Layer 2 = **STREET**
    Layer 3 = **BLDG**
    Layer 4 = **PARKING**
    Layer 5 = **TEXT**
    Layer 6 = **DIMS**
    Layer 7 = **BORDER**

3. Color Layers:
    PROPLIN   = **Lt Mgta**
    STREET   = **Lt Cyan**
    BLDG   = **Lt Cyan**

PARKING = **Lt Grn**
TEXT = **Brown**
DIMS = **Brown**
BORDER = **Yellow**

4. Rectangle size (lay out area):

X = 640'
Y = 460'

5. Plot Scale : **1:20**

6. Set Pens:
Brown = **1**
Lt Grn = **2**
Lt Cyan = **3**
Lt Mgta = **4**
Yellow = **4**

7. Dimension Text and Note Text Size: **2.5 feet**

8. Remember to save your drawing, using the **File I/O, New Dwg, Yes** options.

GETTING READY TO DRAW
USING THE DEFAULT DRAWINGS

Once your default drawings are filed (using the **File I/O, New Dwg, Yes** options), you are ready to begin drawing. To do so, you will want to bring back the original drawing list. This is done by changing the *pathname* again.

Remember, the pathname is a way to describe to the system "what drawer to look in", or what *directory*, for your drawings. Currently, you set your pathname to the DEFAULT directory, which exists in the MTEC drawer. This means that only the default drawings are displayed.

Now you will change it back to DWG directory. This is the directory that came with DataCAD, and it contains some sample drawings.

Step 1 –   At the DataCAD "drawing list" screen, pick the **New Path** option.

New Path

Step 2 –   Type in **DWG**.

DWG

Step 3 –   Notice that the original drawing list appears on the left side of the screen.

DataCAD Exercise 2

Please complete the following exercise by reading each question carefully, then circling the letter that corresponds to the correct answer.

1. You should create:

   a. 5 default drawings. This is as many as anyone would ever need.
   b. At least 1 for every different scale and type of drawing you will need, and for different layer naming schemes.
   c. 10 default drawings. This is the maximum you can create.

2. To change into another directory in order to access other drawing files (such as the DEFAULT directory), you use the:

   a. Directory menu, New Dir option.
   b. File I/O, New Dwg option to retrieve the Drawing List screen (or the first DataCAD menu if you are just starting DataCAD), then pick the New Dir option.
   c. File I/O, New Dwg option to retrieve the Drawing List screen (or the first DataCAD menu if you are just starting DataCAD), then pick the New Path option.

3. Default drawings are created in order to:

   a. Save many steps, increase productivity, help eliminate errors, and establish consistency in all of your CADD drawings.
   b. Increase the time consuming steps in every drawing. Using Default drawings is not recommended.

4. Your default drawings should reside in the:

   a. MTEC\DEFAULT directory.
   b. MTEC\DWG directory.
   c. MTEC\SYM directory.

5. To create layers in your drawing, you use the Layers menus, then pick the:

   a. AddLayer option.
   b. NewLayer option.
   c. On/Off option.

6. Once you have added layers to your drawing, next you should:

   a. Use the Snap option found in the Layers menu, to define a snap setting for each layer.
   b. Name your layers.
   c. Leave the Layers menu. The layers will be automatically named.

7. The actual scale of the drawing:

   a. Is determined once you define a plot scale in your default drawing. All walls and lines are drawn full scale as you create them, then are plotted at the appropriate scale. Text, however, must be sized in accordance to the final plot scale.
   b. Effects the way you create walls and other lines. These type of entities must be scaled as you draw them.

    c. Doesn't effect the text size setting. No matter what your scale is, the text size stays the same.

8. To define the pens your plotter will use as the drawing is plotted, you use the:

    a. Layer menu, Color and Set Pens options.
    b. Plotter menu, Set Pens option.
    c. Plotter menu, Color option.

9. Different pens are assigned to different entities in your drawing by associating pen numbers to:

    a. Line Types.
    b. Colors.
    c. Line Widths.

10. When setting your Dimension variables, you:

    a. Have to define variables for all the different types of dimensions.
    b. Only have to define the variables for Linear and Angular dimensions.
    c. Only have to define the variables for Linear dimensions. These variables will then be set for all of the dimension types.

11. The Text Size that you set in your default drawing is defined at:

    a. The appropriate size in relation to the plotting scale. (E.g., If the drawing is to be plotted at ¼″, text created 6 inches high will be plotted at ⅛″ high.)
    b. The size you want it plotted. It will always turn out the correct size, regardless of the plotted scale.

12. The text size must be set in:

    a. The Text menu only.
    b. Both the Text and Dimensions menu.
    c. The Text, Dimension, and Plotter menus.

13. The most important thing to know about your drawings BEFORE you create your default drawings, is the:

    a. Text size.
    b. Paper size.
    c. Scale you will be plotting your drawing at.

Lesson 3: Basic Drafting Techniques

WHAT YOU WILL BE DOING:

YOU will use DataCAD to create a floor plan. You will add windows and doors, and use different kinds of snapping as well as coordinate input techniques. You will also organize the kinds of items you create (walls, doors, and windows) onto separate layers in your drawing.

Remember to reference *The DataCAD Operations Guide* when instructed. This section is your "quick" guide to DataCAD operations.

OBJECTIVES

Your lesson objectives, then, are to:

- Select a default drawing.
- Create walls.
- Change the snap increment.
- Change layers.
- Add windows.
- Add doors.
- Define a reference point to help place items.
- Use coordinate input

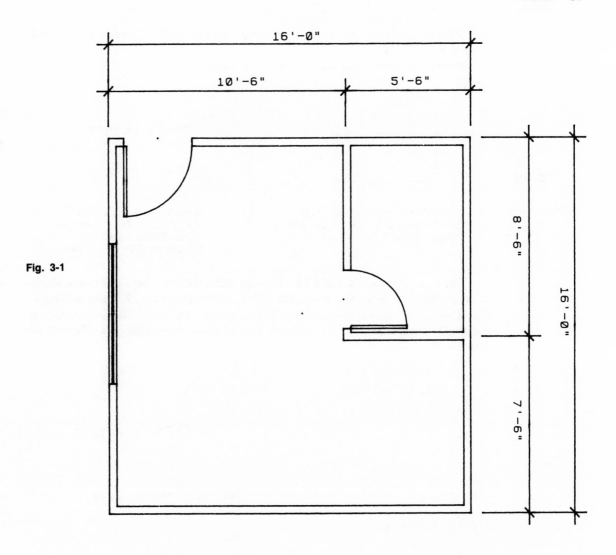

Fig. 3-1

WALLS

Walls are created easily using DataCAD. When you draw a wall, it looks like a double line. The space between the line is the wall "width". This space is accurate to the actual width you define for your wall. In other words, an internal wall may be one width, while an external wall another width, and the difference is accurately represented on your screen. (Fig. 3-2)

Fig. 3-2

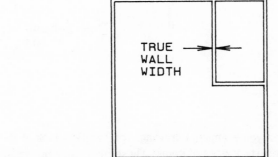

What you don't see when you are drawing your wall, is the "height" of your wall. Your wall is being drawn with the real floor, or "base" elevation, and the real ceiling, or "height" elevation. You are drawing a 3-dimensional wall! (Fig. 3-3)

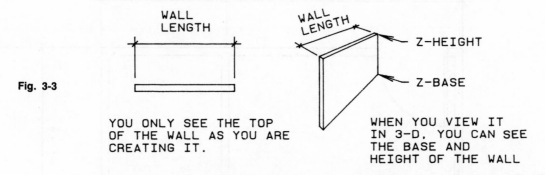

Fig. 3-3

WALL LENGTH

YOU ONLY SEE THE TOP OF THE WALL AS YOU ARE CREATING IT.

WALL LENGTH — Z-HEIGHT — Z-BASE

WHEN YOU VIEW IT IN 3-D, YOU CAN SEE THE BASE AND HEIGHT OF THE WALL

This is all automatic in DataCAD. You can define different base and height elevations for your walls before you draw them. This is referred to as the "Z" base and height. The X and Y coordinates are parallel to the screen in ortho view. The Z coordinate is the height of your walls, which is perpendicular to the screen in ortho view. This is illustrated in Fig. 3-4.

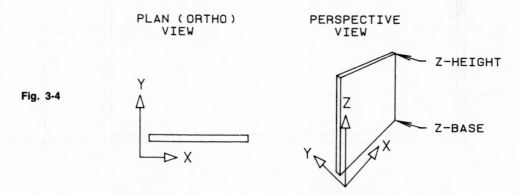

Fig. 3-4

PLAN (ORTHO) VIEW

PERSPECTIVE VIEW

Z-HEIGHT
Z-BASE

The beginning base and height elevations, as shown in Fig. 3-5, are set to:

Z-base = 0.0
Z-height = 8.0

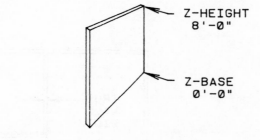

Fig. 3-5

Z-HEIGHT
8'-0"

Z-BASE
0'-0"

LAYERS

When you examine a drawing, you naturally look at the entities (lines, arcs, etc.) as being certain types of items. These items may be walls, doors, windows, property lines, among other types of items that appear in your drawings.

When you create one type of item, such as walls, you will want to separate it from other types in your drawing. This is done by using "layers". You will put your walls on a layer called "Walls". When you create a different type of item, such as doors, you will separate that item onto another layer. Doors will reside on the "Doors" layer. When you create windows, you will put them on the "Windows" layer. This type of item layering helps you organize the entities in your drawing, as illustrated in Fig. 3-6.

Fig. 3-6

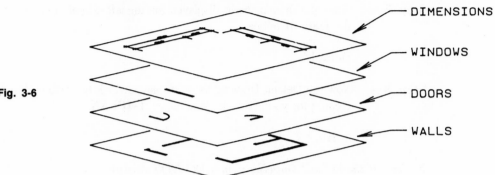

The concept of layering started with the pin graphics technique used in manual drafting, often called overlaying or overlay drafting. This technique permits items pertaining to certain disciplines to be divided onto separate sheets for many different reasons.

The same idea is used in your CADD drawings. When each type of entity is separated onto layers, then a series of layers can be viewed, plotted, and worked on independently or in conjunction with other entities in the drawing. (Fig. 3-7)

Fig. 3-7

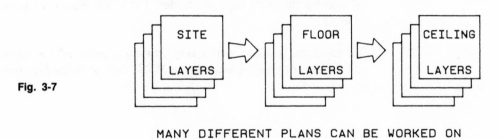

MANY DIFFERENT PLANS CAN BE WORKED ON
USING THE SAME BASE LAYERS, AND TURNING
ON AND OFF LAYERS FOR THAT DISCIPLINE

During this lesson, you will learn how easy it is to apply these techniques and to learn the essential skills for beginning drafting with DataCAD!

STARTING THE FLOOR PLAN

To begin the floor plan (project 001), you will first want to create a drawing file. This drawing file will use the **1-4PLAN** default drawing you created during the **Initial Drawing Set-Up** in the previous lesson.

Step 1 – *If you are not in the DataCAD program,* type in:

      cd \ mtec
      dcad

If you are presently in the DataCAD program, Start a new drawing by selecting:

File I/O (Utility menu)
New Dwg
Yes

Step 2 – When the Drawing list is displayed (on the left side of the screen), select the **Default** option.

Default

Step 3 – Now the Default Drawing list is displayed. Pick the default drawing you created for your ¼ scale floor plans: **1-4PLAN**.

1-4PLAN

Notice - If the Default Drawing names DO NOT appear:

1) *Pick the* **New Path** option.

2) Type in and **[Enter]: default**

3) Now pick the default you will use: **1-4PLAN**

Step 4 – Now that your default drawing has been set, you will want to create a special drawing directory (special "folder") that will hold your personal drawings.

This pathname is where your lesson drawing projects will be stored on your computer (a special folder in the MTEC drawer of the file cabinet). See Fig. 3-8.

Fig. 3-8

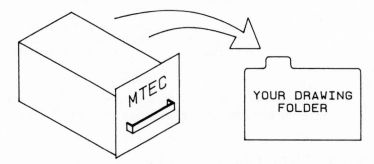

YOUR DRAWINGS WILL GO IN A SPECIAL DIRECTORY

Step 5 – Pick the **New Path** option.

New Path

Step 6 – Type in your first or last name for the directory name. This way, you will always be able to identify whose practice drawings are in this directory. Later, you will name your directories by *project name* instead of your name. (only 8 alphanumeric characters are allowed.) Remember to press **[Enter]**.

yourname

Step 7 –   Since this is a new directory, a prompt will be displayed that informs you
this directory does not exist, as in Fig. 3-9. If this directory already exists
(perhaps you created it before), this prompt will not be displayed.

Fig. 3-9

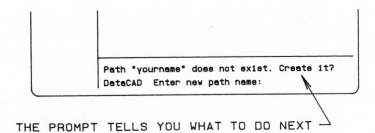

Path "yourname" does not exist. Create it?
DataCAD Enter new path name:

THE PROMPT TELLS YOU WHAT TO DO NEXT ⌐

Step 8 –   Select the **Yes** option to create your new directory.

Yes

Step 9 –   Now that you have defined the directory for your practice drawings, you
do not have to go through these steps again. The directory will stay active until you tell the system you want to use another directory.

Of course, if you are sharing this computer with others that use the
DataCAD program, they may want to switch the path to their own directory. In this case, you will have to reset your pathname before you start
work on your drawings.

Step 10 –   Type in the name of your drawing project: **PLAN1**.

plan1

Step 11 –   Your drawing file will be created, and you are ready to begin drawing!

DRAWING WALLS

Place project PLAN001 (Fig. 3-10) by your workstation for easy reference. Notice
that your project has exterior walls, interior walls, doors, and windows. First, you will
make the exterior walls. This is easily done by using the ''drawing walls'' mode and
either picking the placement of the wall with your cursor, or by using relative cartesian
coordinates.

Step 1 –   Make sure your **Walls** layer is active. If it is not, then press the **[Tab]**
key until ''Walls'' appears in the **Status area** of your screen, as in Fig.
3-10.

[Tab]

Fig. 3-10

"WALLS"
SHOULD
APPEAR
IN STATUS
AREA

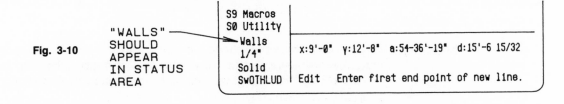

S9 Macros
S0 Utility
Walls
1/4"
Solid
SWOTHLUD

x:9'-0" y:12'-8" a:54-36'-19" d:15'-6 15/32

Edit   Enter first end point of new line.

Step 2 - Press the wall = key. This is the quick key to turn from the "drawing lines" mode, to "drawing walls".

=

*Notice - The lines mode should have been active, and you should get a prompt that asks you to indicate a wall width. If you were set for walls already, you will be toggled to the lines mode ("Now drawing lines"). If you are not presented with a prompt to type in (enter) a wall width, just press the = key again.

Step 3 - The user prompt asks you to establish a wall thickness. Notice that it is already set to **4"**. You will accept this value by pressing [Enter].

[Enter]

Step 4 - You will draw the EXTERIOR walls first. Notice that these walls are dimensioned to the *outside* of the walls. You will want to use an option in DataCAD called SIDES to draw your walls.

Pick the **Architct** option, found in the EDIT menu.

Architct

Step 5 - Pick the **Sides** option, until a * appears in front of the option (*Sides).

*Sides

Step 6 - Press mouse button **3** to quit.

Step 7 - Pick the start point of your wall with your cursor, using mouse button **1**, as indicated in Fig. 3-11. Make sure the start point is inside the border rectangle.

Fig. 3-11

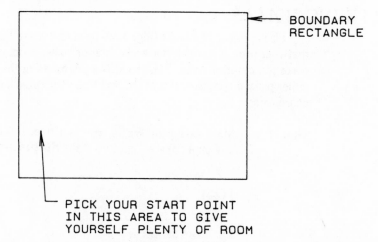

BOUNDARY
RECTANGLE

PICK YOUR START POINT
IN THIS AREA TO GIVE
YOURSELF PLENTY OF ROOM

Step 8 - Pick the second corner of your wall, using the grid as reference for measuring. You will notice that the coordinate readout displays the distance you are picking. "Picking" is one way to determine item placement (such as placing your wall). (Fig. 3-12)

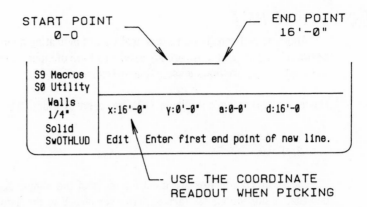

Fig. 3-12

Step 9 - Since you have set the "Sides" option, the system will now prompt you to pick the *other* side of the wall. This will be the *undimensioned* side of the wall, which in this case is the inside. Pick anywhere on the other side you wish the inside wall should be drawn, as illustrated in Fig. 3-13.

Fig. 3-13

ZOOMING IN

Step 10 - Notice that your first wall is drawn, but appears very small. You will want to "zoom in", or "Window in", to see the wall better.

Press the / key. This is the same key that has the **?** on it.

/

Step 11 - Now pick two diagonal points around the wall that you drew, as indicated in Fig. 3-14.

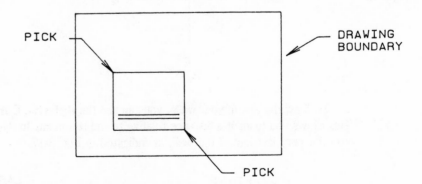

Fig. 3-14

Step 12 - The wall appears bigger on your screen. Press mouse button **3** once, to quit back to drawing walls. Notice that the cursor is still connected to your wall, and you can continue drawing!

COORDINATE INPUT

Another, and usually more practical way of indicating a length for a wall is by using *coordinate input*. You have already used this type of input when you created the border rectangle in the previous lesson (Initial Drawing Set-Up).

There are two major coordinate systems used by DataCAD. They are:

1. Cartesian
2. Polar

Cartesian coordinates are used for most of the simple **X,Y** movements. **X** is the axis that is horizontal, or "across" the screen. **Y** is the axis that is vertical, or "up and down" the screen. (Fig. 3-15)

Fig. 3-15

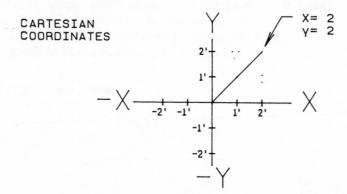

Polar coordinates are typically used for defining angles. An example of polar coordinates is illustrated in Fig. 3-16.

Fig. 3-16

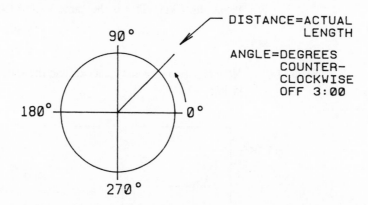

To draw the rest of your walls, you can use the **Relative Cartesian** coordinates. This allows you to input a distance relative to the last point. In this case, the last point was the very last end of the wall, as indicated in Fig. 3-17.

Fig. 3-17

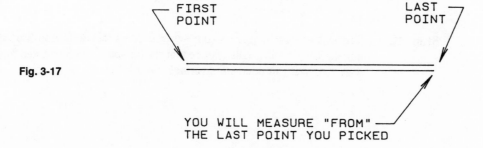

Step 1 – Your coordinates should already be set to **Relative Cartesian**, since that was the last setting you used when you created your Default Drawing. To double check this, press the **[Insert]** key until **Relative Coordinates** appear as the input mode.

   [Insert]

Step 2 – Press the **[Space bar]** to invoke the coordinate mode.

   [Space bar]

Step 3 – You will now be prompted to **Enter the relative X distance**. Since you are creating a vertical wall (X = horizontal and Y = vertical), you will not enter a relative **X** distance. Press **[Enter]**.

   [Enter]

Step 4 – Next, you are prompted to **Enter a relative Y distance**. Type in **16**, and press **[Enter]**.

   16

Step 5 – Pick on the inside of the wall, for the "other side", as indicated in Fig. 3-18.

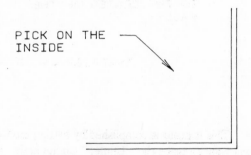

PICK ON THE
INSIDE

Fig. 3-18

Step 6 – Press the **[Space bar]** again.

   [Space bar]

Step 7 – Type in the −**X** distance for the next wall: −**16**.

   X = −16
   Y = 0

Step 8 – Pick on the inside for the other side of the wall.

Step 9 – To finish the exterior walls, place the cursor by the beginning of the first wall, and object snap to it using mouse button **2**.

   Remember to pick on the inside for the other side of the wall.

Step 10 – When your exterior walls are complete, press mouse button **3** to detach the cursor.

Step 11 – Your drawing should look like Fig. 3-19.

YOUR EXTERIOR
WALLS!

Fig. 3-19

DRAWING THE INTERIOR WALLS

You are ready to add the interior walls for your project. Notice that the interior walls are dimensioned to the centers, unlike the exterior walls which were dimensioned to the outside. (See Fig. 3-20)

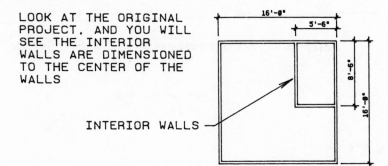

LOOK AT THE ORIGINAL
PROJECT, AND YOU WILL
SEE THE INTERIOR
WALLS ARE DIMENSIONED
TO THE CENTER OF THE
WALLS

Fig. 3-20

INTERIOR WALLS ⟶

This is easily accomplished by setting the **Center** option in the Architct menu. You will want to make the "Center" option active (instead of the Sides option), whenever your walls are dimensioned to centerlines.

Step 1 – Pick the **Architct** option, found in the EDIT menu.

Architct

Step 2 – Pick the **Center** option until it is active (*Center).

Center

Step 3 – Remember to press mouse button **3** to quit.

REFERENCING A CORNER POINT

Now that the Center option is set, you are ready to begin drawing your interior walls. Notice that the interior wall (illustrated in Fig. 3-21) is dimensioned from a corner of your exterior wall. To make placement of this wall easier, DataCAD allows you to measure from this point, by defining the corner as a "reference point".

Step 4 - Press the ~ key. (DO NOT press the [Shift] key with the ~ key, as this would change the action of the key.) This is a quick key to establish a reference point. (Fig. 3-21)

~

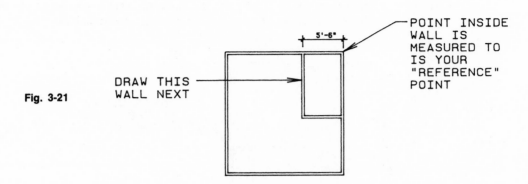

Fig. 3-21

DRAW THIS WALL NEXT

5'-6"

POINT INSIDE
WALL IS
MEASURED TO
IS YOUR
"REFERENCE"
POINT

Step 5 - Object snap to the outside upper right corner of the exterior wall, as illustrated in Fig. 3-22. Be sure to use the mouse button **2**!

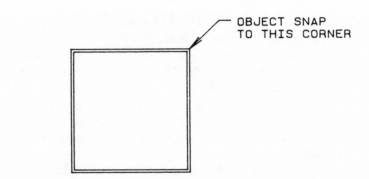

Fig. 3-22

OBJECT SNAP
TO THIS CORNER

Step 6 - Move your cursor back to this corner again, and notice that it now reads out as the 0,0 coordinate location! (Fig. 3-23)

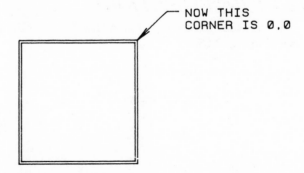

Fig. 3-23

NOW THIS
CORNER IS 0.0

Step 7 - Press the [Space bar] to invoke the relative coordinate mode.

[Space bar]

Step 8 - Type in – **5.6** in the **X** direction (5 feet 6 inches). This will define the start point of the interior wall.

$$X = -5.6$$
$$Y = 0$$

Step 9 – Now type in the length of your wall, –**8.6**.

$$X = 0$$
$$Y = -8.6$$

Step 10 – Finish your wall by picking the last endpoint using mouse button **1**, and using mouse button **3** to quit. Your drawing should look like Fig. 3-24.

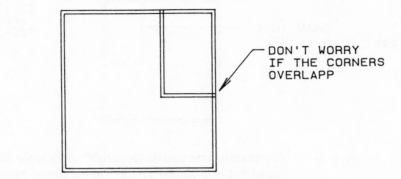

Fig. 3-24

DON'T WORRY
IF THE CORNERS
OVERLAPP

REFERENCING THE DATACAD OPERATIONS GUIDE

Turn to the section called **WALLS** in Appendix A: The DataCAD Operation Guide. It will be close to the end, since the sections are alphabetical. Notice that the name of the operations are listed on the left side of the page, while the "1,2,3" steps to follow are listed on the right side.

This is the page you may want to reference later, when you are creating walls in your own projects. Notice that the steps are written in a short, concise format. These instructions are designed to complement your lesson instructions and to remind you how each operation works.

Notice that one of the operations listed for WALLS is "Cleaning up wall intersections after they are created". These are the steps you will be following next. Examine them briefly before continuing.

CLEANING UP INTERSECTIONS

Once you've created your interior walls, you will want to clean up the intersections noted in Fig. 3-25.

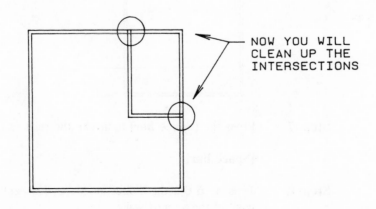

Fig. 3-25

NOW YOU WILL
CLEAN UP THE
INTERSECTIONS

Step 1 – Pick the **Cleanup** option from the EDIT menu.

        Cleanup

Step 2 – Pick the **T Intsct** option. (T-intersection.)

        T Intsct

Step 3 – Pick two points indicating a rectangle around the first intersection you want to clean up, as indicated in Fig. 3-26.

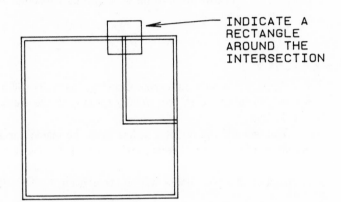

Fig. 3-26

Step 4 – Pick the line of the wall you want the interior wall trimmed to, as indicated in Fig. 3-27.

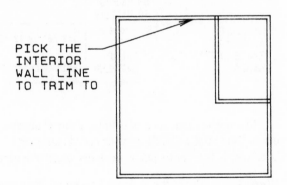

Fig. 3-27

Step 5 – Your wall will be trimmed, as in Fig. 3-28.

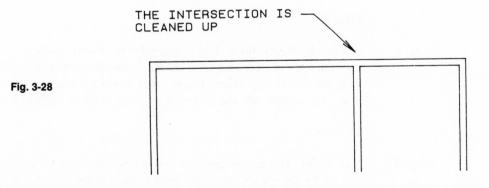

Fig. 3-28

Step 6 -   If your wall is NOT trimmed, and you are given a message that two end-points must be indicated, the system is trying to tell you it found *more* than two endpoints. This could mean that you have a small segment of a line in this area. (Sometimes this happens because you are not practiced with mouse input device, and double pick as you are drawing.)

This is easy to correct, by using the Erase option, and erase by area, indicating a small area around the intersection you are trying to clean up. Only the fully surrounded lines will be erased.

Step 7 -   Follow these same steps (Steps 1 through 5) to clean up the other intersection.

ADDING DOORS

When you add doors to your drawing, the walls will be automatically cut. You can set this so that they are *not cut* (by turning off the Cutout option) but this is usually not desired.

You will add the doors 3 inches from the inside corners of the walls. Again, this is achieved by using the "reference" key [~] and object snap to indicate a corner point.

Remember that your doors will be created on the DOORS layer.

Step 1 -   Press the [Tab] key until the layer is changed to **Doors**. (Fig. 3-29)

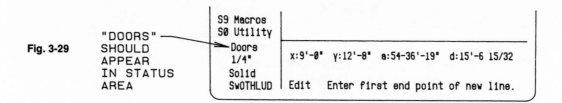

Fig. 3-29   "DOORS"   ——   SHOULD   APPEAR   IN STATUS   AREA

```
S9 Macros
S0 Utility
Doors
1/4"
Solid
SwOTHLUD

x:9'-0"  y:12'-8"  a:54-36'-19"  d:15'-6 15/32

Edit    Enter first end point of new line.
```

In a normal sequence of events, you will always add the walls first, then insert the doors INTO the walls. Since your coordinate mode is already set, and the correct layer is active, it is easy to put your doors exactly where you want them.

Step 1 -   Press the **A** key. This should put you in the Architect menu.

A

Step 2 -   Pick the **DoorSwng** option.

DoorSwng

Step 3 -   Pick the **LyrSrch** option. This option tells the system which layer contains the walls you want cut when you insert the doors on the active layer. (You may have many different layers with different kinds of walls if you wish. This option tells the system which one of those walls to cut.)

LyrSrch

Step 4 -   Pick **Walls**. This is now the layer you will be searching for your walls. You will not have to perform these steps again until you begin a new drawing, as DataCAD will remember that you have set the Walls layer as the layer to cut when you insert doors.

Walls

Step 5 – The prompt asks you to **Enter Hinge side of door**.

Since door jambs are measured off of the inside corner, you will want this as your reference point. Press the ~ key, and **Object snap** to this corner, as indicated in Fig. 3-30.

Fig. 3-30

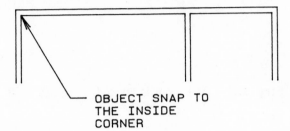

OBJECT SNAP TO
THE INSIDE
CORNER

Step 6 – Once you have indicated this corner as your reference point, press the **[Space bar]**.

[Space bar]

Step 7 – The user prompt will ask you to **Enter relative x distance**. Type in **0.4** for 0 feet, 4 inches. (Remember that you should always press **[Enter]** after you type something in, or press mouse button **2** to enter). You do not want to move in the **Y** direction this time.

X = 0.4
Y = 0

Step 8 – Now the prompt asks you to **Enter strike side of door**. Press the **[Space bar]** again.

[Space bar]

Step 9 – Type in the width of the door: **3** feet, for the relative X distance, and 0 feet for the Y direction.

X = 3
Y = 0

Step 10 – Pick on the inside of the room for the **direction of swing**. (Fig. 3-31)

Fig. 3-31

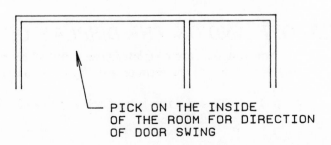

PICK ON THE INSIDE
OF THE ROOM FOR DIRECTION
OF DOOR SWING

Step 11 – Pick on the outside of the building for the **outside of the wall**, as in Fig. 3-32. This pick determines where the centerpoint (for dimensioning) will be placed.

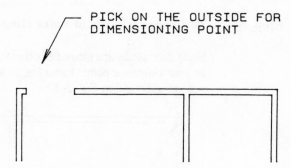

PICK ON THE OUTSIDE FOR
DIMENSIONING POINT

Fig. 3-32

Step 12 – Your door is created, as in Fig. 3-33.

YOUR DOOR IS CREATED

Fig. 3-33

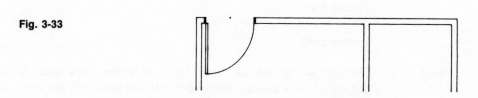

Step 13 – Create the second door, **4″** from the inside corner, this time using the **relative y distance**. This door is 2′6″ in width. (Fig. 3-34)

Remember to use the ~ key, object snap for the reference corner, and the **[Space bar]** to invoke coordinate mode.

CREATE THE
BATHROOM
DOOR

Fig. 3-34

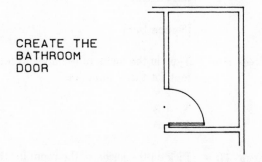

TURNING OFF AND ON THE DISPLAY OF LAYERS

Now that you have completed your walls and doors on two different layers, you may want to try turning them on and off to see how they work.

Step 1 – Press **L**. This is the quick way to enter the Layers option found in the UTILITY menu.

L

Step 2 - Pick the **On / Off** option, to turn the layers "on and off".

On / Off

Step 3 - The layers will be displayed. Notice that most layers have a star * in front of the name. This means they are **displayed**.

The **DOORS** layer will have a **$** in front of it. (Fig. 3-35) This means the layer is **active**. In other words, if you created anything, it would reside and appear in this layer.

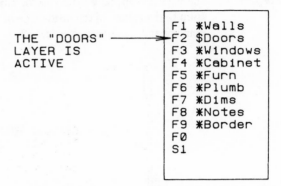

THE "DOORS"
LAYER IS
ACTIVE

```
F1 *Walls
F2 $Doors
F3 *Windows
F4 *Cabinet
F5 *Furn
F6 *Plumb
F7 *Dims
F8 *Notes
F9 *Border
F0
S1
```

Fig. 3-35

Step 4 - Press the **[Tab]** key. Did the **$** move to the next layer? Notice that this layer now appears in the **settings area** of your display screen.

Step 5 - Pick the **WALLS** layer with your cursor. The * will toggle off. The WALLS layer will be turned off from displaying. (Fig. 3-36)

THE WALLS ARE
TURNED OFF, AND
ONLY THE DOORS
ARE DISPLAYED

Fig. 3-36

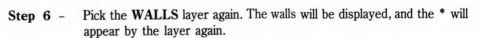

Step 6 - Pick the **WALLS** layer again. The walls will be displayed, and the * will appear by the layer again.

Step 7 - When you are done turning the layers off and on, make sure they are all ON (*). Then press mouse button **3** to quit.

CREATING WINDOWS

The window in your project is located in the center of the wall. You will set the center option in windows, and object snap to the center of this wall for window placement.

Step 1 - Make sure the **Windows** layer is active before you add the windows. Remember to press the **[Tab]** key until **Windows** appears as the active layer.

[Tab]

Step 2 - Press **A** to enter the Architect menu.

A

Step 3 –   Pick **Windows**.

Windows

Step 4 –   Pick the **Sides** option until the * IS TURNED OFF. This will allow you to "create windows about a center", by defining a centerpoint. The message line will say: **Windows defined by center and jamb**.

Sides

Step 5 –   The user prompt now asks you to: **Enter center of window. Object snap** to the center of the inside face of the wall, as indicated in Fig. 3-37. Remember to use mouse button **2**.

Fig. 3-37

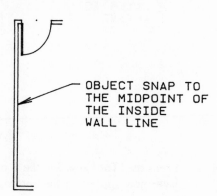

OBJECT SNAP TO
THE MIDPOINT OF
THE INSIDE
WALL LINE

Step 6 –   Now the prompt asks you to: **Enter one jamb of window**. You will use coordinate input. Press the **[Space bar]**.

[Space bar]

Step 7 –   Type in a **relative y distance** of **3** feet.

X = 0
Y = 3

Step 8 –   Now pick a **point on the outside of the wall**, shown in Fig. 3-38.

Fig. 3-38

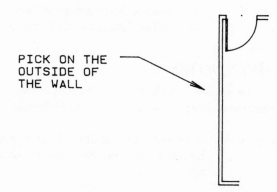

PICK ON THE
OUTSIDE OF
THE WALL

Step 9 – Your window is created, as illustrated in Fig. 3-39. Press mouse button **3** to quit.

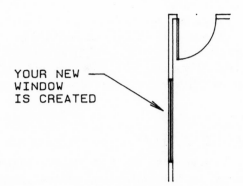

Fig. 3-39

YOUR NEW —
WINDOW
IS CREATED

REFERENCING THE DATACAD OPERATIONS GUIDE

Turn to the section in your *DataCAD Operations Guide* called **DOORS & WINDOWS**. Since the operations are listed *alphabetically*, look for this section under ''D''. Notice that the steps you used to add these components to your drawing are found in this section. This section is your quick reference for adding doors and windows to your own drawings.

To manipulate the layers in your drawing, you will want to reference the section called LAYERS. You will find that there are other kinds of operations that can be accomplished with your layers!

AUTOMATIC SAVE

As you worked on your drawing, you may have noticed that every five minutes or so it was ''AUTOMATICALLY SAVED''. This is a process that saves your current drawing, or ''workfile'' to a save-file.

This save-file is ''temporary''. This means it is created only while you are working on your drawing. When you quit DataCAD normally, it is erased. If you experience a problem with DataCAD (such as a power failure), then DataCAD is not exited normally, and the save-file still exists. You would be able to recover the last ''auto save'' of the drawing you were working on from this temporary save-file when you restart DataCAD.

The Auto save-file is not a replacement for permanently saving your drawing. You can only do this using the File I/O, Save Dwg options.

SAVING YOUR DRAWING

Every hour or so that you work on DataCAD, you should permanently save your drawing. It takes just a few seconds.

Step 1 – Pick the **FILE I / O** option found in the UTILITY menu. This stands for File In and Out (saving and retrieving drawing files).

File I / O

Step 2 – Pick the **Save Dwg** option. Your drawing will be permanently saved to the hard disk, with the name you gave it when you started your drawing. That is all there is to it!

Save Dwg

DATACAD "QUICK KEYS"

You have used some quick keys to enter menus in DataCAD. Quick keys allow you to access menus without having to pick the options from the screen. There are many more quick keys on the *DataCAD Keyboard Layout*, included in this book.

Caution – The quick keys are updated and changed almost everytime the DataCAD software is updated. The DataCAD Keyboard Layout is updated to the most recent 3.6 software. If you have an earlier version of DataCAD, many of these keys will not apply. You could, however, test your keys and create your own Keyboard Layout for your use.

QUITTING DATACAD

If you are going directly to the next lesson, you will not want to exit DataCAD. You may exit DataCAD and continue your lessons later, if you wish, by following these steps.

To assure that your drawing is permanently saved when you leave DataCAD, make sure that you pick the YES option from the Quit menu.

Step 1 –   Press the **[Alt]** and **Q** keys, or pick **Quit** from the UTILITY menu. The Quit menu will be displayed.

[Alt] Q

Step 2 –   Pick **Yes**, and your file will be permanently saved, and you will leave DataCAD.

Yes

USER REMINDER - DO NOT PICK ABORT. Remember that picking **Abort** will "trash" your drawing, and NOT save any changes or additions you made to it.

DataCAD Exercise 3

Please complete the following exercise by reading each question carefully, then circling the letter that corresponds to the correct answer.

Review of the mouse keys:

1. The first (left most) button on the mouse is used to:

    a. Pick an option or pick on the screen.
    b. Object snap or to enter a typed value.
    c. Quit an operation or exit a menu.

2. The second (middle) button on the mouse is used to:

    a. Pick an option or pick on the screen.
    b. Object snap or to enter a typed value.
    c. Quit an operation or exit a menu.

3. The third (right most) button on the mouse is used to:

    a. Pick an option or pick on the screen.
    b. Object snap or to enter a typed value.
    c. Quit an operation or exit a menu.

4. To toggle to the UTILITY menu when you are in the EDIT menu, you press:

    a. Mouse button 3.
    b. Mouse button 2.
    c. = key.

Basic Drafting Review:

5. The quickest way to turn from lines to walls, or from walls to lines, is to use the:

    a. Menu option choices.
    b. < key.
    c. = key

6. To draw the exterior walls in your project, which were dimensioned to the outside of the walls, you used the:

    a. Sides option.
    b. Centers option.
    c. Exterior option.

7. To draw the interior walls, which were dimensioned to the center of the walls, you used the:

    a. Sides options.
    b. Centers option.
    c. Interior option.

8. In order to define a reference point, you press the:

    a. [Space Bar].
    b. ~ key while pressing the [Shift] key.
    c. ~ key.

9. The X,Y type of coordinates you used, is called:

   a. Relative polar.
   b. Absolute Cartesian.
   c. Relative Cartesian.

10. To set the coordinate input *mode*, you press the:

    a. [Ins] key.
    b. [Tab] key.
    c. [Alt] key.

11. To clean up wall intersections after you create them, you use the:

    a. Cleanup menu.
    b. Edit menu.
    c. Erase menu.

12. To erase the last item you created, you use the:

    a. Delete option.
    b. < less than key.
    c. > greater than key.

13. To erase an entire area at one time, you use the:

    a. Erase menu, Area option.
    b. [Shift] < keys together.
    c. [Shift] > keys together.

14. To erase items in your drawing by picking them one-at-a-time, you use the:

    a. Erase menu, make sure the Any option is active, then pick any item to erase.
    b. Erase menu, make sure the Entity option is active, then pick the items to erase.
    c. Change menu, Delete option, then pick the items to delete.

15. The Automatic-Save file is:

    a. Really good for permanently saving your drawing file.
    b. Only temporary. You would only retrieve it if DataCAD was halted abnormally (such as a power failure).
    c. Retrievable even if you quit DataCAD normally.

16. To permanently save your drawing file, you:

    a. Use the File I/O, Save Dwg options every hour or before a major change in your drawing, or pick Yes to save your drawing as you quit DataCAD.
    b. Let the Automatic-Save do it for you.
    c. Quit DataCAD, then pick the Abort option.

Lesson 4: Windowing

WHAT YOU WILL BE DOING:

You will use the several windowing functions available to control the display of your drawing. These techniques will help you get in closer to your drawing, in order to see the littlest details, move around your drawing, and view your drawing in it's entirety.

OBJECTIVES:

Your lesson objectives, then, are to:

- Window in to a small area of your drawing by defining an area to view.
- Window closer by using the Page Down key.
- Move away from your drawing using the Page Up key.
- Move across, up, and down your drawing using the arrows keys.
- Return your drawing to its full view.

Remember to reference the *DataCAD Operations Guide* when instructed. This section will be very useful when you are ready to learn more available windowing techniques.

WINDOWING

The term "*windowing*" means to manipulate the viewing window of your drawing. You are not changing the actual drawing in any way, and you are not "moving" the drawing. You are simply moving to another position to view it.

This might be a new concept to you, since you have always been able to look at the entire drawing you worked on when it was taped down to your board. On your computer, you are given two major ways to look at your drawing.

1. Window extends – A full window of your drawing. This is the easiest way to see everything, since the entire drawing is displayed on your screen. Detailed areas and text may be hard to examine, especially on large drawings.

2. Windowed in – An area is chosen to enlarge (magnify) for viewing. You will use this function often, in order to see the small details in your drawings. This is also called "zooming in".

Once you have defined the window you want to work in, you can quickly move it around your screen using quick keys!

QUICK KEYS FOR WINDOWING

There are 10 keys that are used to control your viewing window. They are illustrated in Fig. 4-1.

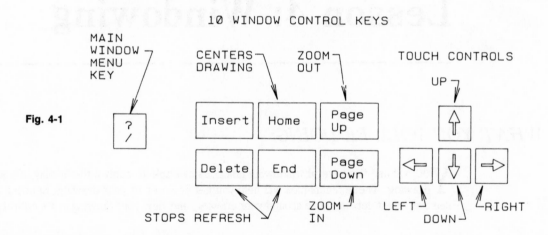

Fig. 4-1

PRACTICING WINDOWING TECHNIQUES

Step 1 – Make sure you have entered DataCAD, and have the floor plan you created displayed on your screen, as in Fig. 4-2.

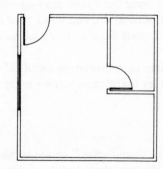

Fig. 4-2

WINDOWING IN

Step 2 – Press the / key, to enter the Window menu. This is a special key that allows you to change your window without leaving the menu you are presently in. You can be performing almost any function, press /, window in, then go back to what you were doing.

/

Step 3 – Pick two points to indicate a rectangle around the items you would want to magnify for viewing, as indicated in Fig. 4-3.

Fig. 4-3

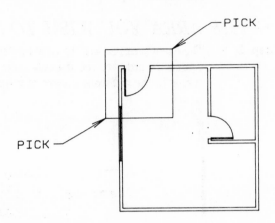

Step 4 – Your new window is displayed! (Fig. 4-4)

Fig. 4-4

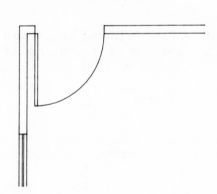

MOVING THE WINDOW

Moving your viewing window is called "panning". The term comes from photography, when the camera eye "pans" the landscape or subjects for the best frame.

Step 5 – Press the **[right arrow]** key. This is the key with the arrow pointing to the right. Your window will be moved to the right. Your drawing will appear to be shifted over to the left slightly.

If your arrow key doesn't work, press the [NumLock] key until the Num-Lock light is turned off.

[right arrow]

Step 6 – Try pressing the **[left arrow]** key. The window will move to the left.

[left arrow]

Step 7 – Now press the **[up arrow]** key. The window will move up.

[up arrow]

Step 8 – The **[down arrow]** key moves your window down.

[down arrow]

CENTERING THE AREA YOU WISH TO SEE

Step 9 – The exact area you wish to view may appear over to the right side of your screen. In order to see it easily, you will want to center it. Place your cursor to the righthand corner of your drawing, as indicated in Fig. 4-5.

Fig. 4-5

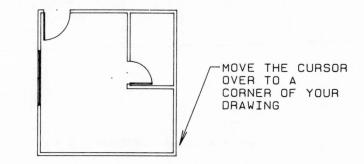

MOVE THE CURSOR
OVER TO A
CORNER OF YOUR
DRAWING

Step 10 – Press the **[Home]** key. The spot where your cursor appeared is now the center of your window! (Fig. 4-6) Just place the cursor on the area you want in the middle of the screen, and press **[Home]**.

[Home]

Fig. 4-6

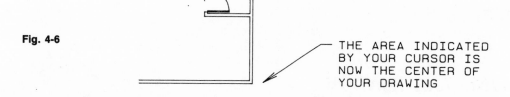

THE AREA INDICATED
BY YOUR CURSOR IS
NOW THE CENTER OF
YOUR DRAWING

GETTING A CLOSER LOOK

Step 11 – Press the **[Page Down]** key. On some keyboards, this key appears as **[Pg Dn]**. Your window will move in closer to your drawing. You can move in until your viewing window reaches its maximum limits. This may be 12″ scale.

You can remember to use [Page down], since you can think of moving your camera "down" to view your drawing. This would, of course, give you a magnified view of your drawing.

[Page Down]

TAKING A STEP BACK

Step 12 - Press the **[Page Up]** key. On some keyboards, this key appears as **[Pg Up]**. Your window will move away from the drawing. You can move out until the window reaches its limits. This may be 1:40 scale.

This is similar to moving your camera ''up'' and away from the drawing, which would, of course, give you a fuller and less detailed view.

[Page Up]

GETTING A FULL WINDOW

The fastest way to get a full view of your drawing is usually achieved by using the / key, and the Extends option.

Step 13 - Press the / key. This is the same key that has the **?** mark on it.

/

Step 14 - Pick **Extends**. The window that was previously calculated as the full window will be displayed. (Fig. 4-7)

Extends

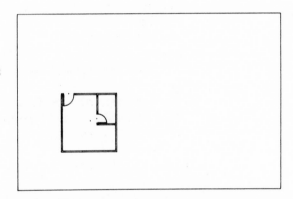

YOUR ENTIRE
DRAWING AND
DRAWING BORDER
IS DISPLAYED

Fig. 4-7

Step 15 - If your drawing is not perfectly centered and fully displayed, you will want to recalculate the window extends. Pick the **Re-Calc** option.

Re-Calc

Step 16 - Now your drawing is completely displayed. After recalculating the window extends, you can pick the Extends option, and it will remember this window. (This is important, since it takes more time to recalculate in big drawings.)

Step 17 - Practice windowing techniques to view different areas of your drawing.

REFERENCING THE DATACAD OPERATIONS GUIDE

The section you will want to reference in the *DataCAD Operations Guide* is called WINDOW VIEWS. This section describes other ways to control the window views that you will be using in your drawing when you become more experienced. A complete explanation is also available in the *DataCAD Users Manual* that came with your DataCAD program.

DataCAD Exercise 4

Please complete the following exercise by reading each question carefully, then circling the letter that corresponds to the correct answer.

1. To quickly enter the Window menu, you press the:

   a. \ key.
   b. / key.
   c. [Alt] / keys.

2. Moving your viewing window across the drawing, is called:

   a. Panning.
   b. Paging.
   c. Windowing in.

3. To move the window in closer to your drawing, you can use the:

   a. [Page Up] key.
   b. [Page Down] key.
   c. [right arrow] key.

4. To move the window to the right of your drawing, you use the:

   a. [left arrow] key.
   b. [Page Up] key.
   c. [right arrow] key.

5. To get a pre-calculated full view of your drawing, you press the:

   a. / key, then pick the Re-Calc option.
   b. / key, then pick the Extends option.
   c. [Page Up] key.

6. The Re-Calc option:

   a. Recalculates the window extends for your drawing, and takes a little longer than using the Extends option.
   b. Should always be used because it is much faster than the Extends option.
   c. Works the same as the Extends option.

Some review questions:

7. The second (middle) button on the mouse is used to:

   a. Pick an option or pick on the screen.
   b. Object snap or to enter a typed value.
   c. Quit an operation or exit a menu.

8. In order to define a reference point, you press the:

   a. [Space Bar].
   b. ~ key.
   c. X key.

9. The X,Y type of coordinates you used, is called:

   a. Relative polar.
   b. Absolute Cartesian.
   c. Relative Cartesian.

10. To set the coordinate input mode, you press the:

    a. [Ins] key.
    b. [Tab] key.
    c. [Alt] key.

11. To type in the actual coordinates, you press the:

    a. [Ins] key.
    b. [Space bar].
    c. [Tab] key.

Lesson 5:
Adding Symbols

WHAT YOU WILL BE DOING:

You will be using templates to add symbols to your drawing. You will also rotate symbols as you add them. During this lesson, you will be using some of the many symbols that are provided with the DataCAD Software. Later, during the **Creating Templates and Symbols** lesson, you will learn how to create your own symbols.

OBJECTIVES:

Your lesson objectives, then, are to:

- Define the correct directories for the templates you will use.
- Call up symbol templates.
- Retrieve symbols from the templates and place them on your drawing.
- Rotate the symbols into a new position as you place them.
- Adjust the height of the symbol.

Remember to reference your *DataCAD Operations Guide* when instructed.

TEMPLATES AND SYMBOLS

During this lesson, you will add the necessary furniture and plumbing to your floor plan. (See Fig. 5-1)

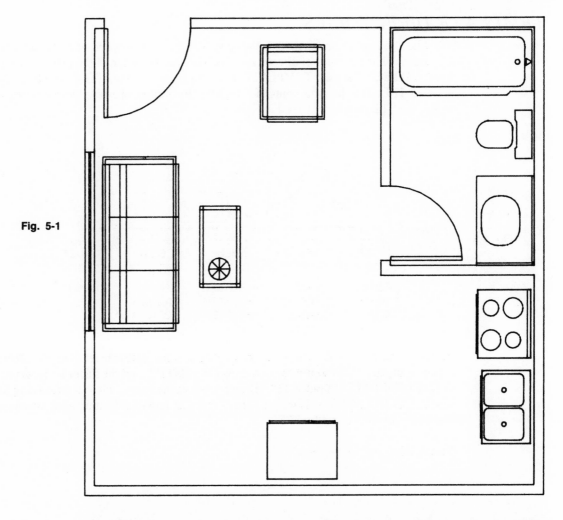

Fig. 5-1

The furniture and other items in your project are all pre-created symbols. DataCAD Symbols are attached to templates, as in Fig. 5-2, similar to the plastic drafting templates you may already use. Templates, then, are a way to organize related symbols together for easy retrieval.

Fig. 5-2

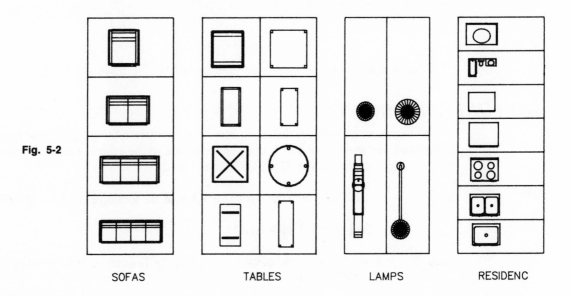

SOFAS   TABLES   LAMPS   RESIDENC

TEMPLATE DIRECTORIES

When you install DataCAD 3.6, the templates that are supplied with the software are organized into a series of directories. The main directory for all the DataCAD software is **MTEC**. The main TEMPLATE directory resides in the MTEC directory, and is called **TPL**. The different types of templates are further organized into directories within the TPL directory. (See Fig. 5-3)

Fig. 5-3

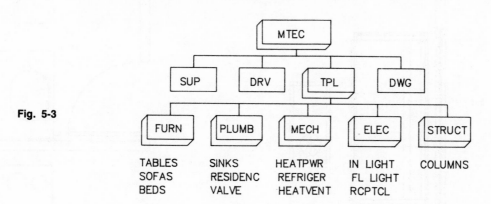

You can think of these directories as they relate to your filing cabinet. The file cabinet is your computer. A drawer of the cabinet is called MTEC, and the folder in the drawer for the TEMPLATES is called TPL. Each section in the folder, which is organizing the types of TEMPLATES, is labeled by that particular type. And within each section of the folder are the TEMPLATES!

This is illustrated in Fig. 5-4.

Fig. 5-4

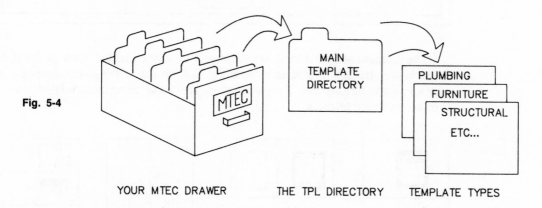

YOUR MTEC DRAWER   THE TPL DIRECTORY   TEMPLATE TYPES

GETTING A TEMPLATE

When you wish to add symbols, you first need to retrieve the template that holds the symbols you wish to use. For your living room, you will be using the template called SOFAS, which resides in the TPL/FURN directories.

Step 1 –   Press **[Tab]** until the layer that will hold the furniture is active: **FURN**.

            [Tab] (to the FURN layer)

Step 2 –   Press **T**. This is the quick way to enter the Template option, found in the UTILITY menu.

            T

Step 3 – Pick the **New Path** option. This option will allow you to define the correct directory for the template you wish to use.

New Path

Step 4 – Type in the directory names for the template, separating each name with the ⟍ key. (Do not add any space.)

tpl ⟍ furn

(Notice that you do not have to start the pathname with MTEC. This is because as you are using the program, you reside in the MTEC directory. Do NOT, however, start the directory pathname with a ⟍. This would cause the program to look for the directory *outside* of the MTEC directory.)

Step 5 – The templates that reside in the FURN directory will be displayed, as in Fig. 5-5.

Fig. 5-5

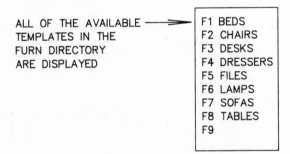

ALL OF THE AVAILABLE
TEMPLATES IN THE
FURN DIRECTORY
ARE DISPLAYED

F1 BEDS
F2 CHAIRS
F3 DESKS
F4 DRESSERS
F5 FILES
F6 LAMPS
F7 SOFAS
F8 TABLES
F9

Step 6 – Pick the template called **SOFAS.**

Step 7 – The symbols attached to the SOFAS template will be displayed, as indicated in Fig. 5-6.

Fig. 5-6

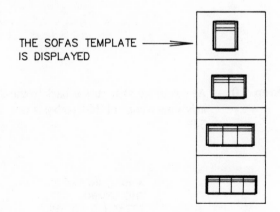

THE SOFAS TEMPLATE
IS DISPLAYED

ADDING SYMBOLS TO YOUR DRAWING

Step 8 –   Move your cursor over to the template symbols. Notice that, as the cursor is positioned over a symbol, the name of the symbol is displayed in the message area of your screen. (Fig. 5-7)

Fig. 5-7

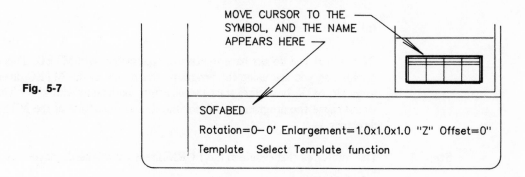

MOVE CURSOR TO THE
SYMBOL, AND THE NAME
APPEARS HERE

SOFABED

Rotation=0—0' Enlargement=1.0x1.0x1.0 "Z" Offset=0"

Template   Select Template function

Step 9 –   Pick the symbol for the **lounge,** as indicated in Fig. 5-8, by pressing mouse button **1.**

Fig. 5-8

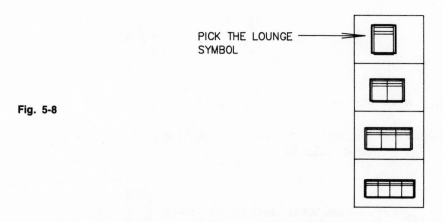

PICK THE LOUNGE
SYMBOL

Step 10 –   As you move your cursor back to the drawing area, you will notice a box indicating a copy of the symbol is now attached to your cursor. (See Fig. 5-9)

Fig. 5-9

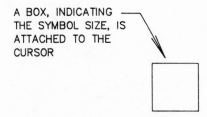

A BOX, INDICATING
THE SYMBOL SIZE, IS
ATTACHED TO THE
CURSOR

Step 11 – Place the lounge symbol in the living room, as in Fig. 5-10, by moving it into position with the cursor then pressing mouse button **1**.

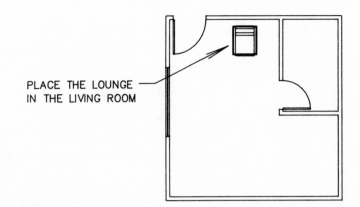

Fig. 5-10

PLACE THE LOUNGE
IN THE LIVING ROOM

Step 12 – Press mouse button **3** to quit placing the symbol.

ROTATING SYMBOLS

The other furniture symbols in your living room will have to be rotated 90 degrees. You can set the rotation value once, then all symbols you bring in will be rotated until you reset the value back to 0.

Step 1 – Pick **DymnRot** from the Template menu twice, in order to specify a rotation angle.

DymnRot
DymnRot

Step 2 – Pick the **90-0'** option.

90-0'

Step 3 – Pick the **sofa** symbol. Place it in the living room. Notice it is positioned at a 90 degrees rotation angle, as in Fig. 5-11.

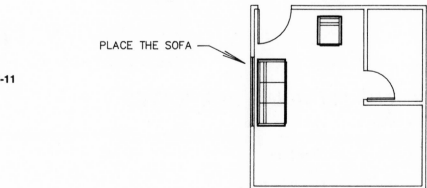

PLACE THE SOFA

Fig. 5-11

GETTING A NEW TEMPLATE

Now you are done with the FURN template. You will want to get the template called TABLES.

Step 1 –   Pick the **New File** option, found in the Template menu.

New File

Step 2 –   Pick the **TABLES** template.

TABLES

Step 3 –   The **TABLES** template is displayed, as in Fig. 5-12.

THE TABLES TEMPLATE →
IS DISPLAYED

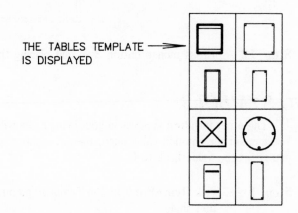

Fig. 5-12

Step 4 –   Place the **Coffee** table symbol in your drawing, as in Fig. 5-13.

PLACE THE COFFEE
TABLE IN THE LIVING
ROOM

Fig. 5-13

GETTING THE PLUMBING TEMPLATES

Step 1 –   Pick **New File.**

New File

Step 2 –   Pick **New Path.**

New Path

Step 3 – Type in the directory pathname for the plumbing templates.

tpl \ plumb

Step 4 – Once the plumbing templates are displayed, pick the **RESIDENC** template.

RESIDENC

Step 5 – The RESIDENC template is displayed, as in Fig. 5-14.

THE RESIDENC TEMPLATE
IS DISPLAYED

Fig. 5-14

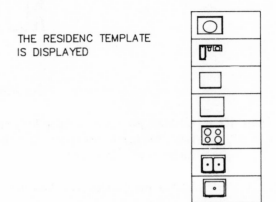

Step 6 – Pick the **BathGrup** symbol. Notice that it comes in at the same 90 degree angle you set for the previous symbols, as illustrated in Fig. 5-15. This is because a **rotation angle you define will stay set until you change it**. Since this is the wrong angle for this symbol, you will need to change the rotation to either **270**, or **–90**. Both angles will give the desired result.

THE BATHGROUP IS
IS STILL ROTATED
AT 90 DEGREES

YOU WILL CHANGE THIS

Fig. 5-15

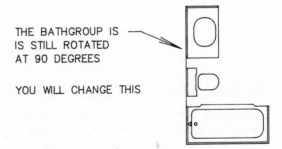

Step 7 – First, press mouse button **3** to drop the symbol.

Step 8 – Pick **DymnRot** twice. The first pick will turn on the Dynamic Rotation (allows you to drag the symbol "dynamically" into a rotation angle). The second pick will allow you to enter a specific angle.

Then, change the angle to **270**.

DymnRot
DymnRot
270

Step 9 –   Pick the symbol again and place it in your drawing. Notice it is now positioned in the correct angle. (See Fig. 5-16)

NOW THE BATHGROUP
SYMBOL FITS

Fig. 5-16

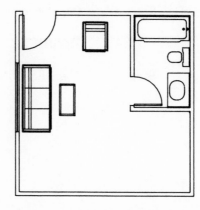

Step 10 –   Continue placing the symbols for your drawing that are found in this template, rotating as necessary. Use the second **Wardrode** symbol as the double door refrigerator.

Your drawing should now look like Fig. 5-17.

ADD THE REFRIGERATOR,
STOVE, AND DOUBLE SINK
TO YOUR PLAN

Fig. 5-17

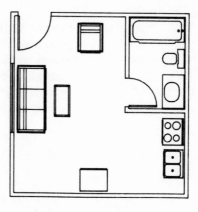

ADDING THE LAMP AT TABLE HEIGHT

There are times that you will want to adjust the **Z-Height** of your symbols. This is particularly true if you are working at multiple floor height, as in a two story building.

You have an occasion for changing the height of the symbol when you set your lamp on the top of the coffee table. The option to do this is called **Z Offset**. The Z Offset option is another option that remains set until you change it, so you will want to remember to do so after placing the lamp.

Step 1 –   Pick **New File.**

New File

Step 2 –   Pick **New Path**

New Path

Step 3 –   Type in the directory pathname for the **Lamps** template.

tpl \ furn

Step 4 –   Now pick the **LAMPS** template.

Lamps

Step 5 –   The Lamps template will be displayed, as in Fig. 5-18.

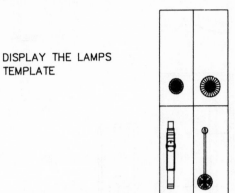

DISPLAY THE LAMPS
TEMPLATE

Fig. 5-18

Step 6 –   Pick the **Z Offset** option.

Z Offset

Step 7 –   Type in the height of the table. In this case, the table is 8½″ high. You will want to raise your lamp off the ground 8½″ also.

0.8.1/2

Step 8 –   Pick the lamp called **Ceramic**, and place it on your table. This is illustrated in Fig. 5-19.

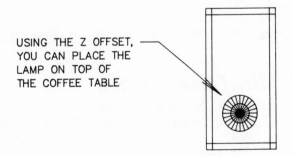

USING THE Z OFFSET,
YOU CAN PLACE THE
LAMP ON TOP OF
THE COFFEE TABLE

Fig. 5-19

Step 9 –   Pick the **Z Offset** option again.

Z Offset

Step 10 –   Change the offset value back to **0**.

0

Step 11 - Your drawing should now look like Fig. 5-20.

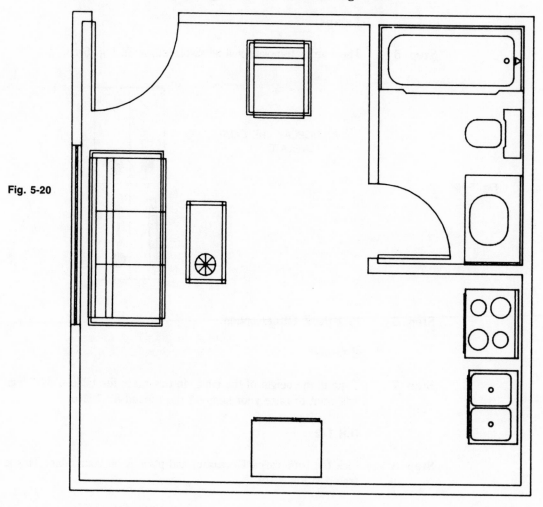

Fig. 5-20

Step 12 - File your drawing, using the **File I/O** menu, and the **Save Dwg** option.

TURNING THE TEMPLATES OFF

Step 13 - To turn the template off when you are through working with it, Pick the **TempOff** option, in the **Template** menu.

TempOff

THE DATACAD OPERATIONS GUIDE

Turn to the **SYMBOLS** section found in your *DataCAD Operations Guide*. Notice how there are many symbol type of operations listed in this section. You will want to use this section as you add symbols to your own projects.

DataCAD Exercise 5

Please complete the following exercise by reading each question carefully, then circling the letter that corresponds to the correct answer.

1. To quickly change layers, you press the:

   a. [Tab] key.
   b. [Alt] L keys.
   c. L key.

2. DataCAD symbols are attached to:

   a. Other symbols.
   b. Symbol libraries.
   c. Templates.

3. To change a template directory, you use the:

   a. New Dir option.
   b. New Path option.
   c. Tem Dir option.

4. To use a symbol, you first have to:

   a. Pick a library.
   b. Pick a template.
   c. Call up a symbol file.

5. The quick way to enter the Template menu, is to press the:

   a. A key.
   b. T key.
   c. [Alt] T keys.

6. To pick a symbol off the template, you use mouse button:

   a. 1.
   b. 2.
   c. 3.

7. To quit placing the symbol, you use the mouse button:

   a. 1.
   b. 2.
   c. 3.

8. To place a symbol at another angle, you use the:

   a. Angle option.
   b. DymnRot option.
   c. NewAngl option.

9. When you have set a rotation angle while placing a symbol, it:

   a. Automatically resets to 0 for the next symbol.
   b. Changes all of the rotation angles for the other symbols already placed in your drawing.
   c. Remains set for all new symbols you are adding, until you change it.

10. To open a new template, when you already have a template displayed, you pick:

   a. New File.
   b. StrtFile.
   c. NewTempl.

11. When you are working on the second floor of a building, before you pick a symbol you would want to set the:

   a. Z Base option in the Template menu.
   b. X Offset option in the Template menu.
   c. Z Offset option in the Template menu.

12. To use coordinate input, you press the:

   a. [Space Bar].
   b. [Alt] C keys.
   c. [Tab].

Lesson 6: Adding Dimensions and Text

WHAT YOU WILL BE DOING:

You will add dimensions to your project. You will also add notes to describe your drawing components.

OBJECTIVES:

Your lesson objectives, then, are to:

- Create horizontal and vertical dimensions.
- Create stringline dimensions.
- Create an Overall dimension.
- Add text to your drawing.
- Draw arrows.
- Change the size of the text.

Remember to reference your *DataCAD Operations Guide* when instructed. You will find many helpful sections that complement this lesson.

ADDING DIMENSIONS AND TEXT TO YOUR DRAWING

Dimensioning your drawing is fast in DataCAD. The text in your dimensions is automatically generated. This is because the system already knows how big or what length you have created your items. All you do is tell the system what you want dimensioned, and where you want the dimension to appear.

When you tell the system what it is you want dimensioned, remember to use OBJECT SNAP! This is to make sure you are "grabbing" onto the object you are dimensioning.

There are certain times, however, when you will not want to object snap to a corner of a wall. In your project, the interior walls are dimensioned to the centers. Although this is not common practice in residential design, it is in commercial design. When you create a dimension to the center, there is not a corner of the wall to grab onto. You will learn, then, how to dimension to a pick point.

Fig. 6-1

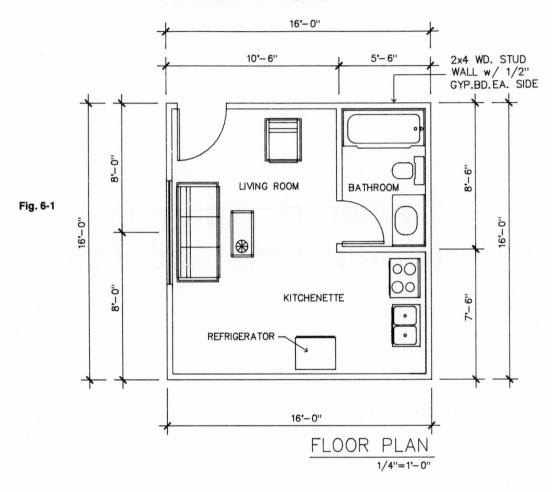

FOUR TYPES OF DIMENSIONS

There are four types of dimensioning available. They are shown in Fig. 6-2.

1. Linear
2. Angular
3. Diameter
4. Radius

Fig. 6-2

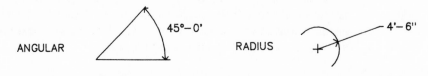

SETTING THE SNAP INCREMENTS

Notice the current cursor snap increments are set to **4″**. In order to pick at the center of the wall, you will want to change the snap to **2″**.

Step 1 – Press the **S** key. This is the quick way to enter the **Grids, GridSize, Set Snap** menus. *DO NOT press the [Shift] key.*

S

Step 2 – The prompt in the message area of your screen, will ask you to type in the X and Y increment values. Type in **0.2** for both the X and Y coordinates. This will set the value to **2 inches**.

X = 0.2
Y = 0.2

CREATING LINEAR DIMENSIONS

Step 1 – Press the **[Tab]** key until the correct layer is active: **DIMS**.

[Tab] (To the DIMS layer)

Step 2 – Press **D**. This is the quick way to enter the Dimension option, found in the UTILITY menu.

D

Step 3 – Pick the **Linear** option.

Linear

Step 4 – Pick the **Horiznt** option until it is active (***Horiznt**).

*Horiznt

Step 5 – Object snap to the first corner point of the wall to dimension, as illustrated in Fig. 6-3. USE MOUSE BUTTON **3**.

USE OBJECT SNAP
TO "SNAP" TO
THIS CORNER,
PLACING THE
CURSOR AS
SHOWN HERE

Fig. 6-3

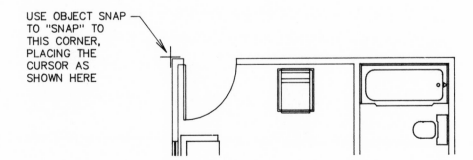

Step 6 -   Press the **X** key until your grid snap is on. The message line will say: **Snapping is ON**, as shown in Fig. 6-4. This will allow you to easily pick at 6″ increments.

X

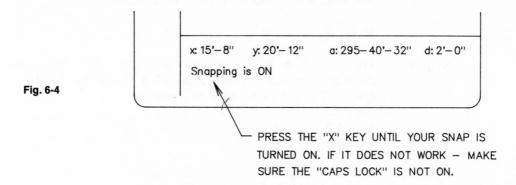

x: 15′– 8″   y: 20′– 12″   a: 295– 40′– 32″   d: 2′– 0″

Snapping is ON

PRESS THE "X" KEY UNTIL YOUR SNAP IS TURNED ON. IF IT DOES NOT WORK — MAKE SURE THE "CAPS LOCK" IS NOT ON.

Fig. 6-4

Step 7 -   Now pick the center point of the interior wall, as shown in Fig. 6-5, using grid snap to help you pick. USE MOUSE BUTTON **1**.

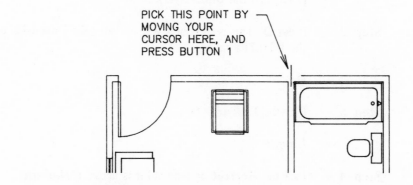

PICK THIS POINT BY MOVING YOUR CURSOR HERE, AND PRESS BUTTON 1

Fig. 6-5

Step 8 -   Move the cursor to place the height of the dimension, and pick with mouse button **1**. (See Fig. 6-6)

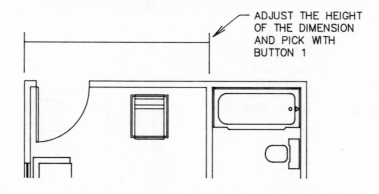

ADJUST THE HEIGHT OF THE DIMENSION AND PICK WITH BUTTON 1

Fig. 6-6

Step 9 -   The text will appear. (It may look like a small box.)

Step 10 -   Pick the **StrngLin** option (String Line).

Strnglin

Step 11 – Now object snap to the last corner, as indicated in Fig. 6-7.

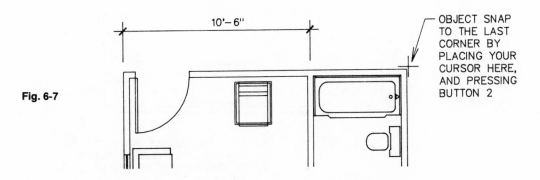

Fig. 6-7

Step 12 – The second dimension will pop up. (Fig. 6-8)

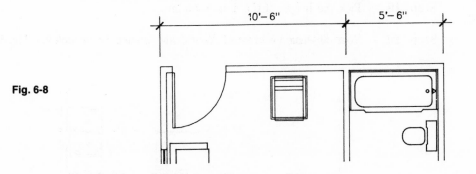

Fig. 6-8

Step 13 – Now press mouse button **3** to quit. You will be returned to the Linear Dimensions menu.

Step 14 – Pick the **OverAll** option.

    OverAll

Step 15 – The overall dimension will appear, as in Fig. 6-9.

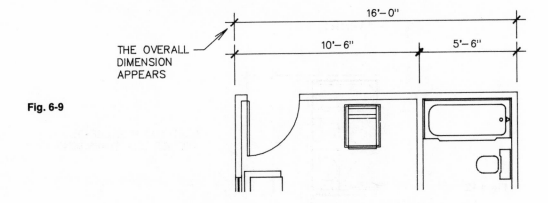

Fig. 6-9

Step 16 – To create the last horizontal dimension, pick the **Entity** option.

    Entity

Step 17 – Pick the line to dimension, as indicated in Fig. 6-10.

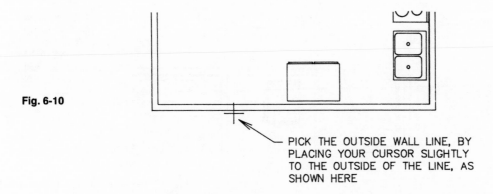

Fig. 6-10

PICK THE OUTSIDE WALL LINE, BY
PLACING YOUR CURSOR SLIGHTLY
TO THE OUTSIDE OF THE LINE, AS
SHOWN HERE

Step 18 – Pick the height of the dimension line.

Step 19 – Your dimension is created! Your drawing should now look like Fig. 6-11.

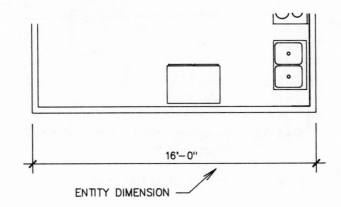

Fig. 6-11

16'–0"

ENTITY DIMENSION

Step 20 – Pick the **Verticl** option until it is active. This option allows you to create
the vertical dimensions in your drawing, as indicated in Fig. 6-12.

*Verticl

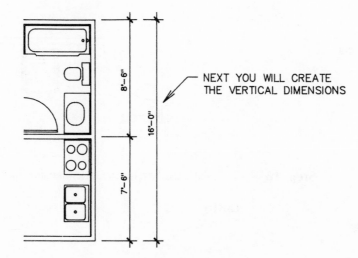

Fig. 6-12

NEXT YOU WILL CREATE
THE VERTICAL DIMENSIONS

Step 21 – Create the vertical dimensions for your project, shown in Fig. 6-13. Follow the same steps for creating the horizontal dimensions. Be sure to object snap when applicable.

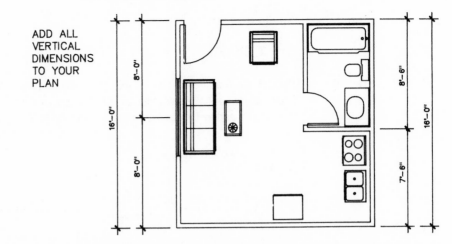

ADD ALL
VERTICAL
DIMENSIONS
TO YOUR
PLAN

Fig. 6-13

Step 22 – Be sure to save your drawing, using **File I/O**, and the **Save Dwg** option.

REFERENCING THE DATACAD OPERATIONS GUIDE

If you turn to the DIMENSIONING section of the *DataCAD Operations Guide*, you will find easy to follow steps for creating single dimensions, string line dimensions, and other dimensioning operations.

To complement the last part of this lesson, you will also find additional operations for creating the notes in your drawing, under the section called TEXT.

ADDING NOTES TO YOUR DRAWING

In DataCAD, notes are referred to as TEXT, and are very easy to create. You just pick a spot to place the text, then type it in!

Step 1 – Press the **[Tab]** key to change the active layer to: **NOTES**. (Reminder: If you use [Shift] and [Tab] together, you can scroll backwards through the layer list.)

[Tab]

Step 2 – Pick the **Text** option, found in the UTILITY menu.

Text

Step 3 – Pick the position for the LIVING ROOM text, as indicated. Notice that the shape of your cursor has changed. The new shape and size of the cursor now represents the size that your text is currently set to. (Fig. 6-14)

FIRST PICK A START POINT FOR YOUR
TEXT. NOTICE THE CURSOR NOW
INDICATES THE TEXT SIZE.

Fig. 6-14

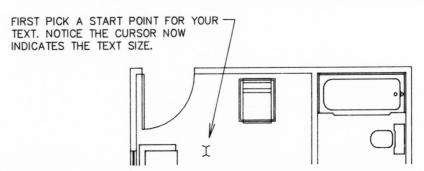

Step 4 –   Press the **[Caps Lock]** key in order to easily type in capitalized letters.

[Caps Lock]

Step 5 –   Type in the text.

LIVING ROOM

Step 6 –   If you desired a second line of text, you would press the **[Enter]** key. Since you do not have a second line of text, press mouse button **3** to quit. The text is added to your drawing, as in Fig. 6-15.

THE TEXT IS ADDED TO
YOUR DRAWING

Fig. 6-15

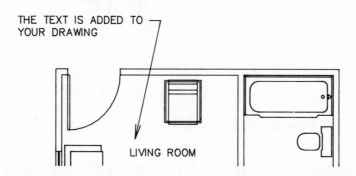

LIVING ROOM

Step 7 –   Notice the text for your REFRIGERATOR also has an arrow. This is easy to do. First, you add the text, then you add an arrow line.

Step 8 –   Pick the starting position for the REFRIGERATOR text, and type it in.

REFRIGERATOR

Step 9 –   Press mouse button **3** once, to quit back to the TEXT menu.

Step 10 –   Pick the **Arrows** option. This option allows you to draw a line that ends with an arrow. The last line picked will be where the arrow appears.

Arrows

Step 11 –   Pick the start point of the leader line, as indicated in Fig. 6-16.

Fig. 6-16

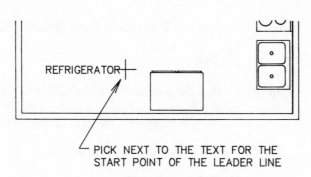

REFRIGERATOR

PICK NEXT TO THE TEXT FOR THE
START POINT OF THE LEADER LINE

Step 12 – Pick the point for the elbow of the line, as indicated in Fig. 6-17.

Fig. 6-17

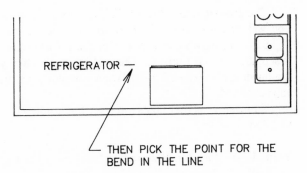

REFRIGERATOR ⌐

THEN PICK THE POINT FOR THE
BEND IN THE LINE

Step 13 – Now pick the last point of the line, in the position you wish the arrow to appear, as in Fig. 6-18.

Fig. 6-18

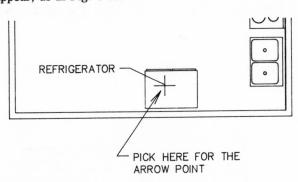

REFRIGERATOR ⌐

PICK HERE FOR THE
ARROW POINT

Step 14 – Press mouse button **3** to quit. The arrow will be drawn on the end of your line! (Fig. 6-19)

Fig. 6-19

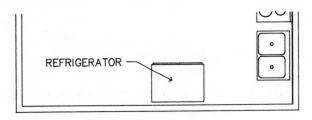

REFRIGERATOR ⌐

THE ARROW APPEARS AT
THE LAST PICK POINT

Step 15 – Continue adding the rest of the small text and necessary arrows for your drawing. This is indicated in Fig. 6-20.

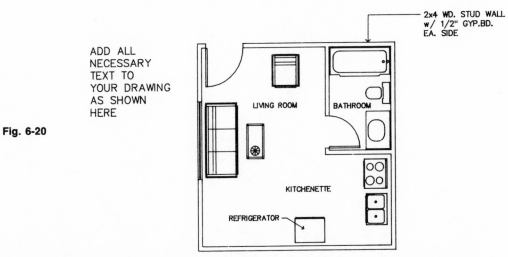

2x4 WD. STUD WALL
w/ 1/2" GYP.BD.
E.A. SIDE

ADD ALL
NECESSARY
TEXT TO
YOUR DRAWING
AS SHOWN
HERE

Fig. 6-20

LIVING ROOM

BATHROOM

KITCHENETTE

REFRIGERATOR ⌐

CHANGING THE SIZE OF YOUR TEXT

The drawing title: FLOOR PLAN, is made in larger text than the rest of the sheet. You will want to change the text size in order to create it.

Since the drawing you are creating is in **full scale**, the text you are currently using is actually set to **6 inches**. (This makes sense when you think about the perimeter of the building as a true 16 feet.) When you plot your drawing at ¼″ scale, 6 inches will appear as ⅛″.

To make your text double in size, then, you will want to set the size of your text to 1 foot.

Step 1 –   Pick the **Size** option from the Text menu.

Size

Step 2 –   Pick the **1′–0″** option. This setting will make your text appear at ¼″ high.

1′–0″

Step 3 –   Finish adding the larger text to your drawing, and any other text that is necessary. (Fig. 6-21)

Fig. 6-21

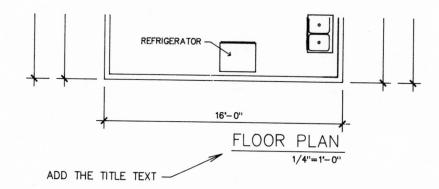

Step 4 –   File your drawing when you are done, using **File I/O**, and picking the **Save Dwg** option.

DataCAD Exercise 6

Please complete the following exercise by reading each question carefully, then circling the letter that corresponds to the correct answer.

1. To quickly change layers, you press the:

    a. [Tab] key.
    b. [Alt] L keys.
    c. L key.

2. To put the items (walls, dimensions, text, etc.) you are creating onto the right layer, you should:

    a. Change to the correct layer BEFORE you create the item.
    b. Change to the correct layer AFTER you create the item.
    c. Just create the item. It automatically goes to the correct layer.

3. To make a horizontal or vertical straight dimension, you would use the:

    a. Angular option.
    b. Radius option.
    c. Linear option.

4. If you are dimensioning a line that is in the Y axis, you would pick the:

    a. Horizontal option.
    b. Vertical option.
    c. Baseline option.

5. To string a series of chained dimensions, you pick the:

    a. Chain option.
    b. Strnglin option.
    c. Series option.

6. To get the total length of the wall dimensioned after you have defined string line dimensions, you use the:

    a. Total option.
    b. Length option.
    c. OverAll option.

7. To dimension an unbroken wall (has no windows or doors) quickly, you use the:

    a. Entity option.
    b. Wall option.
    c. Length option.

8. To create text, you:

    a. Type in the text, then position it on your drawing.
    b. Pick a start point, then type in your text.
    c. Pick a start point, type in your text, then drag the text to a new position.

9. To have text that is plotted at ⅛ inch when you are plotting at a ¼ inch scale, you create your text at the size of:

   a. ⅛ inch.
   b. 1 foot.
   c. 6 inches.

10. To permanently save a drawing to your hard disk, you must:

    a. Save the file using File I/O, and Save Dwg, or pick Yes to save when quitting DataCAD.
    b. Not do anything. The file is automatically saved.
    c. Exit the system, and pick Abort.

Lesson 7: Viewing Your Drawing in 3-D

WHAT YOU WILL BE DOING

YOU will create a 3-D perspective view of your drawing. You will use the hidden line removal function to enhance your 3-D view. Then you will add the 3-D view image to your drawing, and scale it down to fit in your drawing border.

OBJECTIVE:

Your lesson objectives, then, are to:

- Create a 3-dimensional perspective view.
- Save the view as an image.
- Add the image to the drawing.
- Scale the size of the image to make it fit within the drawing boundary.
- Create a perspective image with hidden lines removed.

Remember to reference your *DataCAD Operations Guide* when instructed.

3-D VIEWS

You can create 3-D views for presentations, spatial studies, and illustration purposes, directly from your plan view drawings. You can create three types of 3-D views:

1. Parallel
2. Perspective
3. Oblique

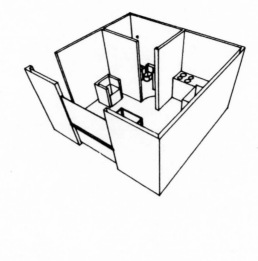

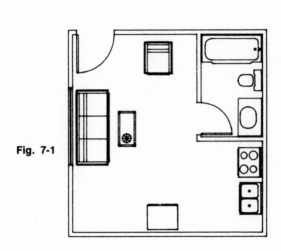

Fig. 7-1

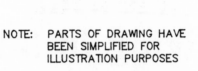

NOTE: PARTS OF DRAWING HAVE
             BEEN SIMPLIFIED FOR
             ILLUSTRATION PURPOSES

During this lesson, you will create a PERSPECTIVE view.

TURNING OFF UNNECESSARY LAYERS

Before you create a 3-D image, you will want to turn off the layers that hold graphics you do NOT want to see in 3-D.

Step 1 – Press **L**, to enter the Layer menu.

        L

Step 2 – Pick **On/Off** option.

        On/Off

Step 3 – Pick the layers called: NOTES, DIMS, and BORDER to turn them off.

        NOTES
        DIMS
        BORDER

Step 4 – Quit by pressing mouse button **3**.

Step 5 – Now, only the plan view is displayed, as illustrated in Fig. 7-2.

MAKE SURE THE
PLAN DRAWING IS
DISPLAYED

Fig. 7-2

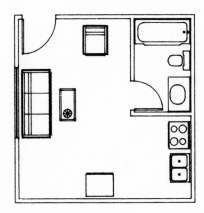

CREATING THE PERSPECTIVE VIEW

Step 6 – Press the **Y** key. *DO NOT use the [Shift] key*. This is the quick way to enter the DCAD 3D menu, 3D Views option, from the UTILITY menu. (If it doesn't work, make sure your [Caps Lock] is OFF.)

Y

Step 7 – Pick the **Prspect** option (Perspective).

Prspect

Step 8 – Now the CONE OF VISION will be displayed, as in Fig. 7-3. This cone graphically represents the formula for your perspective.

Fig. 7-3

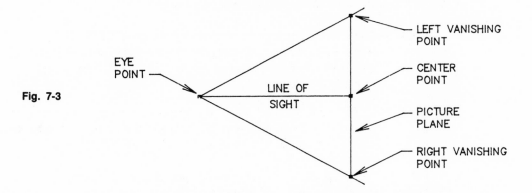

Step 9 – *If the cone of vision is NOT displayed* - It may be that a perspective view has been previously set for your drawing. In this case, pick the **SetPersp** option. This will allow you to set the cone of vision again.

SetPersp

WHAT IS THE CONE OF VISION?

The cone defines:

-Eye point
-Picture plane

-Vanishing points
-Line of sight
-Center point

This is illustrated in Fig. 7-4.

Fig. 7-4

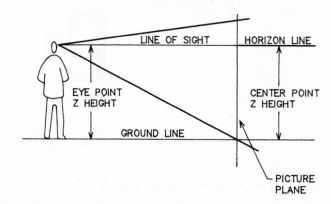

EYE POINT: Your point of vision, also called a station point. The eye point height (horizon line), in normal perspectives (those viewed from a standing position) is located 5'-0" above the ground line.

The height of the EYE POINT is adjustable using the **Eyepnt Z** option. The angle of the eye point (for three point perspectives) is determined by also adjusting the **CentPnt Z** option. (See CENTER POINT.)

PICTURE PLANE: Items appearing in front of the plane look larger, items in back of the plane appear smaller. Items intersecting the plane retain true size.

VANISHING POINTS: These are the vanishing points for your perspective, which are projected to the horizon line.

LINE OF SIGHT: This is the line drawn from the eye point to the picture plane. Where it intersects the plane is the center point. The angle of the line of sight is adjustable by using the **EyePnt Z** and **CentPntZ** options.

CENTER POINT: This is the point where the line of sight meets the picture plane. The result is the horizon line. The height of the center point (and resulting horizon line) is adjustable using the **CentPntZ** option.

For a normal two point perspective (horizon line height is the same as eye level) the center point height is 5'-0", or the same as the eye point setting. This provides you a **level line of sight**.

For a three point perspective (horizon line is at a different level than the eye level), you would adjust the **center point** and the **eye point** heights to provide you an **angled line of sight**. This is the case when the desired effect is looking down at a building, or looking up.

SETTING THE CONE OF VISION

Step 9 –   Press the [left arrow] key until your plan view is moved over to the right hand side. This will give you a better area to work with for positioning your cone of vision. (If it doesn't work, make sure your [Num Lock] is OFF.)

[right arrow]

Step 10 – Press your [down arrow] key until the view is moved into the upper right hand corner.

[down arrow]

Step 11 – Pick a point in the lower left of your drawing, as indicated in Fig. 7-5. This will be your new eye point. (The height for your eye point is pre-set to 5'-0".)

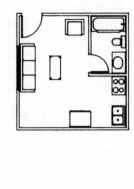

Fig. 7-5

PICK HERE
FOR EYE
POINT

Step 12 – Move your cursor around. Notice that the length of the cone does not change as you move your cursor. This is because the **FixCone** option is active. You will want to turn FixCone *OFF* by picking it until the "*" is gone.

FixCone (until "*" is OFF)

Step 13 – Now you will be able to drag the cone of vision by the center point over to your building. **Object snap** to the lower left corner of the building, as indicated in Fig. 7-6.

Fig. 7-6

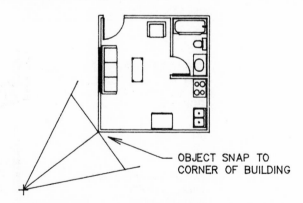

OBJECT SNAP TO
CORNER OF BUILDING

Step 14 – A text-book perspective will be displayed, and should look similar to Fig. 7-7.

Fig. 7-7

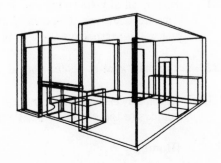

SAVING THE 3-D VIEW

Once you are satisfied with your view, you can save in onto a layer, and add it to your plan view.

Step 15 – Pick the **SaveImag** option (Save Image).

SaveImag

Step 16 – Pick the **NewLayer** option. This will allow you to name a special layer for your 3-D view.

NewLayer

Step 17 – Type in the name for your new layer: **PERSP1**. (Perspective #1.)

PERSP1

Step 18 – Pick **On**, to keep this new layer displayed.

On

Step 19 – Once you are returned to the 3D VIEW menu, pick the **Ortho** option. This will return you to the original plan view, and display the new image as well.

Ortho

Step 20 – Press mouse button **3** until you are returned to the UTILITY menu.

Notice that your perspective view may not be located exactly where you would like it to be. You will want to move it to a better location. You may also want to change the size of your perspective to better fit in the border area. (Fig. 7-8)

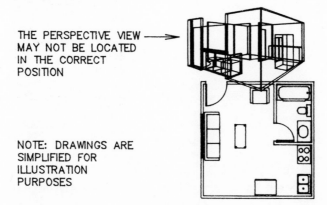

THE PERSPECTIVE VIEW →
MAY NOT BE LOCATED
IN THE CORRECT
POSITION

Fig. 7-8

NOTE: DRAWINGS ARE
SIMPLIFIED FOR
ILLUSTRATION
PURPOSES

Step 21 – Display all of your layers, by using the **L** key, and the **On/Off** option. This will allow you to see all of the objects in your drawing, in order to adjust the perspective view to fit.

Step 22 – You may want to center your drawing again, using the [arrows] keys.

USER HINT > You may also instantly center your drawing by placing the cursor where you desire the center to be, then pressing the **[Home]** key.

[Home]

MOVING ITEMS IN YOUR DRAWING

When an item or items are created in the wrong place, it is an easy task to move them. You will want to move the perspective image to a new location in your drawing.

Step 1 – Press **M** to quickly enter the Move option, found in the EDIT menu.

M

Step 2 – Pick the **Drag** option.

Drag

Step 3 – Make sure the layer that holds your perspective view: **PERSP1**, is active, by using the **[Tab]** key.

[Tab] (to PERSP1 layer)

Step 4 – Make the ***Group** option active, by picking it until there is a star in front of it (*Group). This will allow you to move the entire perspective as a group (perspectives are grouped when they are created.)

*Group

Step 5 – Pick a corner of your perspective. It will become **gray and dashed**.

Step 6 – Now you will be prompted to pick a point to move the perspective by. Pick a point to the left of the perspective, as indicated in Fig. 7-9.

Fig. 7-9

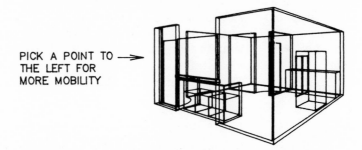

PICK A POINT TO →
THE LEFT FOR
MORE MOBILITY

Step 7 – Now a box outline will appear, and you will be able to drag it to a new location. Pick a spot over to the lower right of the original floor plan, as indicated in Fig. 7-10.

Fig. 7-10

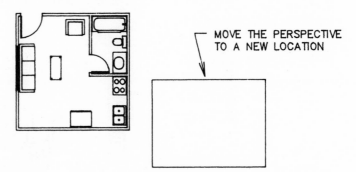

MOVE THE PERSPECTIVE
TO A NEW LOCATION

ENLARGING AND SHRINKING ITEMS IN YOUR DRAWING

You use the same function to enlarge items in your drawing as you do to shrink it.

Step 1 –   Press mouse button **3** to quit the Move menus.

Step 2 –   Pick the **Enlarge** option, found in the EDIT menu.

Enlarge

Step 3 –   Pick in the center of your perspective to establish a center of enlargement, as indicated in Fig. 7-11. This is the point that will stay stationary as the group is enlarged or shrunk.

Fig. 7-11

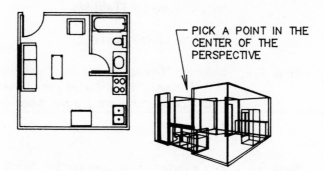

PICK A POINT IN THE CENTER OF THE PERSPECTIVE

Step 4 –   Pick the **Enlrgmnt** option, to enter an enlargement factor.

Enlrgmnt

Step 5 –   Pick an enlargement factor that you want to change the size of the perspective by. For example, **.5** will shrink your items to half the present size. An enlargement factor of **2** will make items twice the present size.

You may want to pick **.75**

.75

Step 6 –   Now press mouse button **2** to enter this factor for the X enlargement size, and again to accept this for the Y enlargement size. (You could also use the [Enter] key if you wish.)

Step 7 –   Notice that the ***Group** option is still active. Pick a corner of your perspective and it will become smaller. (Fig. 7-12)

Fig. 7-12

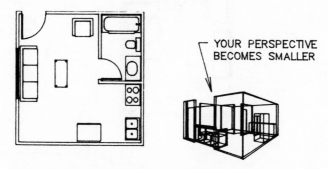

YOUR PERSPECTIVE BECOMES SMALLER

Step 8 –   Once the size of the perspective image is reduced, you may want to "Move" it in your border again.

USER NOTE: The **Inverse** option will change the enlargement to the *opposite* of the set value. Example: If the value was set to 2, for twice the size, the inverse of that would be 0.50, or half the size. You can use this if you want your items back to their previous size.

CREATING A SECOND PERSPECTIVE WITH HIDDEN LINES

Now you will create another perspective view. This time, you will change your eye level and remove the hidden lines.

Step 1 – Use the **Layers** menu to turn off your new layer called **PERSP1** and all other layers except the layers called Walls, Doors, Windows, Furn, and Plumb. Your drawing will be ready for your next perspective.

Step 2 – Press **Y**.

Y

Step 3 – Pick **Prspect**. Your original perspective view is displayed.

Prspect

Step 4 – Pick **SetPersp**. This option allows you to redefine your viewing orientation.

SetPersp

Step 5 – Pick **EyePntZ**, to change your eye point height.

EyePntZ

Step 6 – Pick **Custom**.

Custom

Step 7 – Type in **30**. This will change your eye point height to 30 feet. Now you will be able to look over the walls and into the room when you create your perspective.

30

Step 8 – Pick the points for your cone again, following the original cone displayed, and Object snapping to the corner of the building.

Your new perspective will be displayed, and you will have a bird's eye view of the building, as shown in Fig. 7-13.

Fig. 7-13

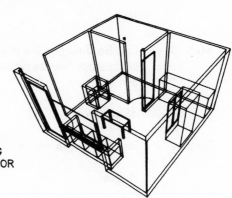

NOTE: DRAWING
IS SIMPLIFIED FOR
ILLUSTRATION
PURPOSES

Step 9 – You can adjust the view, if you wish, with the small globe that is located on the screen. By picking in the globe, you can dynamically change your eye point position. This globe is illustrated in Fig. 7-14.

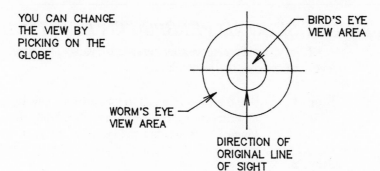

Fig. 7-14

Step 10 – After you have picked different positions on the globe, if you would like to return quickly to your original bird's eye view, you can pick the **Set-Persp** option.

SetPersp

Step 11 – Now pick the **Reset** option. Your original view is returned, as in Fig. 7-15.

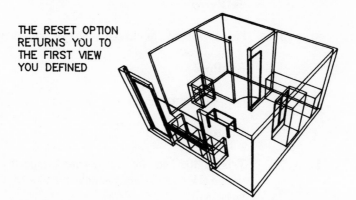

Fig. 7-15

HIDDEN LINE REMOVAL

Once you have achieved the desired view, you will want to remove the hidden lines from your view.

Step 1 – Press mouse button **3** to return to the **3D Edit** menu.

Step 2 – Pick the **Hide** option.

Hide

Step 3 – Pick **SavImag** until it is active (***SavImag**), to save the image you will be creating. You always will want to do this BEFORE you create the hidden line view.

*SavImag

Step 4 – Pick the **Begin** option.

Begin

Step 5 – After the hidden line removal process is complete, pick the **NewLayer** option.

NewLayer

Step 6 – Name this layer: **PERSP2**.

PERSP2

Step 7 – Pick **On**, to keep this layer active.

On

Step 8 – Press the **Y** key to return to the 3D VIEW menu.

Y

Step 9 – Pick the **Ortho** option, to return the plan view.

Ortho

Step 10 – Turn on the other Layers in your drawing.

Step 11 – Use the **[Tab]** key to make the new layer that holds your perspective view active: **PERSP2**.

Step 12 – Finish your drawing by **M**oving your new perspective view, **Dragging** it as a **Group** to a new location,then **Enlarge** it to a reduced size. Follow the same steps described earlier.

Step 13 – Your drawing should now look similar to Fig. 7-16

Fig. 7-16

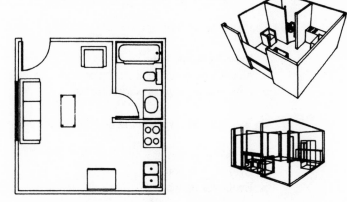

Step 14 – Remember to use **File I/O** and **Save Dwg** to make sure that your drawing is permanently saved to hard disk.

DataCAD Exercise 7

Please complete the following exercise by reading each question carefully, then circling the letter that corresponds to the correct answer.

1. Before creating a 3-D view, you should:

   a. Make sure all of the layers are displayed.
   b. Turn off all layers that you do not want to view in 3-D
   c. Make sure the dimensions layer is displayed.

2. To help you create the perspective, DataCAD displays a:

   a. Cone of Vision.
   b. Option called Line of sight.
   c. View of Vision.

3. To save the 3-D view, you use the:

   a. SaveView option.
   b. NewView option.
   c. SaveImag option.

4. When saving the 3-D view, you:

   a. Must have a pre-defined layer to hold your views on.
   b. Are given the option to create a new layer for your view.
   c. Cannot save in on any layer but the active one.

5. The perspective view:

   a. Usually will have to be moved to a better location.
   b. Pops into your drawing in the exact location you want it to be.
   c. Automatically moves to an upper right hand corner.

6. The Enlarge option:

   a. Enlarges items only.
   b. Allows you to enter a new plot scale for your drawing.
   c. Lets you enlarge or shrink items.

7. To increase the eye level height for viewing the perspective, you use the:

   a. BirdsEye option.
   b. EyePnt Z option.
   c. EyeLevel option.

8. If you want to save the view with hidden lines removed, you must:

   a. First set the SavImag option.
   b. Remove the lines, then pick the SavImag option.
   c. Remove the lines, then pick the SaveView option.

9. To display the plan view of your drawing after creating a perspective, you use the:

   a. Ortho option.
   b. PlanView option.
   c. Mouse button 3. The plan view is automatically displayed.

10. To have text that is plotted at ½ inch when you are plotting at a ¼ inch scale, you create your text at the size of:

    a. ⅛ inch.
    b. 1 foot.
    c. 2 feet.

11. To permanently save a drawing to your hard disk, you must:

    a. Save the file using File I/O, and Save Dwg, or pick Yes when quitting DataCAD.
    b. Not do anything. The file is automatically saved.
    c. Quit DataCAD, and pick Abort.

Lesson 8:
Plotting your Drawing

WHAT YOU WILL BE DOING:

YOU will create a finished plot of your drawing. You will create this plot at a ¼″ scale. Your drawing will be plotted on a D size sheet, 24 × 36. It is assumed that you have a plotter, it is properly set up according to the owner's manual and DataCAD, and it is capable of plotting a D size drawing.

OBJECTIVES:

Your lesson objectives, then, are to:

- Check the plot scale of the drawing.
- Check the location of the plot area (layout).
- Check the colors are set to the proper pen numbers.
- Prepare the plotter.
- Run the plot.

Remember to reference the **PLOTTING** section of your *DataCAD Cookbook*.

PLOTTING

The final plot is the ultimate goal of creating your CAD drawing!

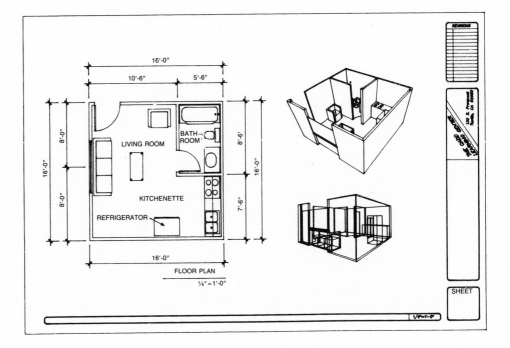

Fig. 8-1

Pre-set plot specifications

As mentioned earlier, the *Standard Default Drawing* that you have been using (1-4PLAN) contains pre-set defaults and standards (such as drawing boundaries, text size, layers, etc.). This drawing also contains information for your plot.

If you created your own default drawing, during the DRAWING SET-UP lesson, you already know what goes into setting up the drawing for plotting. Having the plotting information pre-set makes plotting a one step process. This means you simply pick the Plot option and go!

When first defining these specifications, for the standard default drawing, you follow 5 basic steps:

1. Defining the **scale** of the plot.
2. Identifying the actual **plotting area** of your paper.
3. Defining the **layout**, or the plotting area of your drawing.
4. If you are using different pens, **setting the pens** for your plot.

When your default drawing has this information in it already, then you will follow these 4 steps:

1. Put the correct pens in the plotter.
2. Put the paper in the plotter.
3. Turn the plotter on.
4. Pick PLOT in DataCAD.

During this lesson, to reinforce the process involved in setting up the plot specifications, you will check these settings before you send your drawing to plot. If you find an incorrect setting, you will want to change it as you proceed through the following steps.

Step 1 – Start DataCAD.

Step 2 – Retrieve the drawing you wish to plot.

Step 3 – Once the drawing you wish to plot is displayed, pick the **Plotter** option from the UTILITY menu.

Plotter

CHECKING THE PLOT SCALE

Step 4 – Pick the **Scale** option.

Scale

Step 5 – Check that the current scale is set to ¼". If it is, **quit** back to the Plotter menu. If it isn't, select this setting from the menu.

¼"

CHECKING THE PAPER SIZE

Step 6 – Pick the **PaperSiz** option.

PaperSiz

Step 7 – Make sure the paper size is set to **23 × 32**. If it is, **quit** back to the Plotter menu. If it isn't, pick **Custom** from the menu, and set the correct size.

23 × 32 (X = 32, Y = 23)

CHECKING THE LAYOUT

Next, you will want to check the layout to make sure that the drawing is positioned correctly on the sheet.

Step 8 – Pick the **Layout** option. The current sheet layout will be displayed. It should line up exactly on your rectangle boundary. If it does, **quit** back to the plotter menu. If it doesn't, object snap to the centerpoint of the rectangle to reposition the layout.

CHECKING THE PEN SETTINGS

Step 9 – Pick the **Set Pens** option.

Set Pens

Step 10 – Notice that the names of colors are displayed in the menu area. The colors listed represent the colors that can be displayed on your screen. As mentioned in the earlier lesson, DRAWING SET-UP, you can connect a certain pen number to each color. This pen number is used by your plotter, in order to pick up a certain pen to draw with.

PEN TABLES

It is essential that you standardize color use in your office. This is done by defining a PEN TABLE. Pen tables are used to graphically connect colors and pen numbers to pen widths. This way, you can be confident that a certain color will be plotted with the correct pen.

The following pen table, shown in Fig. 8-2, is currently set for you drawings. This is a good example of a pen table used for training purposes.

Fig. 8-2

PEN TABLE FOR TRAINING PURPOSES			
LINE	PEN SIZE	NUMBER	COLOR
————	.70	4	WHITE YELLOW
————	.50	3	LT MGTA
————	.35	2	GREEN CYAN LT BLUE
————	.25	1	BROWN

Step 11 – If you wish to check that these settings are correct in your Set Pens menu, pick the **White** option.

   White

Step 12 – White should be set to pen number **4**. If necessary, enter this number.

   4

Step 13 – The rest of the colors should be set to:

   Green   = 2
   Cyan   = 2
   Brown   = 1
   Lt Blue = 2
   Lt Mgta = 3
   Yellow   = 4

Step 12 – Press mouse button **3** to quit back to the Plotter menu.

SETTING UP THE PLOTTER

Before you send your drawing to the plotter, make sure that your plotter is ready to draw. This means the paper is properly installed, the pens are wet and in the proper order (see the next step), and the plotter is ON-LINE.

Step 13 – *If you have a multiple pen plotter* – Check that your pens are set in the following order:

#1 = Smallest of pen widths. Recommended - **.25**
#2 = Next size larger. Recommended - **.35**
#3 = Next size larger. Recommended - **.50**
#4 = Largest of pen widths. Recommended - **.70**

Step 14 – *If you have a single pen plotter* – Check that the smallest of your pens is inserted in the pen holder. The plotter will stop when it is time to insert the second pen.

Step 15 – Place a **D** size paper in your plotter (24 × 36). Make sure it is aligned properly, and the paper holder (clamp) is firmly on the paper.

Step 16 – Turn the plotter on. It will probably view the paper and test the pens, depending on the type of plotter you have.

Step 17 – If necessary, press the **On-line** button, or make sure it is ready to plot.

Step 18 – Pick the **Plot** option. Your plotter should start drawing!

IF YOUR PLOTTER DOESN'T PLOT - This may be due to several problems:

- Your DataCAD is not configured to the correct plotter.
- Your plotter is plugged into the wrong port.
- You have not prepared your plotter properly.

Check with the owner's manual, and the DataCAD User Manual to assure that you have installed your plotter correctly, and the procedures you should follow.

Step 19 – If you have made any changes to your drawing, make sure you file it, using the **File I/O** option, then picking **Save Dwg**.

Step 20 – Or, if you are quitting DataCAD, then press **[Alt] Q**.

[Alt] Q

Step 21 – Pick **Yes**.

Yes.

DataCAD Exercise 8

Please complete the following exercise by reading each question carefully, then circling the letter that corresponds to the correct answer.

1. To make plotting an easy, one step process, you:

   a. Change the colors you use for different items, instead of standardizing the colors used for all of your drawings.
   b. Change the pen numbers every time you plot.
   c. Should have all of the information pre-set in your standard default drawing, and never vary your color standards.

2. To set the factor by which your drawing will be plotted, you pick:

   a. The Factor option.
   b. The Scale option.
   c. None of the options. You should always plot full size.

3. To pick the sheet size you will plot your drawing on, you pick the:

   a. Sheet option.
   b. Layout option.
   c. PaperSiz option.

4. To adjust the position of the plotting area on the drawing, you pick the:

   a. Layout option.
   b. Sheet option.
   c. Adjust option.

5. When you are using multiple pens for your plots, it is important that you:

   a. Set your pen numbers for the colors you have used, and have a defined pen table for plotting purposes.
   b. Have all of your colors set to pen 1.
   c. Do not set pen numbers.

6. The final step in plotting your drawing, is:

   a. Setting the scale.
   b. Adjusting the layout.
   c. Picking the Plot option from the Plotter menu.

7. To change from creating "walls" to creating "lines," and back again, you press the:

   a. Mouse button 3.
   b. = key.
   c. L key.

8. To draw walls that are dimensioned to the centers, you use the:

   a. Center option.
   b. Sides option.
   c. Midpt option.

9. If your walls are dimensioned to the outside corners, you use the:

   a. Exterior option.
   b. Outside option.
   c. Sides option.

10. To set your coordinate input mode, you press the:

    a. [Space bar].
    b. [Ins] key.
    c. [Del] key.

11. To use coordinate input, you press the:

    a. [Space bar].
    b. [Ins] key.
    c. [Del] key.

12. If you pick a symbol from a template, and it comes in at a different angle than it should, you:

    a. Have a problem with your symbol.
    b. Probably have a rotated value set. Simply set it back to 0, or to the proper angle, before you place your symbol.
    c. Should place it, then rotate it after it has been placed in your drawing.

13. If you are picking the position for your linear dimension, and it seems locked on the item you are dimensioning so that you cannot drag it away from the item to place it, you should:

    a. Quit to the Linear Dimension menu, and check the vertical or horizontal setting.
    b. Quit, and call someone for help.
    c. Stop creating dimensions. Your drawing has too many already.

14. To have text that is plotted at ⅛ inch when you are plotting at ¼ inch scale, you need to create your text as the size of:

    a. ⅛ inch.
    b. 1 foot.
    c. 6 inches.

15. When you create a 3-D view, you want to:

    a. Make sure all of the layers are displayed.
    b. Turn off all layers that you do not want to view in 3-D.
    c. Make sure the dimensions layer is displayed.

16. When you create a 3-D view, it:

    a. Usually will have to be moved to a better location.
    b. Pops into your drawing in the exact location you want it to be.
    c. Automatically moves to an upper right hand corner.

17. The Enlarge option:

   a. Enlarges items only.
   b. Allows you to enter a new plot scale for your drawing.
   c. Lets you enlarge or shrink items.

18. To permanently save a drawing to your hard disk, you can:

   a. Save the file using File I/O and the Save Dwg option, or pick Yes when you are Quitting DataCAD.
   b. Only save it using File I/O and picking Save Dwg. Quitting DataCAD does not allow you to save your drawing.
   c. Quit DataCAD, and pick Abort.

Lesson 9: Creating Initial Site Plans

WHAT YOU WILL BE DOING:

Y OU will be transferring survey information to your initial site plan drawing. To do so, you will use the **Bearings** type of coordinate input, and the Curve Data menu to create surveyed radii.

Your site plan will be plotted at a 1:20 inch scale. You will use the special standard Default Drawing for your project you created in the earlier lesson, DRAWING SET-UP, which is designed for site drawings.

OBJECTIVES:

Your lesson objectives, then, are to:

- Set the correct Default Drawing.
- Change the angle type to Bearings.
- Use survey formulas to enter coordinates when drawing property lines.

Remember to reference your *DataCAD Operations Guide* when instructed.

SITE DEFAULT DRAWING

When you change the type of drawing you are using, or changing the scale you will be plotting in, you will want to change the default drawing. This is because these settings are already defined in the default drawing, along with the appropriate border and plot scale ratio.

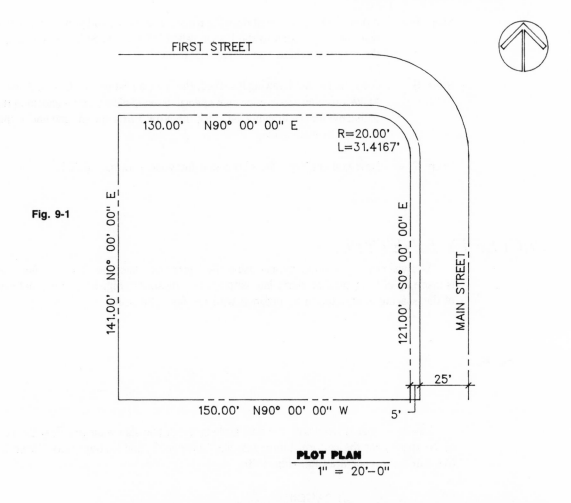

Fig. 9-1

FIRST STREET

130.00'   N90° 00' 00" E

R=20.00'
L=31.4167'

141.00' N0° 00' 00" E

121.00' S0° 00' 00" E

MAIN STREET

25'

150.00'   N90° 00' 00" W   5'

PLOT PLAN
1" = 20'-0"

As an example, when you created your plan layout, it was plotted at ¼″ scale. You used the default drawing that was set up, called 1-4PLAN. The boundary rectangle and text in your drawing was pre-set to be the exact size needed when it was plotted at a ¼″ scale.

Now that you will be creating a drawing to be plotted at a 1:20 scale (Fig. 9-1, 1″ = 20 feet) you will need to call up the default drawing called 1-20SITE. You may have created this default drawing during the lesson called DRAWING SET-UP, or someone may have created it for you. This Default Drawing contains a boundary that is designed for this scale, along with settings adjusted for scale and site work considerations.

CHANGING THE DEFAULT DRAWING

Step 1 –   Start DataCAD. If you are currently using DataCAD, use the **File I/O** option to start a **New Dwg.**

Step 2 –   When the drawing list is displayed, pick the **Default** option.

Default

Step 3 –   The Default Drawing list should be displayed. *If it is not*, check that the New Path name is set to DEFAULT.

Step 4 –   Once the list is displayed, pick the drawing called **1-20SITE**.

1-20SITE

Step 5 – If there is NOT a default drawing named 1-20SITE, and you did not make one earlier, go back to the lesson called DRAWING SET-UP and follow the steps to create this Default Drawing.

Step 6 – Once the Default Drawing is picked, the drawing list will be displayed again. Make sure you are in your own special drawing directory by checking the pathname for the drawing list. Pick the **New Path** option, and check that it is set to your name.

Step 7 – Now you can type the new name for your drawing: SITE1.

        site1

PROPERTY LINETYPE

You will create the property line using the "propline" linetype. This is a line that is made up of the typical property line pattern, as indicated in Fig. 9-2. The exact size of the spacing is adjusted in accordance with the final plot scale.

PROPERTY LINETYPE

Fig. 9-2.

Like text, that is sized with the final scale in mind, you also want to adjust the size of the spacing for the pattern. Linetypes, like "propline", and text are both "descriptive" items in your drawing. (Fig. 9-3)

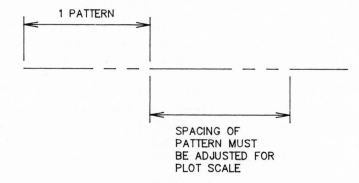

1 PATTERN

Fig. 9-3.

SPACING OF
PATTERN MUST
BE ADJUSTED FOR
PLOT SCALE

DESCRIPTIVE ITEMS VS. REAL ITEMS

As you draw and design with DataCAD, you will find that there are items that *describe* things, (descriptive items) verses *real* items.

Descriptive items are items that are sized in relation to the final plot scale. Examples of this are:

- Text.
- Material description (earth, concrete, steel, etc.).
- Linetype spacing (dashed, dot-dash, etc.).
- Drawing boundaries.
- Hatch pattern spacing.
- Details and detail boxes (drawn in true size, then reduced to scale).

Real items are drawn in true size, and remain in true size. Examples of this are:

- Walls.
- Doors and windows.
- Furniture.
- Plumbing.
- HVAC.
- Streets.
- Parking lots.
- Anything that represents something you can touch in the ''real'' world.

Of course, the property line represents something in the real world, and will represent the true perimeter in full size. But the particular *linetype* that you are going to draw it with is ''descriptive''. (You can't go to the real world site and see a line-dash-dash-line pattern drawn on its perimeter.)

SETTING THE LINETYPE SPACING

Step 1 – Pick the **Linetype** option from the EDIT menu.

Linetype

Step 2 – Pick the **Spacing** option.

Spacing

Step 3 – Change the spacing to **40**. Press [Enter]. This will make the final repeat pattern spaced at 1 inch. See Appendix B for linetype spacing formulas.

40

Step 4 – When you are returned to the LINETYPE menu, pick the **Propline** option. The current linetype will be set to ''property line'', and will appear as the active linetype in the status area of the screen, as in Fig. 9-4.

Propline

Fig. 9-4

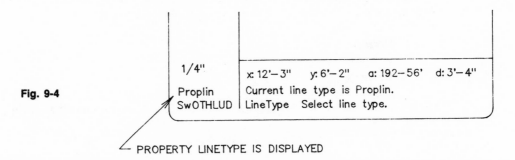

PROPERTY LINETYPE IS DISPLAYED

USING THE DATACAD REFERENCE GUIDE

Turn to Appendix B - DataCAD Reference Guide. Find the **DataCAD Linetypes** chart. This chart illustrates the various linetype you can use, and the formula for the correct *spacing*.

SITE PLANS AND SURVEY DRAWINGS

Site plans are developed from information supplied by the civil engineer, in the form of a survey drawing. Although these types of drawings are routinely traced for site layouts when manually drafting, DataCAD has developed special options to allow the correct input of this information to your drawing.

Correctly drawing the site is especially important when using a computer, since all subsequent plans will be developed from this information, in true scale and accuracy.

Using the exact information supplied by the survey drawing also helps to screen inaccuracies during the initial site development. In manual drafting, when site information is traced, "fudged" areas in error are often transferred to all of the proceeding drawings without being caught until correction of these errors causes major impact to the original investment. Using DataCAD properly helps to eliminate such problems.

Survey drawings are supplied with "Bearings" information calling out the length and direction of lines, in a North/East/South/West type of format. Radii in the drawings are notated with Curve Data information (length, bearings in, bearings out, radius, etc.) This is illustrated in Fig. 9-5.

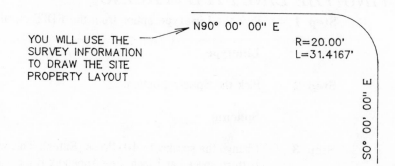

Fig. 9-5

As you reference the survey drawing which will be used for the site layout project during this lesson (Fig. 9-1), you will notice the bearings and radius notations are similar to the survey information you usually find in your civil drawings. You will use this data to create your site layout!

BEARING ANGLE TYPE

"Bearings" is a type of angle you can use for "polar" input. There are three basic angle types you can define, as indicated in Fig. 9-6. They are:

1. Normal
2. Compass
3. Bearings

For replicating survey north-south information, you will use the Bearings angle type.

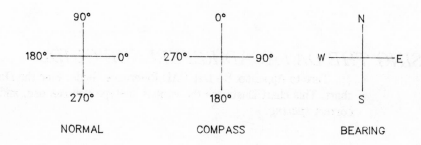

Fig. 9-6

SETTING THE ANGLE TYPE

The polar, or "angle" input type should be set to "Bearings". You can set this by using the Angle Type option.

Step 1 – Pick the **Settings** option from the UTILITY menu.

Settings

Step 2 – Pick the **AngleTyp** option.

AngleTyp

Step 3 – The three angle types are displayed. The current angle is probably set to ***Normal**. Pick the **Bearings** option until a star appears in front of it.

*Bearings

Step 4 – Press mouse button **3** to quit.

CHANGING THE INPUT MODE AND LAYER

The input mode you will learn to use for site plans is **relative polar**. This setting will allow you to input distances and bearing angles.

Step 1 – Set the input mode, press the **[Ins]** key until **Current input mode is relative polar** is displayed.

[Ins] (to set relative polar)

Step 2 – Make sure the correct layer is displayed that will hold your property line: PROPLIN. Press **[Tab]** until the Proplin layer is active.

[Tab] (until PROPLIN layer is active)

SETTING THE Z-BASE AND HEIGHT

Since you will want the property line to be at the 0 elevation only, you must set the Z-base and height to 0.

Step 1 – Press the **Z** key.

Z

Step 2 – Change both the base and height to 0.

Z-Base = **0**
Z-Height = **0**

USING BEARINGS INPUT MODE

Step 1 –   **Pick** a start point for your line, as shown in Fig. 9-7. ALWAYS PICK A START POINT before you use relative input.

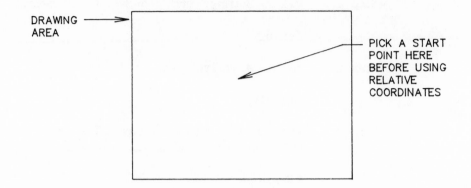

DRAWING AREA

PICK A START POINT HERE BEFORE USING RELATIVE COORDINATES

Fig. 9-7

Step 2 –   Press the **[Space Bar]**.

[Space Bar]

Step 3 –   You will be asked to: **Enter relative distance**. This is the length of the line, at a distance relative to the starting point you picked. Type in the desired length of the first line.

121

Step 4 –   Press **[Enter]**.

[Enter]

Step 5 –   Now you will be prompted to: **Enter relative angle:** A default of N90.0.0E appears at the cursor area. You can either pick from the menu the bearings information for the direction of the line: **S 0-0'E,** or type in the following.

S0E

Step 6 –   Press **[Enter]**.

[Enter]

Step 7 –   Press the **[Space bar]** again, and type in the length for the next line. Remember to press **[Enter]**.

150

Step 8 –   Enter the direction, and press **[Enter]**.

N90W

Step 9 –   Press the **[Space bar]** and type in and [Enter] the length for the next line. Make the direction of this line **NOE**.

Distance = **141**

Direction = **NOE**

Step 10 – Press the **[Space bar]**, and type in the length and direction for the last line.

Distance = **130**

Direction = **N90E**

Step 11 – Your drawing should look like Fig. 9-8. You are now ready to create the curve in your drawing.

Fig. 9-8

CREATING A CURVE USING CURVE DATA

When you are given a drawing from the surveyor, the curves are dimensioned with data that can be used to recreate the curve using the option called CURVE DATA.

Curve Data will create a curve using such survey information (typical on these types of drawings), as:

- Radius,
- Cord length,
- Arc length,
- Delta angle (included angle),
- Bearings in,
- Bearings out, etc.

Step 1 – Pick the **Curve** option, from the EDIT menu.

Curve

Step 2 – Pick the **CurvData** option from the menu.

CurvData

Step 3 – The CURVE DATA menu is displayed, as shown in Fig. 9-9.

THE CURVE DATA ⟶
MENU IS DISPLAYED

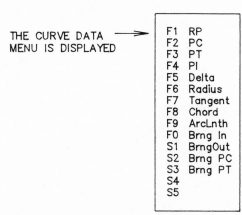

Fig. 9-9

Definitions of options:

RP (Radius Point)
The center of the radius, or "arc" to be defined.

PC (Point of Curve)
The starting point of the arc. *Remember - curve is created in a clockwise direction!*

PT (Point of Tangency)
The ending point of the arc.

PI (Point of Intersection)
The point where the tangent lines through PC and PT intersect. (Lines are tangent to the resulting arc.)

Delta (Delta angle)
The included angle of the arc.

Radius
The radius of the arc.

Tangent
The distance from the start point of the arc, to the PI. This distance will be identical to the distance from the end point to the PI.

Chord
The straight line distance from the starting point to the ending point of the arc.

ArcLnth (Arc Length)
The distance along the arc from the starting point to the ending point.

BrngIn (Bearing In)
The tangent line going into the start of the arc.

BrngOut (Bearing Out)
The tangent line coming out of the end of the arc.

Brng PC (Bearing Point of Curve)
The line created from the center point to the start point of the arc.

Brng PT (Bearing Point of Tangency)
The line created from the center point to the end point of the arc.

As you supply some of the answers to these options, DataCAD will answer any options it can figure out from the data you have supplied! When ALL options are answered (all have a "*" in front of their name), you will be able to "Add" the curve.

Fig. 9-10 illustrates how this data corresponds to the resulting curve.

Fig. 9-10

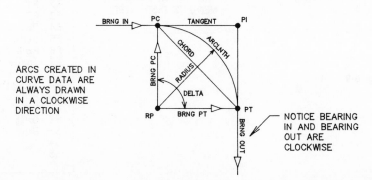

Step 4 –   Pick the **PC** option.

PC

Step 5 –   Pick the start point of your arc, as indicated in Fig. 9-11. Be sure to OBJECT SNAP.

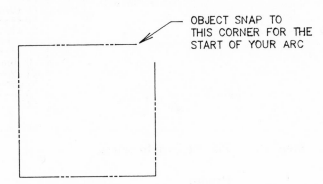

OBJECT SNAP TO
THIS CORNER FOR THE
START OF YOUR ARC

Fig. 9-11

Step 6 –   Pick the **PT** option.

PT

Step 7 –   Pick the ending point of the arc, using OBJECT SNAP again, as in Fig. 9-12.

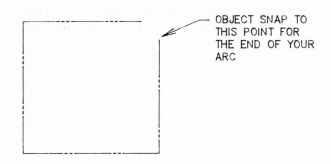

OBJECT SNAP TO
THIS POINT FOR
THE END OF YOUR
ARC

Fig. 9-12

Step 8 –   Pick the **Radius** option.

Radius

Step 9 –   Type in and **[Enter]** the radius for your arc, as indicated in your survey drawing. (R = 20'-0").

20

Step 10 –   Pick the **ArcLnth** option.

ArcLnth

Step 11 –   Type in and **[Enter]** the length of the arc, as indicated on your survey drawing. (L = 31'-5").

31'-5"

Step 12 – Notice that other options are beginning to be answered by DataCAD, as in Fig. 9-13.

AN ASTERISK
APPEARS AS
THE OPTIONS
ARE ANSWERED

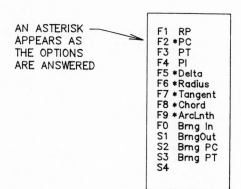

```
F1  RP
F2 *PC
F3  PT
F4  PI
F5 *Delta
F6 *Radius
F7 *Tangent
F8 *Chord
F9 *ArcLnth
FO  Brng In
S1  BrngOut
S2  Brng PC
S3  Brng PT
S4
```

Fig. 9-13

Step 13 – Pick the **BrngIn** option.

BrngIn

Step 14 – The "BrngIn" data will be supplied by the tangent line going into the start of the arc. This means, you will "match" the data supplied by the line. Pick **Match**.

Match

Step 15 – Now you will be prompted to pick the line. Pick the tangent line going into the start of the arc, as indicated in Fig. 9-14.

PICK THIS LINE FOR
TANGENT INFORMATION.

REMEMBER, THE
DIRECTION OF THIS
LINE IS GOING
CLOCKWISE INTO THE
ARC.

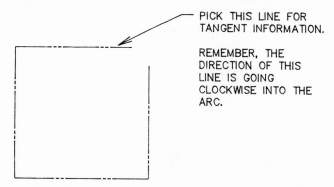

Fig. 9-14

Step 16 – Press mouse button **3** once to quit, then mouse button **2** to accept the bearings value supplied by the line.

Step 17 – Notice now that all of the options have a star by them, as shown in Fig. 9-15. This means that all necessary data is supplied to create the arc. Now the **Add** option appears. This option allows you to add the arc to your drawing.

ALL OPTIONS
HAVE A STAR

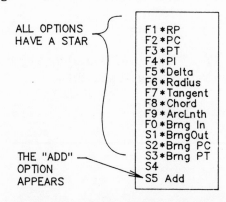

```
F1 *RP
F2 *PC
F3 *PT
F4 *PI
F5 *Delta
F6 *Radius
F7 *Tangent
F8 *Chord
F9 *ArcLnth
FO *Brng In
S1 *BrngOut
S2 *Brng PC
S3 *Brng PT
S4
S5  Add
```

Fig. 9-15

THE "ADD"
OPTION
APPEARS

Step 18 – Pick the **Add** option. The arc is added, as shown in Fig. 9-16.

Add

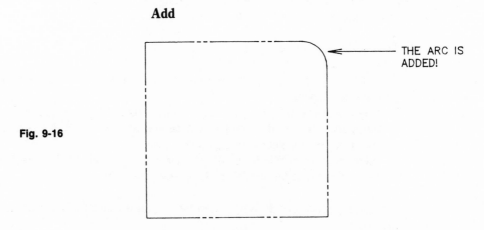

THE ARC IS
ADDED!

Fig. 9-16

Step 19 – Use the **File I/O, Save Dwg** option to save your drawing to hard disk.

DataCAD Exercise 9

Please complete the following exercise by reading each question carefully, then circling the letter that corresponds to the correct answer.

1. Default drawings allow you to:

   a. Change the type of drawing you are going to create, but not the scale or drawing borders.
   b. Pre-set several different "drawing formats" (blank drawing sheets) for the types and scales of drawing you will be creating. This includes setting up special layers for your drawings also.
   c. Have the correct title block already set in your drawing only. The layers and scale cannot be pre-set in the default drawing.

2. To change your default drawing, when the original drawing list is displayed, you pick the:

   a. New Path option.
   b. Default option.
   c. Set Deflt option.

3. Your default drawings should all be stored in the:

   a. MTEC\DWG directory.
   b. MTEC\DEFAULT directory.
   c. MTEC\DWG\DEFAULT directory.

4. The different types of polar input modes are:

   a. Normal, Cartesian, and Bearings.
   b. Relative, Cartesian, and Bearings.
   c. Normal, Compass, and Bearings.

5. Different lines (such as solid, dashed, dot-dash, etc.) are called:

   a. Line Weights.
   b. Linetypes.
   c. Line Scales.

6. There are two basic types of items on your drawings. One represents true life objects, and is called "real items". The second type:

   a. Are the things that are not built yet.
   b. Describes the objects, and is called Descriptive.
   c. Are the walls in your drawing.

7. When you are drawing real items, they are always drawn in:

   a. Relation to the plot scale.
   b. White.
   c. Full size.

8. When you add descriptive items, they are drawn in:

   a. Relation to the plot scale.
   b. Another drawing file.
   c. Full size.

9. To set the polar mode to Bearings, you use the:

   a. [Insert] key.
   b. [Space Bar].
   c. Settings menu, AngleTyp option.

10. To set the input mode to Relative Polar, you use the:

   a. [Insert] key.
   b. [Space Bar].
   c. Settings menu, AngleTyp option.

11. Before you use a relative input mode, you should:

   a. ALWAYS pick a start point.
   b. NEVER pick a start point.
   c. Only pick a start point if the drawing tells you to.

12. When you use Bearings, the following angle could be entered:

   a. 90-0
   b. N90W
   c. 90W

13. The Bearings input mode in DataCAD is usually used:

   a. By Civil Engineers only, in order to create survey drawings. The Architect will never use it.
   b. To quickly input survey information supplied by Civil Engineers, in order to correctly create the site plan.
   c. When first creating the survey drawing only. It is never used while drawing site plans, since you only have to trace the survey drawing on the computer.

14. To recreate Radii found in the survey drawing, you can use the:

   a. Survey menu, Curve option.
   b. Curve menu, Radius option.
   c. CurvData menu.

Some more review questions:

15. The quickest way to turn from lines to walls, or from walls to lines, is to use the:

   a. Menu option choices.
   b. < "less than" key.
   c. = "equal" key.

16. In order to define a reference point, you press the:

   a. [Space Bar].
   b. ~ key.
   c. X key.

17. To clean up wall intersections after you create them, you pick the:

    a. Cleanup option, then pick T or L Intsect.
    b. Cleanup option, then pick Corner.
    c. Architect option, then pick the Clean option.

18. To erase the last item you created, you use the:

    a. Delete option.
    b. < less than key.
    c. > greater than key.

Lesson 10: Creating 3-Dimensional Lines

WHAT YOU WILL BE DOING:

YOU will be creating lines in your drawing that angle through all 3 axes (X,Y,Z). Up until now, your lines have been drawn parallel to the XY axes plane. During the first lessons, you drew wall lines that also were duplicated in the Z depth (Z-Base and Z-Height). You were able to see these lines when you viewed your drawing in 3D View.

When you created your initial site layout, you used a single line located in the Z base of zero, again parallel to the XY axes plane. During this lesson, you will learn how to create lines that are not parallel to the XY axes plane.

OBJECTIVES:

Your lesson objectives, then, are to:

- Draw a building with temporary ridge and hip lines.
- Create a Parallel view.
- Use the 3D Cursor to draw 3D lines.

Remember to reference your *DataCAD Operators Guide* and *DataCAD Reference Guide* when instructed.

3-DIMENSIONAL LINES

Three dimensional lines are drawn as single lines. During this lesson, you will use the three-D lines task to connect two lines that have different heights. This is easy,

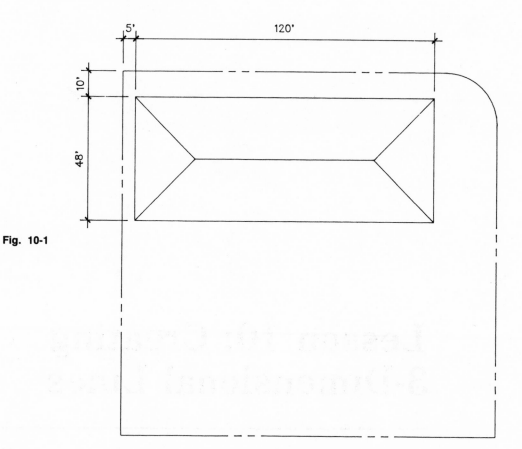

Fig. 10-1

because the 3-D line function allows you to object snap to these line end points, over ruling any currently active Z-height or base settings.

One thing to remember about 3-D lines is that they represent single lines, and not a wall. This means that you cannot "hide" hidden lines behind them, as you do with walls using the "3-D View, Hide" options. (You may still use the Hide function, but lines will not be hidden behind any of your 3-D lines!) You will have to erase any lines you want hidden manually.

Step 1 – You will be adding a building to the site plan you created earlier. See Fig. 10-1. Make sure DataCAD is running, and the SITE1 drawing is displayed on your screen before continuing, as illustrated in Fig. 10-2.

YOU WILL BE ADDING
A BUILDING TO YOUR
SITE PLAN

Fig. 10-2

ADJUSTING YOUR SETTINGS

When you draw the building, you will want to change some of the current settings. This includes the line type, layer, and Z-height and base for your line, and the angle type.

CHANGING THE LINE TYPE

The first thing you will want to do is to change to a solid line.

Step 1 - Press **Q** until the line type displayed is **Solid**. (Hint: Pressing the **[Shift]** key simultaneously with the **Q** key scrolls the line type list *backwards*.)

Q or **[Shift] Q**

CHANGING THE LAYER

Step 2 - Press **[TAB]** until the **BLDG** layer is active. (Again, pressing the **[Shift]** key along with **[Tab]** scrolls backwards through the layer list.)

[Tab]

CHANGING THE Z-BASE AND HEIGHT

Step 3 - Press **Z**.

Z

Step 4 - Type in **0** for the Z-base elevation, then press **[Enter]**.

0

Step 5 - Type in **26** for the Z-height elevation, then press **[Enter]**.

26

CHANGING THE ANGLE TYPE

You no longer need to use the Bearings angle type. You can set it back to the "normal" polar setting.

Step 6 - From the **Utility** menu, pick the **Settings** option.

Settings

Step 7 - Pick **AngleTyp**.

AngleTyp

Step 8 - Pick **Normal**.

Normal

Step 9 - Press mouse button **3** to quit.

DRAWING THE BUILDING OUTLINE

Now that your settings are ready, you will draw the outline of your building. To make it easier in adding your 3-D line, you will complete the roof last.

Step 1 – Notice that the building shape is a simple rectangle, as in Fig. 10-3. This is very common when making building layouts. You will learn how to make rectangles easily with DataCAD.

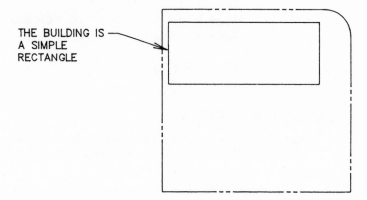

THE BUILDING IS A SIMPLE RECTANGLE

Fig. 10-3

Step 2 – Pick the **Polygon** option, found in the EDIT menu.

Polygon

Step 3 – Since this building is located from the upper left corner of the property line, you will reference this corner to define the dimensions of your building. See Fig. 10-4.

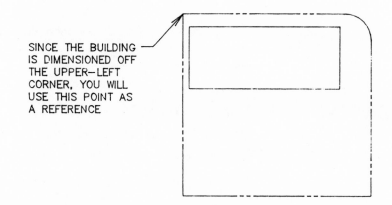

SINCE THE BUILDING IS DIMENSIONED OFF THE UPPER–LEFT CORNER, YOU WILL USE THIS POINT AS A REFERENCE

Fig. 10-4

Step 4 – Press the ~ key.

~

Step 5 – Object Snap to the upper left corner of the property line, as indicated in Fig. 10-5. (Layer Snap should be active in the Object Snap menu. If it isn't, you won't be able to snap to the lines on the PROPLINE layer.)

USER HINT: You can set Layer Snap using your Object Snap menu. (Press [Shift] X.)

Fig. 10-5

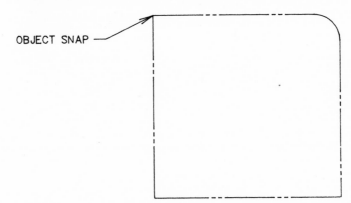

OBJECT SNAP

Step 6 – Press the **[Insert]** key until the Relative Cartesian Coordinate mode is active.

[Insert] (to set relative cartesian mode)

Step 7 – Press the **[Space bar]**.

[Space bar]

Step 8 – Type in the X distance from the reference corner **(5)** and press **[Enter]**.

5

Step 9 – Type in the **Y** distance from the reference corner (–10) and press **[Enter]**. You have now defined the first corner of your building. Notice the rectangle is connected to your cursor, as in Fig. 10-6.

–10

Fig. 10-6

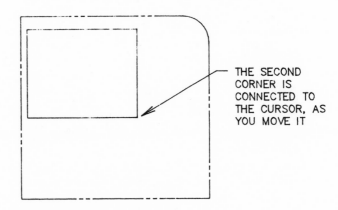

THE SECOND CORNER IS CONNECTED TO THE CURSOR, AS YOU MOVE IT

Step 10 – Press the **[Space bar]** again.

[Space bar]

Step 11 – Type in the coordinates for the opposite corner of your building.

$$X = 120$$
$$Y = -48$$

Step 12 – Your rectangle is created, and should look like Fig. 10-7.

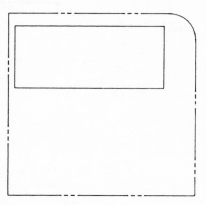

Fig. 10-7

MOVING THE BUILDING

DataCAD is an excellent design tool for this stage of project development. You can easily drag buildings around until you are happy with their locations.

Step 1 – Press **M** to enter the Move menu.

M

Step 2 – Pick the **Drag** option.

Drag

Step 3 – Make sure the **Group** option is active. **(*Group.)**

*Group

Step 4 – Object snap to the upper left corner of your building, as indicated in Fig. 10-8.

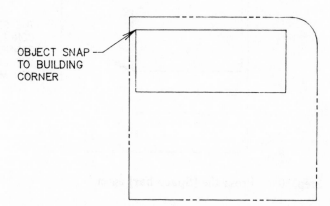

OBJECT SNAP
TO BUILDING
CORNER

Fig. 10-8

Step 5 – Notice that you can drag the building with your cursor!

Step 6 – Press the ~ key.

~

Step 7 – Object snap to the upper left corner of your property line again, as in Fig. 10-9.

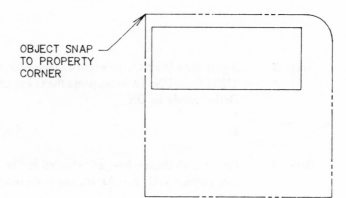

Fig. 10-9

Step 8 – Press the **[Space bar]**, and enter new coordinates to move your building **5** feet in the X and the – Y direction from the corner of your property line.

X = **5**
Y = **–5**

Step 9 – Your building should now be located as dimensioned in Fig. 10-10. Remember to press mouse button **3** to quit.

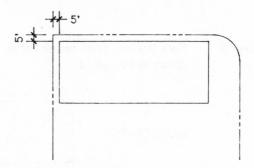

Fig. 10-10

DRAWING TEMPORARY HIP LINES

You will draw temporary lines for your hips, then replace them with 3-D lines later. Since these lines are temporary, you will not worry about the Z-base and height settings.

Step 1 – Object snap to the first corner of your building, as indicated in Fig. 10-11.

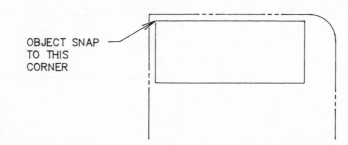

Fig. 10-11

Step 2 –   Drag you line out in the right direction. It should lock onto a horizontal, then 45 degree axis rotations as you move your cursor around the screen, as in Fig. 10-12.

Fig. 10-12

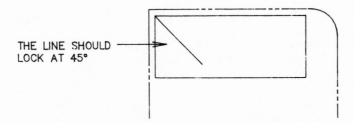

THE LINE SHOULD
LOCK AT 45°

Step 3 –   If your lines DO NOT lock into 45 degree axis, you will want to turn OR-THO LOCK ON. To do so, press the **O** key until the message is displayed: **Ortho mode is ON.**

O

Step 4 –   Create a 45 degree line, as indicated in Fig. 10-13. Make sure that it is long enough to OVERLAP the opposing temporary hip line you will draw next.

Fig. 10-13

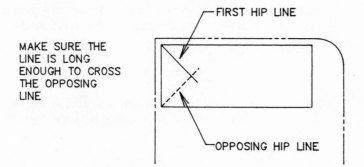

FIRST HIP LINE

MAKE SURE THE
LINE IS LONG
ENOUGH TO CROSS
THE OPPOSING
LINE

OPPOSING HIP LINE

Step 5 –   Place this line, press mouse button 3, and object snap to the next corner, shown in Fig. 10-14.

Fig. 10-14

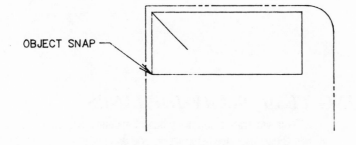

OBJECT SNAP

Step 6 –   Draw a 45 degree line again, as in Fig. 10-15.

Fig. 10-15

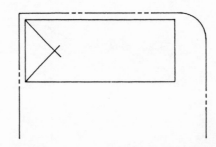

Step 7 – Create the other 2 lines for your hips, as indicated in Fig. 10-16.

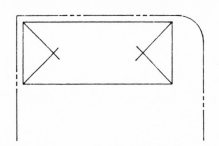

Fig. 10-16

Step 8 – Now you are ready to draw your ridge line. (Fig. 10-17)

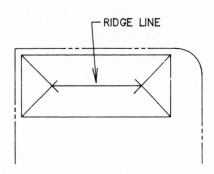

Fig. 10-17

DRAWING THE RIDGE LINE

Step 1 – Press **Z** to change the base and height of the line.

Z

Step 2 – Change both the base and height to **38** feet.

38

Step 3 – Use the **[Shift] X** keys to enter the Object Snap menu. Pick **Intsect** until it is Active (***Intsect**).

*Intsect

Step 4 – Turn OFF **Mid Pnt** and **End Pnt** by picking the options until the star (*) disappears. This will help to make sure that you correctly snap to an intersection point of two lines, and NOT the midpoint or endpoint of one of the lines.

Mid Pnt (* should disappear)

End Pnt

Step 5 – Press mouse button **3** to quit, then Object snap to the intersection of the temporary hip lines, as indicated in Fig. 10-18.

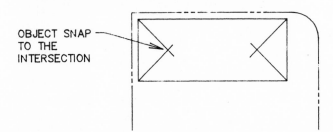

Fig. 10-18

Step 6 – Draw the ridge by object snapping to the opposite hip lines intersection. (Fig. 10-19)

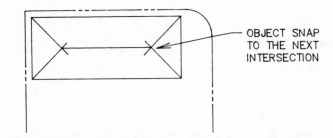

Fig. 10-19

OBJECT SNAP TO THE NEXT INTERSECTION

Step 7 – Erase the temporary hip lines, as shown in Fig. 10-20. (*USER HINT:* use the **E** key to enter the erase menu, then use the ***Entity** setting to erase the individual lines.

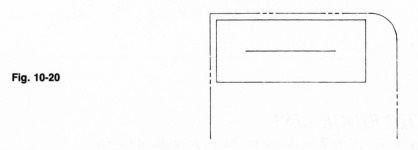

Fig. 10-20

Step 8 – You are ready to draw your 3-D lines!

CHANGING TO A PARALLEL VIEW

You will draw your 3-D lines while viewing in a 3-D angle (3-D view). The first thing you will do, then, is change your view to PARALLEL.

Step 1 – Press **Y**.

Y

Step 2 – Pick **Parllel**.

Parllel.

Step 3 – Pick a viewing location on the globe that appears on the screen. (You may have to try different areas on the globe for better viewing.) See Fig. 10-21.

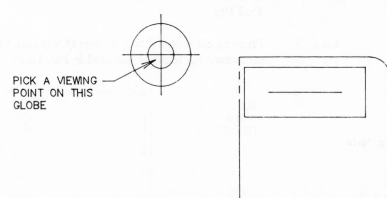

PICK A VIEWING POINT ON THIS GLOBE

Fig. 10-21

Step 4 – Your view should expose all four upper corners of the building, AND the two endpoints of the ridge line, as in Fig. 10-22. This is important since you will be picking these endpoints to attach your 3-D lines.

THE VIEW SHOULD
EXPOSE ALL FOUR
CORNERS OF THE
BUILDING, TO MAKE
PICKING EASIER

Fig. 10-22

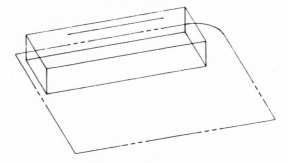

Step 5 – Press mouse button **3** to quit back to the 3D Edit menu.

DRAWING THE 3-D LINE

Step 6 – Pick the **3D Line** option.

3D Line

Step 7 – Pick the **3D Cursr** option until it is active **(*3D Cursr)**.

*3D Cursr

Step 8 – Notice that your cursor is now displayed as an XYZ axis. This option enables the ability to object snap in 3-D. (Fig. 10-23)

Fig. 10-23

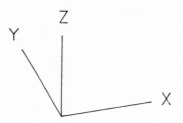

Step 9 – The axis point is the pick point of your cursor, as indicated in Fig. 10-24.

Fig. 10-24

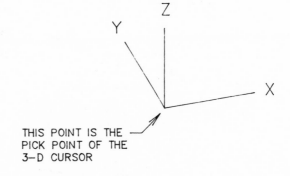

THIS POINT IS THE
PICK POINT OF THE
3-D CURSOR

Step 10 – Object snap to the first corner of the building for the hip, as indicated in Fig. 10-25. Reset the Object Snap menu to *End Pnt.

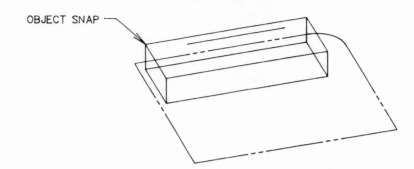

Fig. 10-25

Step 11 – Object snap to the ridge line endpoint, as shown in Fig. 10-26.

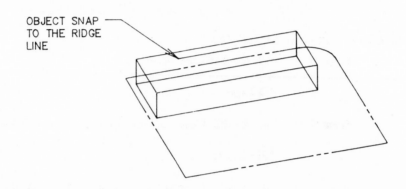

Fig. 10-26

Step 11 – Your 3D line will be drawn! Your drawing should now look like Fig. 10-27.

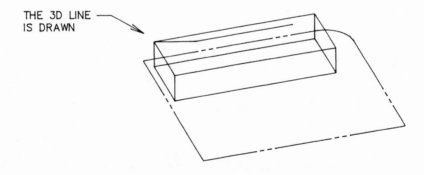

Fig. 10-27

Step 12 – Connect the end points of the other corners to the ridge line, as indicated in Fig. 10-28.

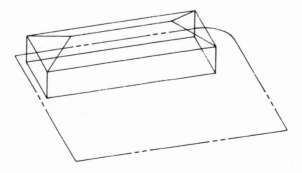

Fig. 10-28

Step 13 – Return to the plan view of your site, by using the **3D View** menu, then selecting the **Ortho** option.

3D View

Ortho

Step 14 – Your building is done! See Fig. 10-29. Remember, if you use Hide to remove hidden lines from the 3D view, your "3D lines" will not hide lines like a wall.

THE BUILDING
IS DONE!

Fig. 10-29

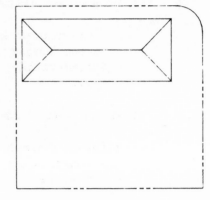

Step 15 – Save your drawing, by using the **File I/O, Save Dwg** options.

DataCAD Exercise 10

Please complete the following exercise by reading each question carefully, then circling the letter that corresponds to the correct answer.

1. To draw a line angled through all three axis (X,Y,Z) you use:

   a. Z-height and base settings.
   b. 3D Line.
   c. AngLine.

2. When you use 3D Lines in your drawing, you:

   a. Cannot remove hidden lines behind them automatically when using the "Hide" function. You simply erase them manually.
   b. Can remove hidden lines behind them automatically when using the "Hide" function.

3. When drawing a building that is a simple rectangle, you can use the:

   a. Polygon, Rectangle options.
   b. Rectangle, 4Corners options.
   c. 3D Line, Rectangle options.

4. Before picking a reference point to measure from, you press the:

   a. R key.
   b. > key.
   c. ~ key.

5. In order to object snap to items not on the current active layer, you use the:

   a. Middle button on the mouse. It does not matter if Layer Snap is on or not.
   b. The Object Snap menu to turn on Layer Snap, then use the middle mouse button.

6. The quick way to enter the Object Snap menu, is to press the:

   a. [Shift] X keys.
   b. [Shift] O keys.
   c. X key.

7. When you want to move a rectangle by dragging it with your cursor, you use the:

   a. Move menu, make the Entity option active, pick the rectangle, then drag it to the new location.
   b. Move menu, pick Drag, make the Entity option active, pick the rectangle, then drag it to the new location.
   c. Move menu, pick Drag, make the Group option active, pick the rectangle, then drag it to the new location.

8. To enter the Move menu quickly, you press the:

   a. D key.
   b. M key.
   c. [Alt] M keys.

9. To turn on the mode that locks your line in 45-degree angles as you draw it, you press the:

   a. O key until the message says: Ortho mode is on.
   b. A key until the message says: Angle lock is on.
   c. L key until the message says: Ortho lock is on.

10. When you wish to easily snap to the intersection point of two lines, in the Object Snap menu, you should make the option Intsect active, and:

    a. The Mid Pnt option active also.
    b. Turn Mid Pnt and End Pnt off.
    c. The End Pnt and Mid Pnt options active.

11. In order to object snap to entities in different Z elevations, in 3D Line you use the:

    a. 3D Cursr option.
    b. Entity option.
    c. Z Off option.

12. The 3D Line option is found in the:

    a. Architect menu.
    b. Parallel menu.
    c. 3D Edit menu.

13. Before creating your 3D line, you should:

    a. Window in for better viewing.
    b. Create a 3D view in order to see all of the line endpoints you will be connecting.
    c. Make sure you are in Ortho view.

14. To return to the plan view of your drawing, you use the:

    a. 3D View, Ortho option.
    b. 2D View, Ortho option.
    c. 3D View, Plan option.

Lesson 11:
Copying Techniques

WHAT YOU WILL BE DOING:

YOU will use copying techniques to create new entities in your drawing. You will copy lines in a repeated pattern, mirror this pattern, offset lines, and change existing lines to another linestyle.

OBJECTIVES:

Your lesson objectives, then, are to:

- Offset copies of existing lines.
- Offset copies of arcs.
- Changing attributes of items.
- Copying in a rectangular pattern.
- Mirroring copies of items.
- Trimming lines.
- Extending lines.
- Adding fillets to round the corners of existing lines.

Remember to reference your *DataCAD Operations Guide* when instructed.

COPYING TECHNIQUES

WHENEVER POSSIBLE, *you would always copy!* Why? Because copying existing geometry saves time, eliminates steps, increases accuracy, and reduces error.

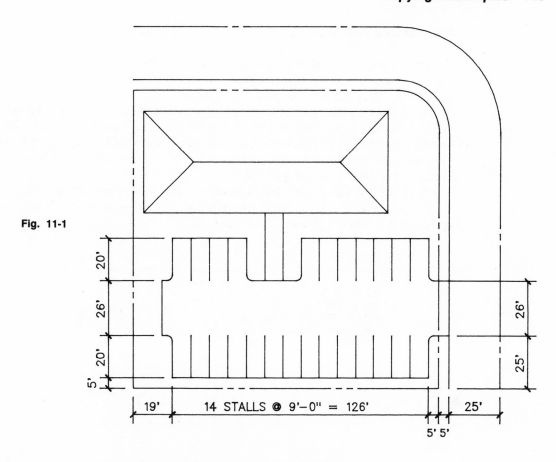

Fig. 11-1

Copying techniques includes such things as:

- Copying in a rectangular pattern
- Copying in a circular pattern
- Moving and copying
- Mirroring and copying
- Offsetting copies

It may even include making symbols of items or a part of a building, and using the symbol in several drawings!

How copying saves time and steps

Copying reduces the amount of time it would take to recreate duplicate geometry. You may want to copy when geometry is not exactly duplicated, but only requires minor changes. Copying from "look alike" sets of entities would be better than starting from scratch.

How copying increases accuracy and reduces errors

Once you have created an item or a set of items correctly, then every time you copy it, it is correct! There will be no errors in subsequent copies, if there is none in the original.

Also, in the case of a copied pattern, you will find that it is much easier and more accurate to define the repeat of the pattern and the spacing, and let the computer do your work, than if you created each piece manually.

Pre-planning your drawing

If you spend a few minutes organizing your steps prior to starting your drawings, you will be able to scan the items for repeated patterns and the "best" way to create the drawing. This technique is called "pre-planning".

Good users of CAD systems always pre-plan their drawings. How long it takes depends on the experience of the user and the complexity of the project. Some users have found it very effective to rough out a "quick and dirty" sketch of the drawing, only penciling the major steps of the drawing creation. Later, when the user is more experienced, sketches only have to be made mentally.

All of the drawings you are guided through in your lessons have been pre-planned for you. It is good, though, to take a minute to look at your project for this lesson, and analyze how it was pre-planned, as in Fig. 11-2.

Fig. 11-2

SOMETIMES A
QUICK SKETCH
HELPS YOU TO
PRE—PLAN YOUR
DRAWING

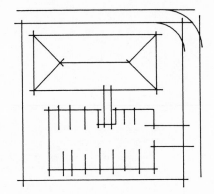

Step 1 –   Examine your project for repeated geometry.

In this case, the street lines are lines and an arc moved a certain constant distance from the property lines. This can be achieved by "copying" the property lines, "offset" at an equal distance.

Although the line types are not the same, it becomes an easy task to simply change the line type of the copied lines. See Fig. 11-3.

THESE LINES CAN
BE OFFSET COPIES
FROM THE ORIGINAL
LINES AND ARC

Fig. 11-3

ORIGINAL
PROPERTY
LINES

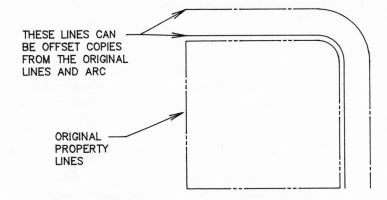

Step 2 – Look for repeated patterns in your drawings.

Notice that the parking lot is a very good example of a repeated pattern. (Fig. 11-4)

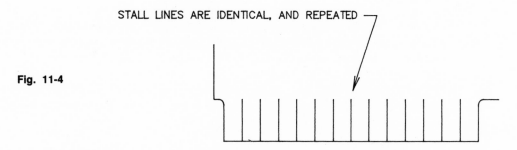

STALL LINES ARE IDENTICAL, AND REPEATED

Fig. 11-4

Step 3 – Look for ways of eliminating steps.

For instance, although the entire parking area could be made by two repeat patterns, establishing the second repeat pattern items, then creating the pattern consumes many more steps than involved in just mirroring the first pattern over to the other side. This is shown in Fig. 11-5.

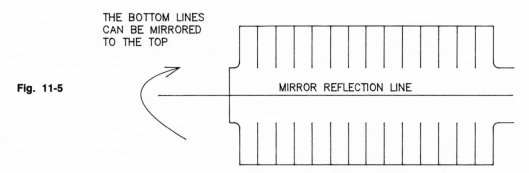

THE BOTTOM LINES CAN BE MIRRORED TO THE TOP

MIRROR REFLECTION LINE

Fig. 11-5

Step 4 – Figure how you will start, and what the progression will be in creating the geometry. What is your first step? What will you do next? Can you lump together some related steps to perform at one time, without having to change back and forth through menus?

It would be faster, for instance, to offset all of the street lines in one step. Then the second step would be to change the offset copies to the correct line type all at one time, as in Fig. 11-6. This avoids needless changes of menus and unnecessary steps.

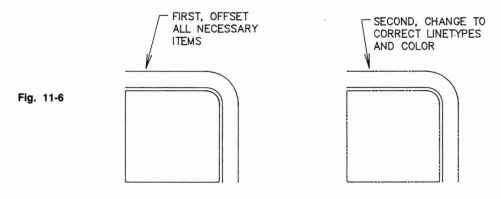

FIRST, OFFSET ALL NECESSARY ITEMS

SECOND, CHANGE TO CORRECT LINETYPES AND COLOR

Fig. 11-6

Examine the following pictorial, Fig. 11-7, which graphically illustrates the creation steps used for this drawing. Each step is story-boarded to help you understand the pre-planning that went into the drawing.

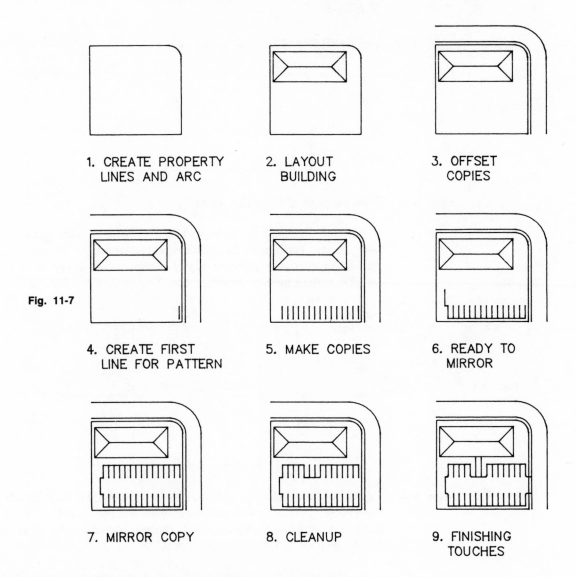

Fig. 11-7

1. CREATE PROPERTY LINES AND ARC

2. LAYOUT BUILDING

3. OFFSET COPIES

4. CREATE FIRST LINE FOR PATTERN

5. MAKE COPIES

6. READY TO MIRROR

7. MIRROR COPY

8. CLEANUP

9. FINISHING TOUCHES

OFFSETTING THE PROPERTY LINES

The ''Offset'' function is found in the Geometry menu. Offset allows you to make a copy of an item at a defined distance. You will use Offset to create copies of the property lines to draw lines for your sidewalk and street. You will not have to draw these lines from scratch with input coordinates, or figure out the correct radius for the arc. DataCAD does it for you!

Step 1 –   Make the **STREET** layer active.

Step 2 –   Pick the **Geometry** option found in the EDIT menu.

Geometry

Step 3 –   Pick the **Offset** option.

Offset

Step 4 –   Make sure the **LyrSrch** option is active.

*LyrSrch

Step 5 –   Make sure the **Dynamic** option is INACTIVE (no star *).

Dynamic

Step 6 –   Pick the **PerpDist** option. (This option is only displayed if the Dynamic option is turned off.)

PerpDist

Step 7 –   Type in and [Enter] the distance for the sidewalk lines.

5

Step 8 –   Pick the first line you will offset, as indicated in Fig. 11-8.

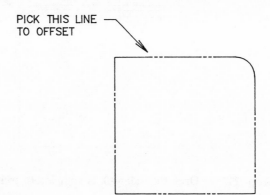

Fig. 11-8

PICK THIS LINE
TO OFFSET

Step 9 –   Pick anywhere on the side of the line you wish the offset copy to appear, as in Fig. 11-9.

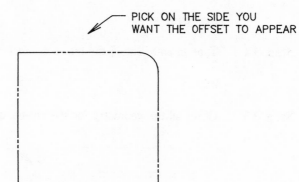

Fig. 11-9

PICK ON THE SIDE YOU
WANT THE OFFSET TO APPEAR

Step 10 – The copy will be created! (Fig. 11-10)

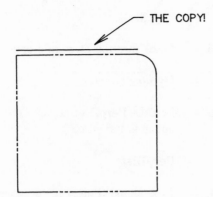

Fig. 11-10

Step 11 – Offset copies for the arc and other line, as indicated in Fig. 11-11.

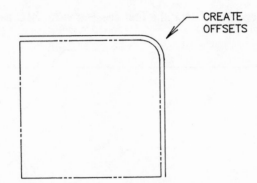

Fig. 11-11

Step 12 – Once the sidewalk is completed, pick the **New Dist** option.

New Dist

Step 13 – Pick **PerpDist** again.

PerpDist

Step 14 – Type in and [Enter] the offset distance for the street.

25

Step 15 – Offset all the geometry for the street, as shown in Fig. 11-12.

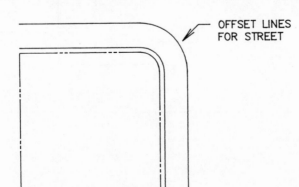

Fig. 11-12

CHANGING THE ATTRIBUTES OF EXISTING ITEMS

Step 1 – Pick the **Change** option, found in the EDIT menu.

Change

Step 2 – Pick **LineTyp.**

LineTyp

Step 3 – Set the line type to **CentrLn.**

CentrLn

Step 4 – Pick **Color.**

Color

Step 5 – Set the color to **Lt Cyan.**

Lt Cyan

Step 6 – Make sure **Entity** or **Group** is active (either will work).

*Entity

Step 7 – Pick all of the items you want changed to the new color and line type, indicated in Fig. 11-13.

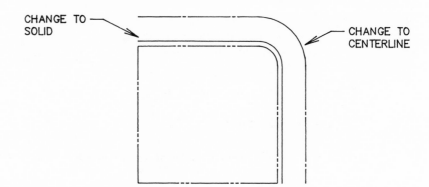

Fig. 11-13

CREATING THE PARKING LOT

Step 1 – Press the **[Tab]** key to change the active layer to **PARKING.**

[Tab]

Step 2 – Set the **Z base and height** to **0** by pressing the Z key and entering 0.

Z

Step 3 – Make sure the coordinate input mode is set to **Relative cartesian coordinates.** (Use the **[Insert]** key.)

[Insert]

Step 4 – The parking lot outline is dimensioned off the lower right corner of the property line, indicated in Fig. 11-14. You will use this corner as your **reference point**.

Fig. 11-14

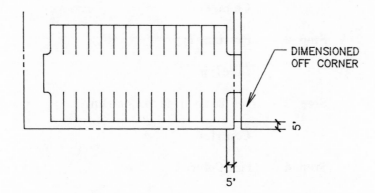

DIMENSIONED
OFF CORNER

5'

5'

Step 5 – Press the ~ key.

~

Step 6 – Pick the reference corner. (Fig. 11-15)

Fig. 11-15

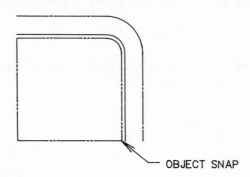

OBJECT SNAP

Step 7 – Press the **[Space bar]** to use Relative coordinates.

[Space bar]

Step 8 – Type in the coordinates for the distance from your reference corner.

(See project for dimensions)

Step 9 – Press the space bar again, and type in the coordinates for the length of the line indicated in Fig. 11-16.

Fig. 11-16

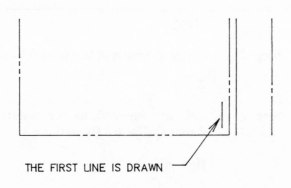

THE FIRST LINE IS DRAWN

Step 10 – This is the only line you need to create for your pattern. Press mouse button **3** to quit.

COPYING IN A RECTANGULAR ARRAY

You can copy all the stripes for your parking lot from this single line.

Step 1 – Press **C** to enter the Copy option found in the EDIT menu.

C

Step 2 – Pick the **RectArry** option.

RectArry

Step 3 – Pick a start point anywhere (Fig. 11-17). It doesn't matter exactly where you pick, since the *distance* you define will be the important factor.

Fig. 11-17

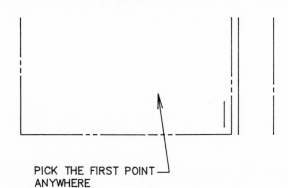

PICK THE FIRST POINT
ANYWHERE

Step 4 – Press the **[Space bar]**, and type in the coordinates defining the distance for the first copy. This will be the distance between the stripes.

X = –9
Y = 0

Step 5 – Now type in the number of repetitions for the **X** direction. This is the TOTAL number of stripes you will want created, INCLUDING the original.

Since it is often hard to predetermine the real number of stripes for your parking lot, you will usually define more than enough, then delete the stripes you *don't* need. In this case, try the number **20** to see how they fit.

20

Step 6 – Now press **[Enter]** to accept the **Y** default of **1**.

Step 7 – Pick the line you will want to copy as shown in Fig. 11-18.

Fig. 11-18

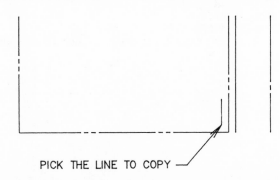

PICK THE LINE TO COPY

Step 8 – The new lines will appear! (Fig. 11-19)

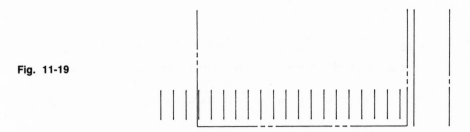

Fig. 11-19

Step 9 – Press the < key to erase any extra lines.

<

Step 10 – Create a line to close the bottom of the lot outline, as shown in Fig. 11-20, by object snapping to the bottom of the two end lines.

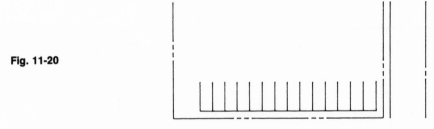

Fig. 11-20

Step 11 – Use object snap and relative cartesian coordinates to create the 5 foot line and the 26 foot line, as indicated in Fig. 11-21.

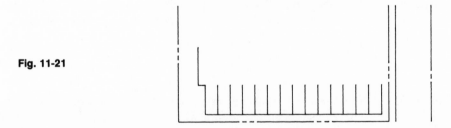

Fig. 11-21

MIRRORING THE PARKING STRIPES

You can mirror the stripes to the other side of the lot. When you mirror, you need to define a mirror axis line. The items you mirror will be reflected to the other side of this line, as though you were holding a mirror there.

You can use the mid point of the line indicated in Fig. 11-22, as the beginning point for your reflection line, then drag your line out on the X axis.

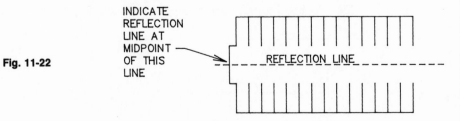

INDICATE
REFLECTION
LINE AT
MIDPOINT
OF THIS
LINE

REFLECTION LINE

Fig. 11-22

Step 1 –   Pick the **Mirror** option, found in the EDIT menu.

Mirror

Step 2 –   Press **[Shift] X** and set the Object Snap to **Mid Pnt**.

*Mid Pnt

Step 3 –   Object snap to the mid point of the line shown in Fig. 11-23, to define the starting point of your reflection line.

Fig. 11-23

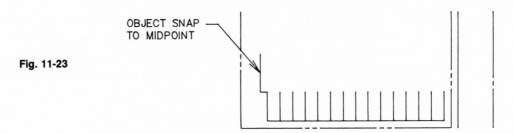

Step 4 –   Pick the second point for your reflection line, making sure the line is straight on the X axis, as in Fig. 11-24. (Ortho mode helps you do this.)

Fig. 11-24

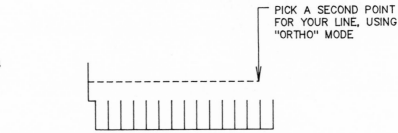

Step 5 –   Make sure the **Area** option is active.

*Area

Step 6 –   Also make sure the **AndCopy** option is active.

*AndCopy

Step 7 –   Pick for the first and second corner points to indicate a rectangle around the area you wish to copy. Make sure you include only a part of the line you used to object snap to for your reflection line, as indicated below.

Any line that is only *partially* included in your rectangle will NOT be copied! Only lines completely surrounded by the rectangle will be mirrored. (Fig. 11-25)

Fig. 11-25

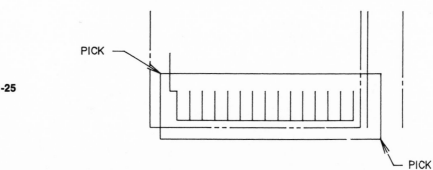

Step 8 - The copy is created, as illustrated in Fig. 11-26.

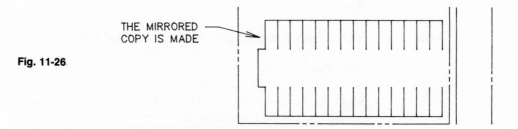

THE MIRRORED
COPY IS MADE

Fig. 11-26

Step 9 - Use the Object snap to connect the fourth line to the seventh line of the mirrored pattern, as indicated in Fig. 11-27.

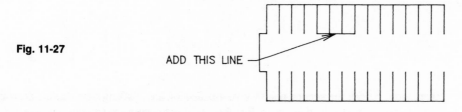

Fig. 11-27

ADD THIS LINE

MAKING A PARTIAL ERASE

Step 1 - Press **E** to erase.

E

Step 2 - Pick the **Partial** option.

Partial

Step 3 - Pick the line indicated in Fig. 11-28. This is the line you will erase only a part of.

PICK THIS LINE

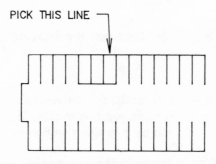

Fig. 11-28

Step 4 - Make sure your Object Snap menu is set to **Intsect**, and that **Mid Pnt** is inactive.

*Intsect
Mid Pnt

Step 5 – Object snap to the intersections of the fourth and seventh line, as indicated in Fig. 11-29. This will define the part of the line you want to get rid of.

Fig. 11-29

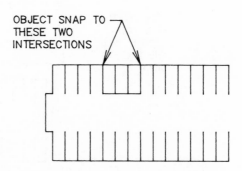

Step 6 – The line will be cut and erased! (Fig. 11-30)

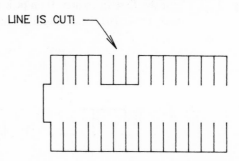

Fig. 11-30

ONE LINE TRIM

Step 1 – Pick the **CleanUp** option, found in the EDIT menu.

CleanUp

Step 2 – Pick the **1LnTrim** option.

1LnTrim

Step 3 – Make sure **Entity** is active.

*Entity

Step 4 – Also make sure **LyrSrch** is active.

*LyrSrch

Step 5 – Pick the bottom line of the building, as indicated in Fig. 11-31. This is the line you will want to trim TO.

Fig. 11-31

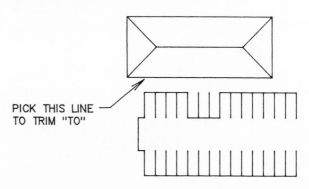

Step 6 – Pick anywhere on the other side of the line, where you DON'T want the line drawn, as indicated in Fig. 11-32.

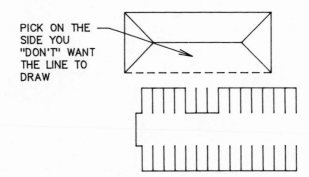

PICK ON THE
SIDE YOU
"DON'T" WANT
THE LINE TO
DRAW

Fig. 11-32

Step 7 – Pick the **Entity** option, then pick the lines you want trimmed (or in this case, *extended*). This would be the two lines indicated in Fig. 11-33.

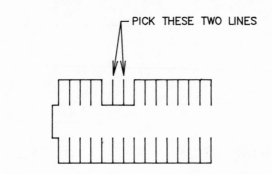

PICK THESE TWO LINES

Fig. 11-33

Step 8 – The lines you pick will be stretched, or extended, to the building. (Fig. 11-34)

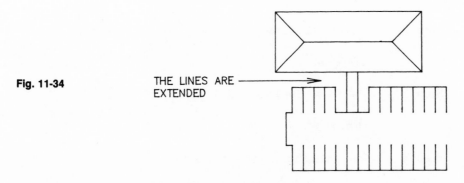

THE LINES ARE
EXTENDED

Fig. 11-34

ADDING LINES FOR THE DRIVEWAY

Step 1 – Object snap to the end of the line indicated in Fig. 11-35.

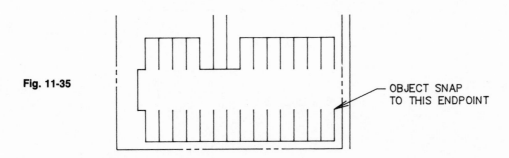

OBJECT SNAP
TO THIS ENDPOINT

Fig. 11-35

Step 2 – Drag a horizontal line out, overlapping the property line as indicated in Fig. 11-36. You will trim this later.

Fig. 11-36

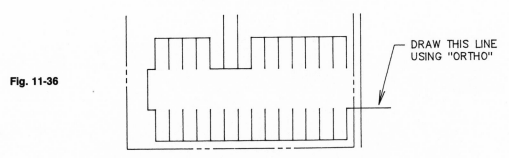

Step 3 – Press **M** to Move this line to the other side of the driveway.

M

Step 4 – To define a moving distance, object snap to the first endpoint, then to the second, as indicated in Fig. 11-37.

Fig. 11-37

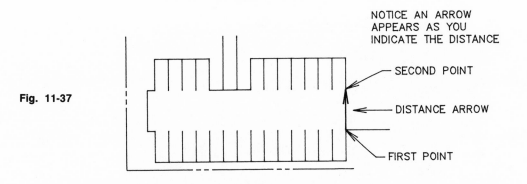

Step 5 – Make sure **AndCopy** is active.

*AndCopy

Step 6 – Pick the line to copy, and the copy is created! (Fig. 11-38)

Fig. 11-38

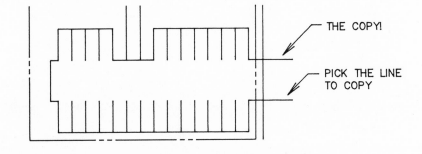

Step 7 - Use the **1 Line Trim** procedure to trim back the overlapping lines of your driveway, as shown in Fig. 11-39.

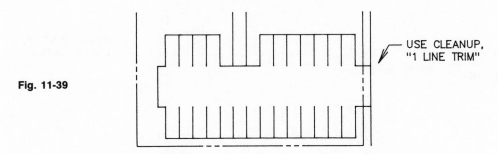

Fig. 11-39

USE CLEANUP, "1 LINE TRIM"

CREATING THE FILLETS

"Fillets" are the little arcs used to round the corners of the parking lot.

Step 1 - Press the **[Alt] U** to enter the CleanUp menu.

[Alt] U

Step 2 - Pick the **Fillets** option.

Fillets

Step 3 - Pick the **Radius** option.

Radius

Step 4 - Set the radius of the fillet to **2** feet.

2

Step 5 - Pick the first line of the "corner" to fillet, as indicated in Fig. 11-40.

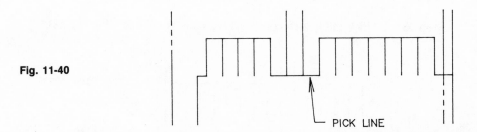

Fig. 11-40

PICK LINE

Step 6 - Pick the second line of the corner to fillet, shown in Fig. 11-41.

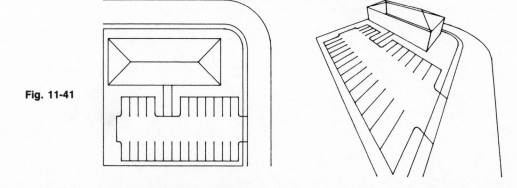

Fig. 11-41

Step 7 – Your fillet will be created. (Fig. 11-42)

Fig. 11-42

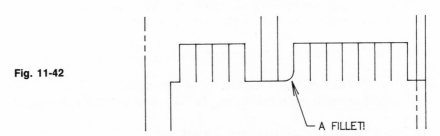

A FILLET!

Step 8 – Continue picking lines of the corners you wish to fillet, until your drawing is completed.

Step 9 – Using **3-D View, Prspect** option, create a BIRD'S EYE VIEW of your drawing, setting the **EyePnt Z** to **50** feet. **Save** this image, using the **Offset** option to control where the image will be placed on your drawing. Create a **NewLayer**, calling this layer: **BIRDSEYE**.

Adjust this 3D view, if necessary, until it is positioned correctly. This is illustrated in Fig. 11-43.

Fig. 11-43

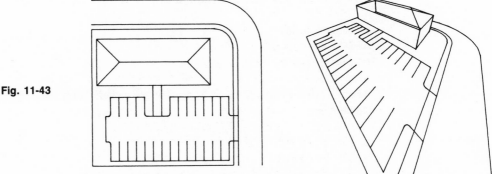

IF YOU NEED A QUICK REVIEW OF 3-D PERSPECTIVES . . .

Just in case you are unable to recall the steps you went through to create your 3-D view, look back at the lesson called: CREATING 3-D VIEWS, or look in the VIEWS - 3-D section of your Appendix A - DataCAD Operations Guide, **Creating a birds-eye perspective view**.

Step 10 – Save your file, using the **File I/O, Save Dwg** options.

DataCAD Exercise 11

Please complete the following exercise by reading each question carefully, then circling the letter that corresponds to the correct answer.

1. Before starting to create your project, you should:

   a. Pre-plan the steps you will use in drawing it.
   b. Not waste time pre-planning the steps you will take in drawing it.

2. Part of the pre-planning stage consists of:

   a. Creating the walls in your drawing.
   b. Looking for repeated patterns, and the "best" way to create your drawing.
   c. Looking for repeated patterns in your drawing. There is never a "best" way to create it.

3. To copy geometry in a repeated pattern, in the X and Y directions, you use the:

   a. Move, AndCopy options.
   b. Copy, RectArry options.
   c. Copy, Repeat options.

4. To reflect entities, or copies of entities, to another location, you use the:

   a. Reflect option.
   b. Mid Pnt option.
   c. Mirror option.

5. When defining an area to copy, items that are included only partially in the rectangle will:

   a. Not be copied.
   b. Will be copied.
   c. Will only be copied if the Include option is active.

6. In order to delete PART of a line only, you use the:

   a. CleanUp, Partial options.
   b. Erase, Partial options.
   c. CleanUp, 1LnTrim options.

7. To extend, or stretch, a line to another line, you use the:

   a. Erase, Partial options.
   b. CleanUp, Stretch options.
   c. CleanUp, 1LnTrim options.

8. If you wish to define a distance for placing a single copy of an entity by picking two points, you use the:

   a. Move option, pick two points defining the move distance, make sure the AndCopy option is active, then pick the item(s) to copy.
   b. Move, Drag options, pick two points defining the move distance, make sure the AndCopy option is active, then pick the item(s) to copy.
   c. Copy option, pick two points defining the move distance, then pick the item(s) to copy.

Some review questions:

9. Default drawings allow you to:

   a. Change the type of drawing you are going to create, but not the scale or drawing borders.
   b. Pre-set several different "drawing formats" (blank drawing sheets) for the types and scales of drawings you will be creating. This includes setting up special layers for your drawings also.
   c. Have the correct title block already set in your drawing only. The layers and scale cannot be pre-set in the default drawing.

10. To change your default drawing, you must retrieve the Drawing list (either by starting DataCAD, or using the File I/O, New Dwg options), then:

    a. Enter the name of your default drawing.
    b. Change the current directory using the New Path option.
    c. Pick the Default option and pick the name of your default drawing.

11. The different types of polar input modes are:

    a. Normal, Cartesian, and Bearings.
    b. Relative, Cartesian, and Bearings.
    c. Normal, Compass, and Bearings.

12. Different lines (such as solid, dashed, dot-dash, etc.) are called:

    a. Line Weights.
    b. Line Types.
    c. Line Scales.

13. To set the polar mode to Bearings, you use the:

    a. [Insert] key.
    b. [Space Bar].
    c. Settings menu, AngleTyp option.

14. To set the input mode to Relative Polar, you use the:

    a. [Insert] key.
    b. [Space Bar].
    c. Settings menu, AngleTyp option.

15. Before you use a relative input mode, you should:

    a. ALWAYS pick a start point.
    b. NEVER pick a start point.
    c. Only pick a start point if the drawing tells you to.

16. The quickest way to turn from lines to walls, or from walls to lines, is to use the:

    a. Menu option choices.
    b. [<] "less than" key.
    c. [=] "equal" key.

17. In order to define a reference point, you press the:

    a. [Space Bar].
    b. ~ key.
    c. X key.

18. To clean up wall intersections after you create them, you:

    a. Press [Alt] C, to enter the Cleanup menu.
    b. Press A, to enter the Cleanup menu.
    c. Pick the Cleanup menu, and use the T or L intersection options.

19. To erase the last item you created, you use the:

    a. Delete option.
    b. < less than key.
    c. > greater than key.

20. To erase an entire area at one time, you use the:

    a. E key to enter the Erase menu, then pick the Area option.
    b. [Shift] < keys together.
    c. [Shift] > keys together.

Lesson 12:
Detail Drawings

WHAT YOU WILL BE DOING:

You will create details and add them to a detail sheet. Details are first drawn true size, scaled, then made into symbols for use in all of your detail sheets.

OBJECTIVES:

Your lesson objectives, then, are:

- Set-up a default drawing for your 1½″ = 1′ details.
- Create a hatch boundary.
- Define a hatch pattern and a scale for the pattern.
- Explode the dimensions in your detail.
- Reduce the size of the detail

Remember to reference your *DataCAD Operations Guide* when instructed.

DEFINING THE DEFAULT DRAWING FOR YOUR DETAIL

Before you begin your detail, you will want to set-up a default drawing. You will be able to use this default for all of your details that are 1½″ = 1′ scale. Of course, you will set up other default drawings to create details in different scales.

This section is a good review of lesson 2 - DRAWING SET-UP. You may wish to reference this lesson for further explanation.

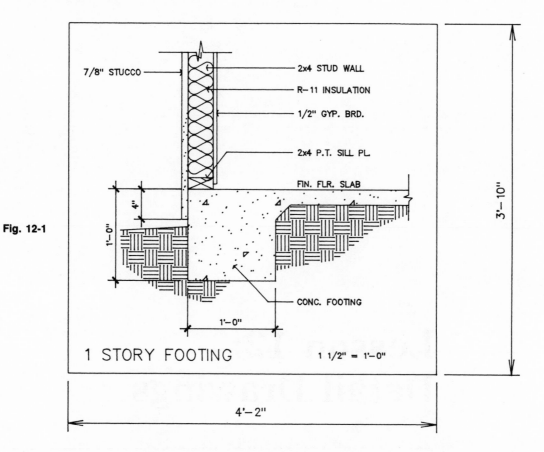

Fig. 12-1

7/8" STUCCO

2x4 STUD WALL

R-11 INSULATION

1/2" GYP. BRD.

2x4 P.T. SILL PL.

FIN. FLR. SLAB

CONC. FOOTING

4"

1'-0"

1'-0"

3'-10"

4'-2"

1 STORY FOOTING   1 1/2" = 1'-0"

Step 1 – Retrieve the DataCAD drawing list, either by starting DataCAD, or by using **File I/O, New Dwg**.

Step 2 – When the drawing list is displayed, select the **Default** option.

Default

Step 3 – Press the **[Space bar]** once, to clear any default drawing. This will return you to the DataCAD defaults.

[Space bar]

Step 4 – Now pick the **New Path** option, to enter the Default directory.

New Path

Step 5 – Type in the name of the default directory: **DEFAULT**

default

Step 6 –   Your default drawing list should be displayed, as in Fig. 12-2.

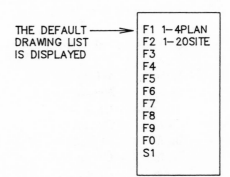

Fig. 12-2

Step 7 –   Now type in the new name of your default drawing: **DET1-1-2**. This will stand for: Detail 1½″ scale.

det1-1-2

Step 8 –   When your new drawing file is displayed, press the **L** key to go to the LAYERS menu.

L

Step 9 –   Use the **NewLayer** option, to add **8** layers (9 layers total).

Step 10 –   Name these layers, as indicated in the following list:

Walls
Wood
Concrete
Earth
Insul
Dims
Notes
Misc
Box

A FAST WAY TO GIVE THE LAYERS COLORS

You will keep the Walls layer color set to white, but the rest of your layers will have other colors associated with them.

Step 1 –   Press **[Tab]** until the **Wood** layer is active.

[Tab]   (until Wood is active)

Step 2 –   Press the **K** key until the current color is set to **Brown**.

K   (until Brown is set)

Step 3 –   Press the **[Tab]** key until the **Concrete** layer is displayed.

[Tab]   (until Concrete is active)

Step 4 –   Press the **K** key until the **Dk Gray** is set.

  K   (until Dk Gray is set)

Step 5 –   Continue until all of the layers are assigned colors:

  Walls   = **White**
  Wood   = **Brown**
  Concrete = **Dk Gray**
  Earth   = **Brown**
  Insul   = **Lt Mgta**
  Dims   = **Green**
  Notes   = **Green**
  Misc   = **Lt Cyan**
  Box   = **Yellow**

SETTING THE DIMENSION VARIABLES

  Since dimensions are *Descriptive* items in your drawing, you need to adjust the variables to the correct settings for 1½″ = 1′ scale.

  The options you will be setting for your dimensions are illustrated in Fig. 12-3.

Fig. 12-3

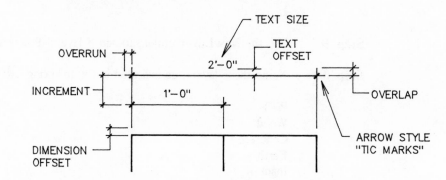

Step 1 –   From the EDIT menu, select the **Dimension** option.

  Dimension

Step 2 –   Pick the **Linear** option.

  Linear

Step 3 –   Select **TextStyl**.

  TextStyl

Step 4 –   Pick **TextSize**.

  TextSize

Step 5 –   Turn to the **DataCAD Scales & Sizes** section of Appendix B *DataCAD Reference Guide*, and find the correct size for "Text Size Notes" at a 1½″ scale.

Step 6 –   Change the current text size to the size you found in this section: **1″**

  1″

Step 7 – Change the text **Offset** option to **1″** also. This will set the offset to ⅛″.

Offset

1″

Step 8 – Press the mouse button **3** to quit back to the DIMENSION menu, and pick **Dim Styl.**

Dim Styl

Step 9 – Change the **Offset** to **1″**.

Offset

1″

Step 10 – Change the **Overlap** to **1″**.

Overlap

1″

Step 11 – Change the **Incrment** to **4″**.

Incrment

4″

Step 12 – Pick **FixdDis** until the option is *OFF* (no star *).

FixdDis   (until * is off)

Step 13 – Press mouse button **3** once to quit back to DIMENSION menu, then pick **ArroStyl.**

ArroStyl

Step 14 – Change the arrow style to **Tic Marks.**

Tic Marks

Step 15 – Change the **Weight** of the drawn tic marks to **2.**

Weight

2

Step 16 – Press mouse button **3** to quit out of DIMENSIONS.

DETAIL BOX

You will draw a detail box that will hold your detail. Again, this is a descriptive item, and you will have to draw it in accordance with the final scale of the drawing.

Refer to the **DataCAD Available Drawing Sheet Areas** section in the *DataCAD Reference Guide*. The size you will use for the detail box is listed under the **Typical**

Detail Box column. The sizes described here will result in a 6¼″ × 5¾″ box when scaled for plotting.

Step 1 – Make sure the **Box** layer is active.

Step 2 – Press the **Z** key, to change your Z-base and Z-height.

Z

Step 3 – Change the base and height to **0**.

Z-base = **0**
Z-height = **0**

Step 4 – Return to the EDIT menu, and pick the **Polygon** option.

Polygon

Step 5 – Pick the **Rectangl** option.

Rectangl

Step 6 – Pick a start point for your box, then use the **Relative cartesian coordinate input mode** to enter the X and Y values for your detail box. (See Fig. 12-4.)

USE COORDINATES
TO CREATE THE
DETAIL BOX

Fig. 12-4

Y = 3′–10″

X = 4′–2″

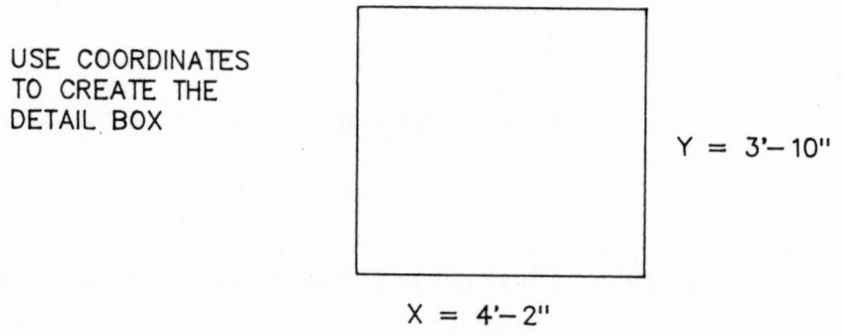

Step 7 – If necessary, recalculate the extents of your window, using the / key.

/

Recalc

SETTING THE SNAP INCREMENT

Your snap increment is presently set to **4″**. This is too large of an increment when you are working on a small scale. You will want to adjust the Snap distance to **1″**.

Step 1 – Press the **S** key. This quick key will put you in the **Grids, SetGrid, GridSnap** menus.

S

Step 2 –   Change the settings for your snap to **1″**, or 0.1.

X = **0.1**
Y = **0.1**

Step 3 –   Save your default drawing and return to the Drawing list, using the **File I/O, New Dwg, Yes** options.

File I/O

New Dwg

Yes

RETURNING TO YOUR ORIGINAL DRAWING LIST

Now the drawing list for the Default drawings is displayed. You will want to change the directory to your own drawing list.

Step 1 –   Pick the **New Path** option.

New Path

Step 2 –   Type in the directory pathname for your drawings. Remember, you named it your first or last name.

yourname

Step 3 –   Now your drawings should appear (PLAN1, SITE1, and any other drawing you may have created during your lessons).

If they do not appear, and you get the message **"Path 'name' does not exist. Create it?"**, pick the **No** option. Then check the spelling of the pathname you are typing in. It should match the name you defined in lesson 3 - **Basic Drafting Techniques** *exactly*.

Step 4 –   Once your drawing names appear, you can define which default drawing you want active. Pick the **Default** option.

Default

Step 5 –   Pick the name of the detail Default Drawing:

DET1-1-2

Step 6 –   Now type in the new name for your drawing: DETAIL1.

DETAIL1

CREATING THE DETAIL

Once the detail box (defined in the Default drawing) is displayed on the screen. You can begin drawing your detail. See Fig. 12-1.

Step 1 –   Apply the skills you have learned in your previous lessons to create the detail, following the procedure illustrated in Fig. 12-5.

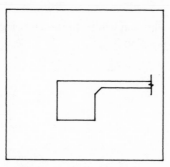

1. CHANGE TO THE CONCRETE LAYER, ADD CONCRETE OUTLINE USING CORRECT COORDINATES.

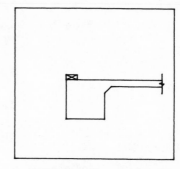

2. USE POLYGON TO CREATE THE RECTANGLE SILL PLATE ON THE WOOD LAYER.

Fig. 12-5

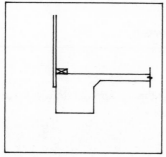

3. TAB TO WALL LAYER, AND USE THE WALL KEY TO ADD .0.7/8 WIDTH WALL FOR STUCCO.

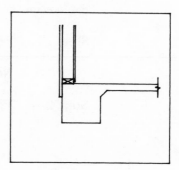

4. CHANGE WALL WIDTH TO .0.1/2 AND DRAW GYP BOARD.

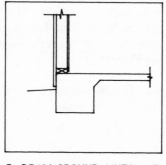

5. DRAW GROUND LINES AND BREAK LINES.

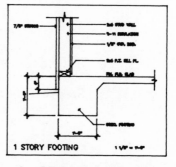

6. ADD DIMENSIONS AND NOTES ON DIMS LAYER.

SAVING YOUR DRAWING

It is a wise idea to ALWAYS ''save'' your drawing before you create the hatch pattern. In fact, you should always save your drawing before you begin a process that requires a lot of computing. You should also make a habit of saving it at least every hour!

Step 1 –   Pick **File I/O** from the UTILITY menu.

  File I/O

Step 2 –   Pick **Save Dwg.**

  Save Dwg

CREATING THE HATCH BOUNDARY

Texture patterns, called "crosshatching", are created in DataCAD using the Hatch option.

Before you create your hatch, you must first create a boundary that will contain your hatch. You can think of this as the "fence" to contain the hatching pattern. Your fence must be "closed". If the fence is open in any place, the hatch may flow out. Fig. 12-6 illustrates this.

Fig. 12-6

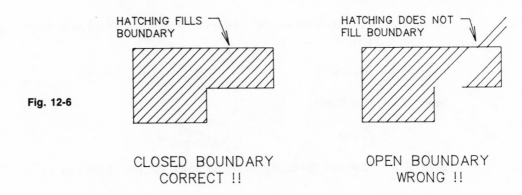

HATCHING FILLS BOUNDARY

HATCHING DOES NOT FILL BOUNDARY

CLOSED BOUNDARY
CORRECT !!

OPEN BOUNDARY
WRONG !!

Many times, the boundary you draw for your hatch will be exactly on top of existing items in your drawing. It is still important to create new lines for two reasons:

1. To make sure the boundary is closed.
2. To avoid using a partial entity in the boundary.

Step 1 – In the Object snap menu, make sure that ***EndPnt** and ***LyrSnap** are active.

     [Shift] X

     *EndPnt

     *LyrSnap

Step 2 – Remember to **[Tab]** to your **Earth** layer.

     [Tab] (to the Earth layer)

Step 3 – Draw the boundary indicated below. Be sure to use OBJECT SNAP to make sure the boundary is exactly on the existing lines. Also, make sure you use **object snap to close the boundary**.

Fig. 12-7

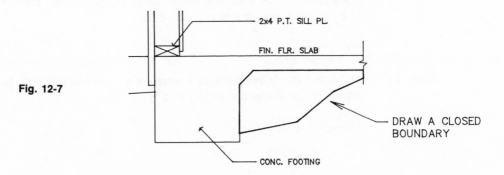

2x4 P.T. SILL PL.

FIN. FLR. SLAB

DRAW A CLOSED BOUNDARY

CONC. FOOTING

Step 4 – Press **H** to enter the Hatch option, found in the UTILITY menu.

H

Step 5 – Pick the **Pattern** option, to define the type of crosshatching pattern you will use.

Pattern

Step 6 – Pick the **ScrlFwrd** option (Scroll Forward) until the **Earth** option is displayed.

ScrlFwrd

Step 7 – Pick **Earth**.

Earth

Step 8 – Now pick the **Scale** option, to adjust the size of the pattern.

Scale

Step 9 – The true size of the hatch pattern is approximately ¹⁄₃₂″, as indicated in Fig. 12-8. You will want to scale it up, in order for it to look right in the drawing.

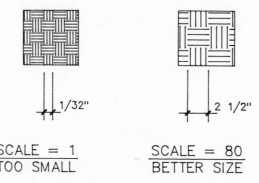

Fig. 12-8

SCALE = 1
TOO SMALL

SCALE = 80
BETTER SIZE

Step 10 – The scale of your patterns will vary according to the plot scale. Hatch patterns are *descriptive*. Hatch patterns, however, do not rely on a particular formula for sizing. You will depend upon your own experimentation with the finished results for approximate scale sizes.

A **80** value for the scale size will result in an approximate pattern size of 2″, which looks very nice in this detail.

80

Step 11 – Make sure the **∗Group** option is active, since you will pick your boundary by group. If it is not active, pick it.

∗Group

Step 12 – Now, pick anywhere on your boundary. The entire boundary should become dashed, as in Fig. 12-9. Make sure all of the boundary is dashed. If your boundary is not one group, use Entity to pick the remaining lines.

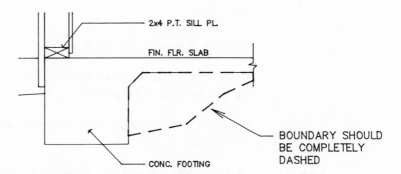

Fig. 12-9

Step 13 – Pick **Begin** to start the crosshatching process.

Begin

Step 14 – The boundary area will fill in with the earth texture pattern, as in Fig. 12-10.

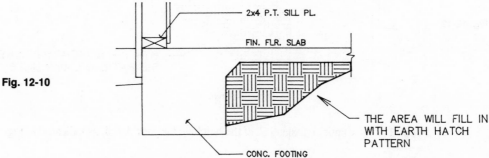

Fig. 12-10

Step 15 – If there is an error in the crosshatching (because of the wrong scale or an overflow outside of the boundary), you will want to delete the hatch and start again.

If the pattern overflowed the boundary, or has "holes" in it as in Fig. 12-11, there is a gap somewhere in your boundary. (You may not have used OBJECT SNAP to close it!)

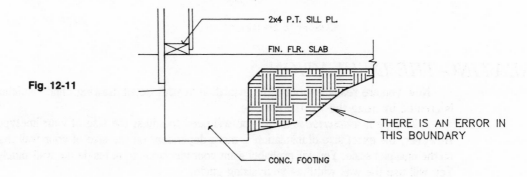

Fig. 12-11

IF YOUR HATCH HAS AN ERROR -

Press **[Shift]** < to erase the last group.

- Or

Press the **E** to enter the Erase menu.

Make sure the ***Group** option is active, then pick a line of the crosshatching. The hatching will disappear.

If necessary, fix the boundary or the scale, and try creating the crosshatching again.

Step 16 –   Once your hatch pattern is successfully created, **Erase** the boundary for your hatching. Be sure to use the Erase menu, ***Group** option, in order to erase the boundary in one pick as a group, if possible. (See Fig. 12-12.)

Fig. 12-12

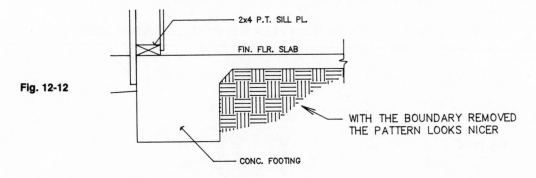

Step 17 –   Continue making all of the hatching for your detail, as indicated in Fig. 12-13.

Fig. 12-13

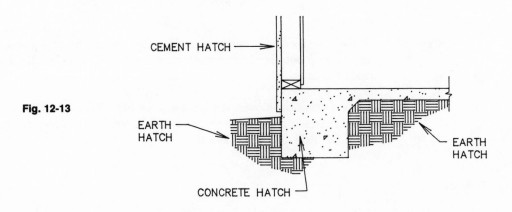

CREATING THE INSULATION

Now you are ready to create the insulation in your detail drawing. The insulation is created by using the INSUL linetype.

A linetype is a *descriptive* item. You will need to adjust the size of your linetype. However, the exact size of insulation is more dependent on the size of your wall than on the final plot scale. You will probably want your insulation to fit inside the wall snugly. You will use the wall width as your sizing guide.

The size of a linetype is adjusted using the ''spacing'' option. The term ''spacing'' refers to the measurement from the start of the pattern, to the end of the pattern. This is illustrated in Fig. 12-14. Notice that one-half of the width of the insul linetype is equal to one pattern spacing.

Fig. 12-14

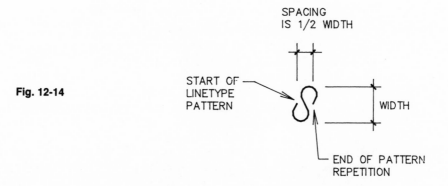

FINDING THE PROPER SPACING FOR INSULATION

As shown in Fig. 12-14, the ''insul'' linetype spacing can be accurately adjusted by calculating the desired final width of the pattern, and dividing it by two. We know that the width of the wall, as indicated by the width of the sill plate, is 4 inches. (See Fig. 12-15) This means you will define the spacing for your linetype as 2''.

Fig. 12-15

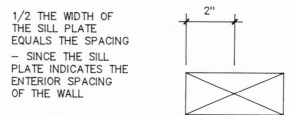

MEASURING THE LENGTH OF A LINE

To double check the sill plate width, you can ''measure'' the length of a line in your drawing.

Step 1 –   Pick the **Measures** option from the UTILITY menu.

    Measures

Step 2 –   Select the **Line** option, to measure the length of a line.

    Line

Step 3 –   Pick the top line of the small sill plate, as indicated in Fig. 12-16.

Fig. 12-16

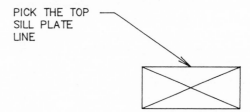

Step 4 – What does the message say the length of the line is? Look at your message, as indicated in Fig. 12-17.

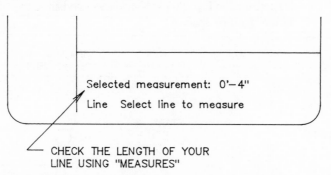

Fig. 12-17

Selected measurement: 0'–4"

Line   Select line to measure

CHECK THE LENGTH OF YOUR
LINE USING "MEASURES"

Step 5 – If you originally created the line at 4" (2 × 4 P.T. SILL PLATE), then this line would now be 4". If it is different than this, it may be you did not create a full size sill board. If you have a different size, make sure you write it down to use in the next steps.

Step 6 – Divide the size of your sill in half. If your sill is now 4", then half of that would be 2". If your sill is another size, then divide that in half, and use it in the next few steps.

SETTING UP THE LINETYPE

Step 1 – Pick the **LineType** option, from the EDIT menu.

LineType

Step 2 – Pick the **Insul** linetype from the menu.

Insul

Step 3 – Pick the **Spacing** option.

Spacing

Step 4 – Change the spacing to the appropriate value. If your sill was 4", then you would enter **0.2**.

0.2

Step 5 – Make the ***MidPnt** option active in the Object Snap menu. Remember how to get into the Object Snap menu?

*MidPnt

Step 6 – Object snap to the midpoint of the top line of the sill plate, as indicated in Fig. 12-18.

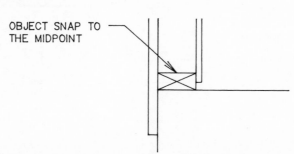

OBJECT SNAP TO
THE MIDPOINT

Fig. 12-18

Step 6 – Draw the line, using Ortho mode to create a vertical line, as in Fig. 12-19, using mouse button **1** to pick the second point of your line. (If Ortho is NOT on, press **O** until it is.)

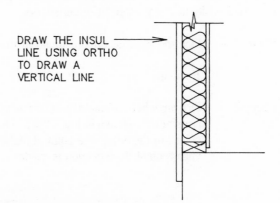

DRAW THE INSUL
LINE USING ORTHO
TO DRAW A
VERTICAL LINE

Fig. 12-19

EXPLODING THE DIMENSIONS

Before you scale the detail (reduce its actual size), you will explode the dimensions. This will allow the dimensions to keep with the original dimension text, and not change to the new reduced dimensions.

Step 1 – Pick the **Dimension** option, found in the EDIT menu.

Dimension

Step 2 – Pick the **Linear** option.

Linear

Step 3 – Pick the **Explode** option.

Explode

Step 4 – Make sure ***Area** is active.

*Area

Step 5 – You can **[Tab]** to the **Dims** layer, or use **Layer Snap** to pick the dimension entities.

Step 6 – Indicate two points to box in the entire drawing, as shown in Fig. 12-20. This will capture all dimensions. The prompt will be displayed **"3 items selected.** *If no entities were found*, then either the Dims layer was not active, or Layer Snap was not on.

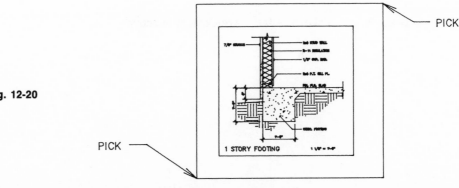

PICK

Fig. 12-20

PICK

1 STORY FOOTING

SCALING THE DETAIL

Once you have created the detail drawing, and exploded the dimensions, you are ready to reduce it to the finished plotting scale. This new size will allow the detail to be added easily in many different detail sheets.

Step 1 –   Pick the Enlarge option, found in the EDIT menu.

        Enlarge

Step 2 –   Pick anywhere around the center of your drawing for the "Center of Enlargement", shown in Fig. 12-21. This pick will indicate the "stationary point" of the detail (the point of the drawing that will not move when the enlargement or reduction is made).

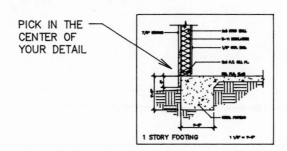

PICK IN THE
CENTER OF
YOUR DETAIL

Fig. 12-21

1 STORY FOOTING

Step 3 –   Pick the **Enlrgmnt** option.

        Enlrgmnt

Step 4 –   Referring to the scales formulas found in the **DataCAD Scales & Sizes** section of Appendix B, find the correct "Enlargement Factor" for a 1½" detail.

        "Anticipated Plot Scale" = 1.1/2″
        "Detail Enlargement Factor" = .125

Step 5 –   Enter the enlargement factor for the **X**.

        .125

Step 6 –   Enter the enlargement factor for the **Y**.

        .125

Step 7 –   Enter the enlargement factor for the linetype spacing.

        .125

Step 8 –   Make sure the ***Area** option is active.

        *Area

Step 9 – Pick two points to indicate a rectangle around the entire detail, including the detail box, as shown in Fig. 12-22.

Fig. 12-22

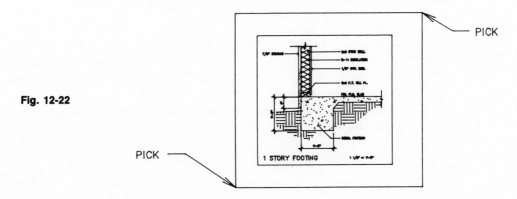

Step 10 – The drawing will be reduced in size, as in Fig. 12-23.

Fig. 12-23

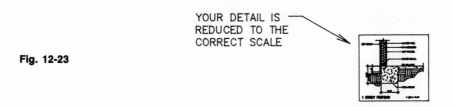

Step 11 – You may want to use the / key to **Recalc** your drawing window.

Step 12 – Use the **File I/O, Save Dwg** option to save your drawing.

DataCAD Exercise 12

Please complete the following exercise by reading each question carefully, then circling the letter that corresponds to the correct answer.

1. When you are creating a drawing, you should make it a practice to "save" the drawing using File I/O, every:

   a. Day.
   b. Time you quit DataCAD.
   c. At least every hour, or before a major change in your drawing, such as adding hatching.

2. Before creating the hatching pattern in your drawing, you must:

   a. Create an open or closed boundary.
   b. Create a closed boundary.
   c. Delete any existing boundaries.

3. If your hatch boundary is open:

   a. Your hatch pattern may flow out of the "fence".
   b. Your hatching will turn out okay anyway.
   c. The system will prompt you to close it.

4. If you wish to delete the hatch pattern, you should use the:

   a. Erase, *Entity option.
   b. Erase, *Group option.
   c. [,] key.

5. Hatch patterns reduce:

   a. Differently than the rest of your entities, and so should be created after you scale the detail.
   b. At a ½ scale than the rest of your drawing. You must use a special formula when scaling them.
   c. Perfectly with your drawing, and can be added before you scale it.

6. To reduce your detail, you use the:

   a. Enlarge menu.
   b. Scale menu.
   c. Reduce menu.

7. Linetypes:

   a. Should be added after you scale your detail, since their size is determined by "spacing".
   b. Reduce perfectly, and can be added before you scale your detail.
   c. Must be exploded before reducing.

8. Associated dimensions should always be:

   a. Created after you scale your detail.
   b. Exploded before reducing the size of your detail. Otherwise, the dimensions will change to the new line sizes.
   c. Reduced along with the rest of your detail, without having to explode them.

9. When you explode dimensions by area, you can:

  a. Indicate an area around your whole drawing. It will only explode dimensions.
  b. Only indicate an area around the dimensions. You must be careful so you do not explode the objects in your drawing.

10. To find the length of a line, you use the:

  a. Length menu.
  b. Measures menu.
  c. Distance menu.

Lesson 13: Creating Templates and Symbols

WHAT YOU WILL BE DOING:

YOU will create a new template, and define symbols to add to that template. You will also add report information to the template and symbol, then extract a report and add it to your drawing.

OBJECTIVES:

Your lesson objectives, then, are to:

- Create a template.
- Add a record field to the template report.
- Add your detail to the template as a symbol.
- Give the symbol an "item name", and other information for your report.
- Add the new symbol to your drawing.
- Extract a sample report and add it to your drawing.
- Modify a report field.

Remember to reference your *DataCAD Operations Guide*.

TEMPLATES AND SYMBOLS

You have already used templates and symbols in the earlier lesson: **Adding Symbols**. In this lesson, you will learn the steps to create your own templates, and how to make symbols out of items in your drawings to add to your template.

To create symbols, you have to:

1. Create the drawing that contains your symbols, and have the drawing displayed on the screen.
2. Create your new template. (Or call up an existing template you will be using.)
3. Add your symbols to the template.

You will create a template called **FTGDTL** (Footing Details). This template will hold your footing details. See Fig. 13-1.

YOUR SYMBOL
ADDED TO YOUR
FOOTING TEMPLATE

Fig. 13-1

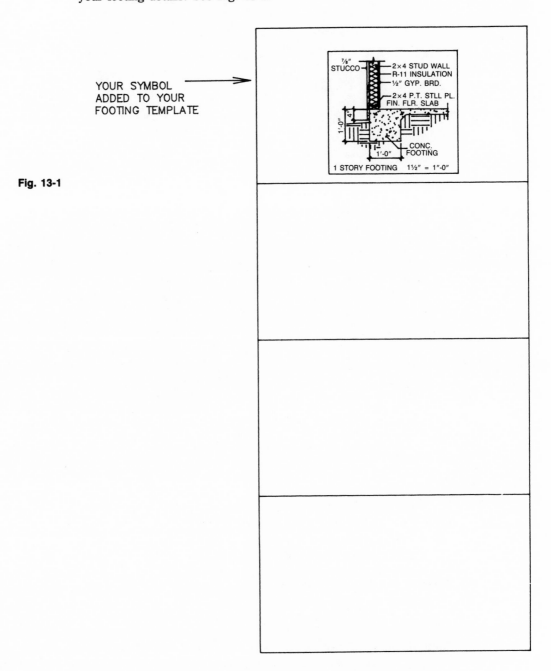

TEMPLATE DIRECTORY

When you create your template (which in essence is a series of boxes that will later hold your symbols), you will put it in your TEMPLATE directory, called **TPL**. This directory resides in the MTEC directory, so it is a "sub-directory" of MTEC, (a folder in your MTEC drawer) as indicated in Fig. 13-2.

Fig. 13-2

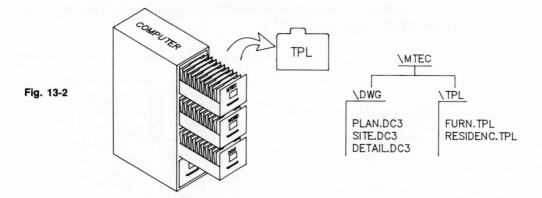

Step 1 – Make sure the footing detail drawing you created in the previous lesson is displayed on your screen. This is the detail you will be adding as a symbol to your template. (Fig. 13-3)

YOU WILL ADD THE FOOTING DETAIL TO THE TEMPLATE AS A SYMBOL

Fig. 13-3

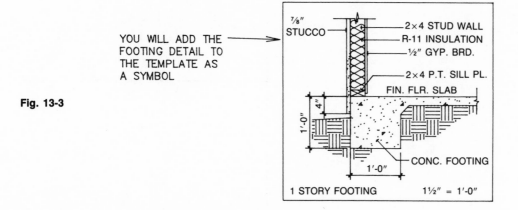

CREATING A NEW TEMPLATE

Step 1 – Press **T** to enter the Template menu.

T

Step 2 – Pick the **New Path** option.

New Path

Step 3 – Check that your directory path name is set to: **\ mtec \ tpl ** . If this directory path is already set, simply press **[Enter]** to continue. If it isn't set to this path, then type in: **TPL**

tpl

(This will automatically change your directory to \ MTEC \ tpl.)

Step 4 – If you had to type the directory path in, and if this is a new directory, pick **Yes** to create it.

Yes

Step 5 – The user message prompts you to: "Enter file name:" for your template. Type in and [Enter] the name for your new template.

FTGDTL

Step 6 – Since this is a new template, the message will say: **"file 'c:\ mtec\tpl\ftgdtl.tpl' does not exist. Create new file?"** Pick **Yes** to create it.

Yes

TEMPLATE FIELDS

Now you will be prompted to add any additional fields to the template form. "Fields" refer directly to the information areas in the schedules that you are able to attain for the symbols in your drawing. Fields 1 through 6 are already defined. They are:

1. Item name
2. Manufacturer
3. Model number
4. Remark 1
5. Remark 2
6. Cost

An example of a report containing these fields is illustrated in Fig. 13-4.

Fig. 13-4

```
Title
Item Name  Manufact   Model No   Remark 1   Remark 2   Qty. Unit Cost   Total Cost

Recliner | La-Z-Boy| L385-12 | Stock   | Leather |   1|    995.00|      995.00
Sofa     | Stylus  | STY336-2| Custom  | Fab./Oak|   2|   1595.00|     3190.00
Coffee Ta| Stylus  | STY184-3| Custom  | Oak/Glas|   2|    295.00|      590.00
Tub/Showe| Am.Std. | 2146.223| Stock   | Fbrgls  |   1|    790.00|      790.00
W/C      | Am.Std. | 2109.405| Stock   | China   |   1|    140.00|      140.00
Lavatory | Am.Std. | 0470.039| Stock   | China   |   1|    187.00|      187.00
Oven/Rnge| GE      | JB600GH | Stock   | Electric|   1|    799.00|      799.00
Dbl.Sink | Am.Std. | 7018.012| Stock   | Cst.Iron|   1|    499.00|      499.00
Refrig.  | GE      | TA7SG   | Stock   | 6.6 c.f.|   1|    259.00|      259.00

                                     TOTAL ITEMS:   11
                                                        TOTAL COST:     7449.00
                                                          Tax (4%):      297.96
                                                       GRAND TOTAL:     7746.96
```

Step 7 – To practice creating your own field, you will add one called "Steel Square Inch". Type in **Steel Square Inch** for "Field 7 Field name:". This field will allow you to type in the number of square inches of steel in your cross section.

Steel Square Inch

Step 8 – Pick the **Number** option to define the field type.

Number

Step 9 – Press mouse button **3** to quit defining fields.

Step 10 – Your new template will appear, as shown in Fig. 13-5.

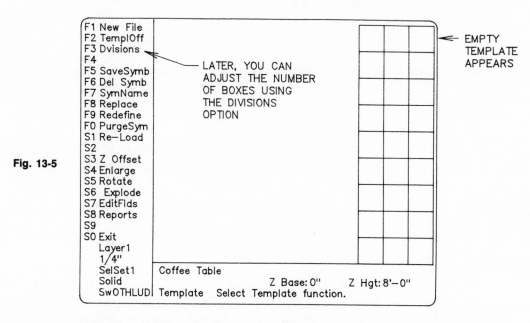

Fig. 13-5

SYMBOLS AND THE SYMBOL DIRECTORIES

Just like templates, symbols reside in a special directory. This helps keep your symbols properly organized. This is very important, since the template file needs to know where the symbols are. This is done by directories and pathnames. The main directory for all of your symbols is called **SYM**. (Fig. 13-6)

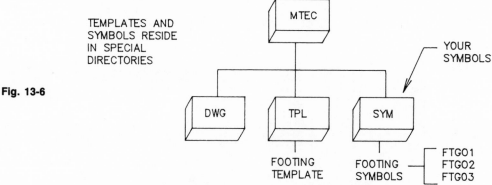

Fig. 13-6

Your symbols are further organized under the SYM directory, into their own specific directory for the template they are attached to. This second "sub-directory" *must match the template name!* This organization is very important in the correct operation of your DataCAD template and symbols. (See Fig. 13-7)

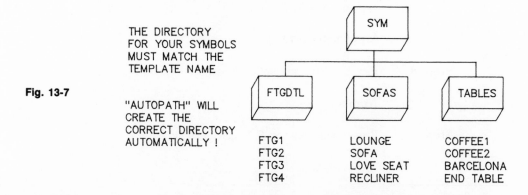

Fig. 13-7

The creation of the correct directories for your symbols is done automatically for you, using the Autopath option!

ADDING A SYMBOL TO YOUR NEW TEMPLATE

Step 1 – The template you will be adding the symbol to must be displayed on your screen, as in Fig. 13-8.

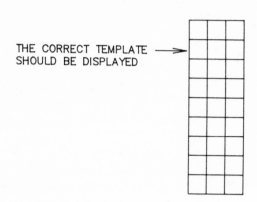

THE CORRECT TEMPLATE
SHOULD BE DISPLAYED →

Fig. 13-8

Step 2 – In the Template menu, pick the **SaveSymb** option.

SaveSymb

Step 3 – Make sure the **AutoPath** option is active (***AutoPath**). If it is NOT, pick it until a star "*****" appears in front of the name. (If you do not have an up-to-date version of DataCAD, it may not have AutoPath. You will have to create the path manually, using NewPath, and typing in: sym \ f + gd + 1)

*AutoPath

Step 4 – You will be prompted to "**Save to which symbol file:**". Type in the name of your new symbol: FTG1 (Footing #1).

FTG1

Step 5 – Make sure the ***Area** and ***LyrSrch** options are active.

*Area
*LyrSrch

Step 6 – Pick two points to indicate a rectangle around the entire detail, EXCLUDING THE DETAIL BOX, as indicated in Fig. 13-9.

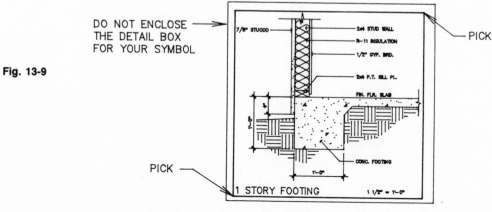

DO NOT ENCLOSE
THE DETAIL BOX
FOR YOUR SYMBOL →

Fig. 13-9

PICK

Step 7 –   Your detail will become dashed. Make a visual check that all pieces of your detail are included, and that the detail box is NOT included. Fig. 13-10 illustrates this.

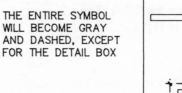

THE ENTIRE SYMBOL WILL BECOME GRAY AND DASHED, EXCEPT FOR THE DETAIL BOX

Fig. 13-10

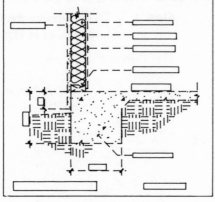

Step 8 –   If everything is correct, pick **Continue**. (If necessary, pick two points to indicate a rectangle of items to add to the symbol, or start over.)

Continue

Step 9 –   Now you will be prompted to **"Enter reference point for your symbol."** Object snap to the lower left hand corner of your detail box, as shown in Fig. 13-11. This will be the point you will use to place your symbol whenever you use it in your detail sheets.

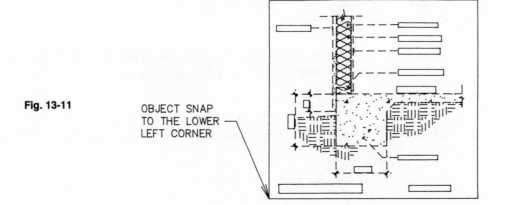

Fig. 13-11

OBJECT SNAP TO THE LOWER LEFT CORNER

Step 10 –   Your symbol is added to the new template. (Fig. 13-12)

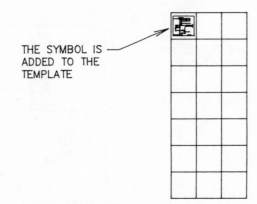

THE SYMBOL IS ADDED TO THE TEMPLATE

Fig. 13-12

Step 11 – Now you are prompted to enter the information for the fields. Since this report is just an example of the kind of report schedules you can create, you can put in your own information if you wish.

The first field is the "Item name". Type in **1 Story Footing.**

1 Story Footing

Step 12 – The next field is Manufacturer. For an example, you can type in **Conc Ctr** for Concrete Contractor. You are limited to 8 characters for this field.

Conc Ctr

Step 13 – Now the field is Model number. Type in: **N/A**, since footings typically do not have a model number.

N/A

Step 14 – For Remark 1, type in: **1 #4 T&B** for 1 number 4 reinforcing bar at the top and bottom. Again, you are limited to 8 characters for this field.

1 #4 T&B

Step 15 – For Remark 2, type in: **2000 PSI** for concrete strength. There is an 8 character limit.

2000 PSI

Step 16 – The next field is Cost. Type in **200**. This field will only allow you to add numbers (no text), and will also display total costs. You may want to put your own, more accurate cost estimate here.

200

Step 17 – The last field is the new one you added: Steel Square Inch. Type in **.40**. Again, this field is limited to numbers.

.40

Step 18 – Now you are prompted to save the next symbol. Notice that the name is automatically changed to **ftg2**. At this point, you would save your second detail if you had one, following the same procedure.

Step 19 – Press mouse button **3** to quit, since you are through making a symbol out of your detail.

Step 20 – Notice that when you move your cursor to the template box that contains your new symbol, the coordinate readout now says: **1 Story Footing**. This is the "Item name" you gave your symbol. If you do not use reports, you would still want to give your symbol an item name. This way, you can always tell what the symbol is by placing your cursor on the template box! (Fig. 13-13)

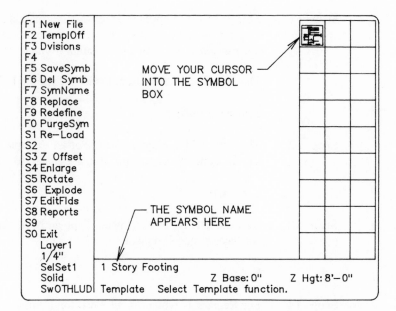

Fig. 13-13

F1 New File
F2 TemplOff
F3 Dvisions
F4
F5 SaveSymb
F6 Del Symb
F7 SymName
F8 Replace
F9 Redefine
F0 PurgeSym
S1 Re—Load
S2
S3 Z Offset
S4 Enlarge
S5 Rotate
S6 Explode
S7 EditFlds
S8 Reports
S9
S0 Exit
   Layer1
   1/4"
   SelSet1
   Solid
   SwOTHLUD

MOVE YOUR CURSOR
INTO THE SYMBOL
BOX

THE SYMBOL NAME
APPEARS HERE

1 Story Footing

Z Base: 0"   Z Hgt: 8'—0"

Template   Select Template function.

REFERENCING THE DATACAD OPERATIONS GUIDE

You will want to turn to the TEMPLATES AND SYMBOLS section of Appendix A, the *DataCAD Operations Guide*.

This section guides you through the creation of templates and adding symbols to the templates, in easy-to-read steps. It also provides you with the steps you would follow to change a symbol in a template, replacing symbols on your drawing with new symbols, and other important operations.

RETRIEVING REPORTS

You may want to see what your report looks like. You must add some symbols to your drawing before you can run a report.

Step 1 –   In the Template menu, make sure that the **Explode** option IS **NOT** active. If it is, your symbols will come in without any report information!

Explode   (option NOT active!)

Step 2 –   Pick the template box that contains your new footing detail symbol, and then pick 2 or 3 places on your drawing to add this detail symbol, as in Fig. 13-14.

Fig. 13-14

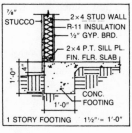
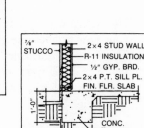
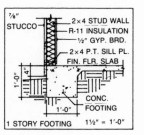

Step 3 – Once a few symbols have been added, pick the **Reports** option.

Reports

Step 4 – The available reports should be listed. (Fig. 13-15)

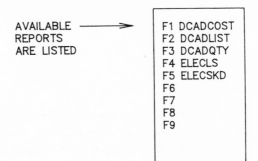

AVAILABLE ——————▷   F1 DCADCOST
REPORTS   F2 DCADLIST
ARE LISTED   F3 DCADQTY
                      F4 ELECLS
                      F5 ELECSKD
                      F6
                      F7
                      F8
                      F9

Fig. 13-15

Step 5 – If the reports are not listed, you will have to change the pathname. This is done by selecting **New Path**, then typing in:

frm

(This changes the pathname to \ mtec \ frm.

Step 6 – Once your report forms are listed, you may pick one. Pick the report called **DCADCOST**.

DCADCOST

Step 7 – The report will be displayed on your screen. Notice how each of your inputs appear in the correct box. Notice also that the item name: **1 Story Footing**, does not fit in the Item Name box. Count the number of characters that did fit. You will find that this area is probably limited to 9 characters. (Fig. 13-16)

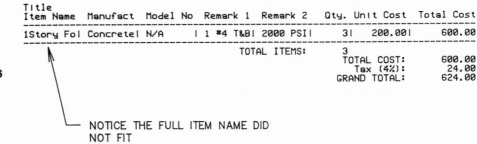

```
Title
Item Name  Manufact  Model No  Remark 1  Remark 2   Qty. Unit Cost  Total Cost
------------------------------------------------------------------------------
1Story Fo| Concrete|  N/A      | 1 #4 T&B| 2000 PSI|   3|   200.00|     600.00
------------------------------------------------------------------------------
                                          TOTAL ITEMS:   3
                                                          TOTAL COST:    600.00
                                                            Tax (4%):     24.00
                                                         GRAND TOTAL:    624.00
```

Fig. 13-16

⌐ NOTICE THE FULL ITEM NAME DID
  NOT FIT

Step 8 – Press the **[Spacebar]** to continue.

[Spacebar]

Step 9 – Now you are given options for the destination of the report. Pick the **ToDrwing** option.

ToDrwing

Step 10 – Drag the cursor out on your screen. Notice that the cursor has changed to represent the text size of your report, as in Fig. 13-17. You may want to pick the **Size** option to make the text bigger or smaller.

THE CURSOR REPRESENTS
THE SIZE OF TEXT THE
REPORT WILL APPEAR IN

Fig. 13-17

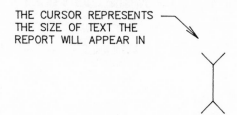

Step 11 – Once the text **Size** is adjusted to what you desire, pick a place for your report on your drawing. Keep in mind that your pick will indicate the upper left-hand corner of the report, as in Fig. 13-18. The report will be added to your drawing.

THE CURSOR PICK INDICATES THE
UPPER LEFT HAND CORNER OF
THE REPORT

Fig. 13-18

```
Title
Item Name  Manufact  Model No  Remark 1  Remark 2   Qty. Unit Cost  Total Cost
-----------------------------------------------------------------------------
1Story Fo| Concrete| N/A     | 1 #4 T&B| 2000 PSI|   3|   200.00|    600.00
-----------------------------------------------------------------------------
                              TOTAL ITEMS:    3
                                          TOTAL COST:       600.00
                                             Tax (4%):       24.00
                                          GRAND TOTAL:      624.00
```

Step 12 – Press the mouse button **3** to quit back to the Template menu.

CORRECTING REPORT INFORMATION

It is an easy task to correct the field information in your report. You will want to change the text in the "Item name" field so that it will fit in 8 character spaces. If you will not be using reports, you do not have to change the item name. You would keep it as "1 Story Footing". For practice, however, you will modify it.

Step 1 – Pick the **EditFlds** option from the Template menu.

    EditFlds

Step 2 – Pick the template box that contains the footing detail, as in Fig. 13-19.

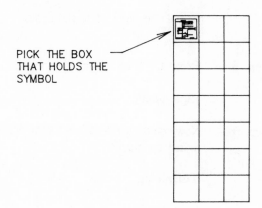

PICK THE BOX
THAT HOLDS THE
SYMBOL

Fig. 13-19

Step 3 - Pick the **ItemName** option.

ItemName

Step 4 - Type in and [Enter] a shortened name for your detail: **1 St Ftg.** This name is 8 characters long (spaces included).

1 St Ftg

Step 5 - Press mouse button **3** to quit back to the Template menu.

Step 6 - Pick the **Reports** option. You can add the same report, or try another type of report for your drawing, if there is one. Notice that the Item Name is corrected. (Fig. 13-20)

Fig. 13-20

```
Title
Item Name   Manufact   Model No   Remark 1   Remark 2   Qty.  Unit Cost   Total Cost
----------------------------------------------------------------------------------
1 St Ftg |  Concrete|  N/A     | 1 #4 T&B|  2000 PSI|    3|    200.00|      600.00
----------------------------------------------------------------------------------
                                          TOTAL ITEMS:    3
                                                          TOTAL COST:     600.00
                                                            Tax (4%):      24.00
                                                         GRAND TOTAL:     624.00
```

DataCAD Exercise 13

Please complete the following exercise by reading each question carefully, then circling the letter that corresponds to the correct answer.

1. A "template" is a:

   a. Series of boxes that will hold your symbols.
   b. Special directory for your forms.
   c. Report form.

2. When you make a template, you:

   a. Shouldn't put it in any special directory.
   b. Should put it in the TPL directory by defining a pathname.
   c. Should put it in the SYM directory by using the AutoPath option.

3. When you make a symbol, you:

   a. Should put it in the TPL directory by defining a pathname.
   b. Should put it in the SYM directory by using the AutoPath option.
   c. Don't have to worry about directories at all.

4. When you create a symbol that is on more than one layer, you should make sure:

   a. LyrSnap is active in the Object Snap menu.
   b. All but one layer is turned off.
   c. LyrSrch is active in the SaveSymb menu.

5. If you enter the Template menu to pick a new template file, do not have a template active, and no template names are displayed in the menu area, you should:

   a. Call someone for help before you do anything.
   b. Check the current pathname, by picking New Path.
   c. Do nothing. All of your templates are deleted.

6. When you have a template active, and wish to get another template, you use the:

   a. New File option in the Template menu.
   b. New Template option in the Template menu.
   c. Template menu. The template names are automatically displayed.

7. Template fields are:

   a. Information areas for reports that you are able to attain from the symbols in your drawing.
   b. An area in your drawing used in landscaping.
   c. Information that cannot be added to your drawing.

8. You can output the report in 3 ways. They are:

   a. To drawing, to plotter, and to printer.
   b. To drawing, to file, and to printer.
   c. To file, to printer, and to plotter.

9. In order to create a name for your symbol that can be read when you move your cursor to the symbol box in the Template, you:

   a. Define an "item name" for your symbol after adding it to the template. This name can be changed later if you wish.
   b. Have to give the symbol a name that you want before adding it to template. This name cannot be modified.
   c. Define an "item name" for your symbol after adding it to the template. This name cannot be changed once you define it.

10. To reduce your detail, you use the:

    a. Enlarge menu.
    b. Scale menu.
    c. Reduce menu.

11. Linetypes:

    a. Should be added after you scale your detail, since their size is determined by "spacing".
    b. Reduce perfectly, and can be added before you scale your detail.
    c. Must be exploded before reducing.

12. Associated dimensions should always be:

    a. Created after you scale your detail.
    b. Exploded before reducing the size of your detail. Otherwise, the dimensions will change to the new line sizes.
    c. Reduced along with the rest of your detail, without having to explode them.

13. If you want to save a 3-D view with hidden lines removed, you must:

    a. Remove the lines, then pick the SavImage option.
    b. Remove the lines, then pick the SaveView option.
    c. Pick the SavImage option first, then remove the lines.

14. To display the plan view of your drawing after creating a 3-D view, you use the:

    a. PlanView option.
    b. Ortho option.
    c. Mouse button 3. The plan view is automatically displayed.

15. To have text that is plotted at ⅛ inch when you are plotting at a ¼ inch scale, you have to create the text at the size of:

    a. ⅛ inch.
    b. 1 foot.
    c. 6 inches.

16. To set the linetype size, in the Linetype menu you use the:

    a. Size option.
    b. Pattern option.
    c. Spacing option.

Lesson 14: Creating Your Default Drawings

WHAT YOU WILL BE DOING:

YOU will create your standard default drawings during this lesson. Earlier, you developed basic default drawings. During this lesson, you will learn about the other common settings that can be predetermined and standardized for your daily use. The first steps presented during this lesson are the most common settings used for a 1:40 SITE plan.

During this lesson, you should begin to incorporate the standards for your own office, customizing the drawing variables for the most efficient use.

OBJECTIVES:

Your lesson objectives, then, are to:

- Pre-plan your default drawing.
- Create and attribute the layers for your drawings.
- Define the scale type, angle type, and other Settings values.
- Adjust the dimension standards.
- Set the text size.
- Set the display options.
- Adjust the Grid and snap values.
- Define the linetype spacing.
- Set typical Object Snap options.
- Pre-set common options in other menus (Polygon/Rectangle, Walls/Width/Side, Z-Base/Z-Height, etc.)

- Create Border line work and title block.
- Adjust the plotter settings.

Remember to reference your *DataCAD Operations Guide* when instructed.

DEFAULT DRAWINGS

Default drawings save you steps, increase through-put, and help to eliminate errors. They also help to establish consistent standards in all of your CADD drawings! This means increased productivity for your company. In fact, well planned default drawings can **save you over 100 steps in creating a drawing**.

Default drawings are simply drawing files that have certain switches and settings pre-defined in them for ease of use. You have learned the use of Default drawings in your previous lessons, and have created some basic ones.

A typical, well planned default drawing can contain the following:

1. Plotting settings, such as Scale, Paper size, and Pens.
2. Scale Type, Angle Type, and other options found in the Settings menu predetermined.
3. Dimension standards set.
4. Text font and size defined.
5. Layers named and attributed.
6. Display options set.
7. Grids and Grid Snap defined.
8. Line Type spacing set.
9. Object Snap settings activated.
10. Other typical defaults set in each menu, such as:
    Polygon/Rectangle
    Walls/Width/Side or Center
    Z-Base and Height
11. Border line work.
12. Title block, if not brought in as a symbol.

As you already know, default drawings reside in the MTEC \ DEFAULT directory. Before you create a new drawing, you pick a Default Drawing, which will serve as a base, or foundation for your new drawing.

HOW MANY DEFAULT DRAWINGS DO YOU NEED?

You will need at least one *default drawing for every different scale* you will be plotting in (e.g., ¼″ = 1′, ⅛″ = 1′), and for *different layer naming schemes*. The idea of a default drawing is to save you steps, and these two general types of changes (scale and layering schemes) entail a large number of steps!

YOUR "1:40 SITE" DEFAULT DRAWING

The first default drawing you will create in this lesson can be used for your 1″ = 40′ site layouts. This default drawing will be similar to the one you created for the 1:20 site layout, but with greater detail paid to the default settings.

TURNING OFF THE CURRENT DEFAULT DRAWING

As before, you will first "turn-off" the current default drawing that may be assigned. You do not have to follow this part of the procedure every time you set up a new default drawing. If you already had the same type of default drawing created, you could name it as your default drawing for creating the new one! This way, all of your layers would already be named properly and other desired settings would already be active.

However, this lesson will guide you from scratch. This way, all of the steps you need to follow will be documented here. You can easily refer to this lesson for creating all of your default drawings.

Step 1 –   Start DataCAD, and display the drawing list. *If you are currently working on a drawing in DataCAD*, use the **File I/O, New Dwg** options to start a new dwg.

Step 2 –   When the drawing list is displayed, pick the **Default** option.

        Default

Step 3 –   Press the **[Space bar]** once, to clear any current default drawing, then press **[Enter]**

        [Space bar]

        [Enter]

CHANGING THE PATHNAME

You must remember to change the pathname to DEFAULT, *before* creating your Default Drawing.

Step 1 –   Pick the **New Path** option.

        New Path

Step 2 –   Type in and [Enter] the path name for your default drawing.

        default

Step 3 –   Now, only the default drawings will be displayed. The default drawings currently on your system include:

        1-4PLAN - ¼″ = 1′ scale plan layout
        1-20SITE - 1″ = 20′ scale site layout
        DET1-1-2 - 1½″ = 1′ detail

Step 4 –   The new name for your site layout will be **1-40SITE**, which stands for 1:40 scale site layout. Type in and [Enter] this new name for your default drawing.

        1-40SITE

CREATING THE LAYERS

Now you are ready to start setting the defaults in your drawing file. You will start with Layers.

Step 1 –   Press **L** to enter the Layers menu.

        L

Step 2 – Pick the **NewLayer** option.

NewLayer

Step 3 – Pick the **6** option, and **[Enter]**.

6

Step 4 – Pick the **Name** option, to name your layers.

Name

Step 5 – Pick **Layer1**.

Layer1

Step 6 – Type in and the new name for this layer: **Proplin** and press [Enter].

Proplin

Step 7 – Pick **Layer2**.

Layer2

Step 8 – Type in and the new name for this layer: **Street** and press [Enter].

Street

Step 9 – Continue naming the layers for your default drawing, as indicated below.

Layer1 = **Proplin**
Layer2 = **Street**
Layer3 = **Bldg**
Layer4 = **Parking**
Layer5 = **Text**
Layer6 = **Dims**
Layer7 = **Border**

Step 10 – Press mouse button **3** to quit back to the Layer menu.

Step 11 – Using the **[Tab]** key to change your layers, and the **K** key to change the colors, give each layer the colors listed below.

[Tab] (to layer)

K (to color)

Proplin = **Lt Mgta**
Street = **Lt Cyan**
Bldg   = **Lt Cyan**
Parking = **Lt Grn**
Text   = **Brown**
Dims   = **Brown**
Border = **Yellow**

DEFINING THE "SETTINGS"

Step 1 -   From the UTILITY menu, pick the **Settings** option.

Settings

Step 2 -   Pick the **ScaleTyp** option.

ScaleTyp

Step 3 -   Pick the ***Decimal** option until it is active.

***Decimal**

Step 4 -   The only other option that should be active is ***Units**.

***Units**

Step 5 -   Press mouse button **3** to quit back to the Settings menu.

Step 6 -   Pick the **AngleTyp** option.

AngleTyp

Step 7 -   Change the type to ***Bearing**.

***Bearing**

Step 8 -   Quit back to the Settings menu, and pick the **MissDist** option. This option allows you to set the distances you can miss an object by and still be able to pick it.

MissDist

Step 9 -   Pick the number **10** (10 screen pixels), and press **[Enter]**. This number will be the approximate distance described by the size of your cursor.

10

Step 10 -   Pick the **ScrlDist** option. This is the distance the viewing window changes when you press the arrow key.

ScrlDist

Step 11 -   Change this distance to **50**. This will move the viewing window 50% when you press the arrow keys.

50

Step 12 -   Pick the **SaveDlay** option, to set the timed intervals between the automatic saves.

SaveDlay

Step 13 -   Change the number of minutes to **20.**

20

Step 14 – Pick the **BigCurs** option. TWICE (until the CURSOR SIZE menu is displayed). This will allow you to adjust the size of your screen cursor.

BigCurs
BigCurs

Step 15 – Change the number of pixels to **10**. This way the size of your cursor will be the same as the Miss Distance.

10

Step 16 – Pick **NegDist** until it is active. This option makes the coordinate display show the negative sign (–) when you are moving the cursor in the minus direction.

*NegDist

Step 17 – Pick **Show Z** until it is active also. This option will display the current Z-base and Z-height settings in the message area of your screen.

*Show Z

Step 18 – Now pick the **Beeps** option until it is active. Setting this option makes your computer beep when you pick an item!

*Beeps

Step 19 – Check your menu before you exit, ONLY the following items should be active:

*Beeps
*NegDist
*Show Z

DEFINING THE GRIDS

Step 1 – Press **G** to enter the Grids menu.

G

Step 2 – Pick the **GridSize** option.

GridSize

Step 3 – Pick the **Set Snap** option.

Set Snap

Step 4 – This next menu allows you to set the snap for each **individual layer**. You simply make the layer active, then select the snap spacing for that layer.

Press **[Tab]** until the **Proplin** layer is active.

[Tab] (to Proplin layer)

Step 5 –   Set the snap for this layer to **10** feet.

10

Step 6 –   Press **[Tab]** until **Street** is active.

[Tab] (to Street layer)

Step 7 –   Set the snap for this layer to **5** feet.

5

Step 8 –   Continue setting the snap distances for all the layers, as described below:

Proplin = **10′**
Street   = **5′**
Bldg   = **2′**
Parking = **1′**
Text   = **0**
Dims   = **1′**
Border   = **0**

Step 9 –   When all of the snaps have been set, press mouse button **3** to quit back to the Grids menu.

Step 10 –   Pick the **SetDisp1** option. This option allows you to define the display characteristics of the small grid.

SetDisp1

Step 11 –   Pick **Custom** to enter a custom spacing.

Custom

Step 12 –   Enter the spacing size of **10** for both X and Y small grid.

X = 10
Y = 10

Step 13 –   Pick **SetDisp2** to define the large grid.

SetDisp2

Step 14 –   Pick **Custom**.

Custom

Step 15 –   Set the X and Y large grid to **40**.

X = 40
Y = 40

Step 16 –   Press mouse button **3** once to exit back to the original Grids menu.

Step 17 – Pick the **GridColr** option.

GridColr

Step 18 – You could use this menu to change the color of the grid, which is presently set to light red for small grid, and light blue for large grid. However, you won't be changing the color. Instead, you will use this menu to adjust the displayed ''mark'' size of the large grid (size of the displayed ''+'').

Pick the **SetDisp2** option.

SetDisp2

Step 19 – Pick the **MarkSize** option.

MarkSize

Step 20 – Set the mark size (in pixels) of large grid to **2**.

2

Step 21 – Press mouse button **3** to quit.

SETTING THE DISPLAY VARIABLES

Step 1 – From the UTILITY menu, pick the **Display** option.

Display

Step 2 – The following options should be active:

*ShowTxt
*ShowDim
*ShwHtch
*ShowWgt
*UserLin
*ShowIns

Step 3 – The other options should be set to:

SmallTxt =**3**
BoxColor =**NoChange**
SmallSym =**3**
ArcFactr =**1**

OBJECT SNAP MENU

It is a good idea to set the most used options in this menu.

Step 1 – Press **[Shift] X** to enter the Object Snap menu.

[Shift] X

Step 2 –   Make sure only the following options are active:

*End Pnt
*Mid Pnt
*LyrSnap
*Quick

DIMENSION VARIABLES

You can set the variable once, in the Linear menu, and they will be set for all of the dimension types.

Step 1 –   Press **D** to enter the Dimension menu.

D

Step 2 –   Pick the **Linear** option.

Linear

Step 3 –   Pick **TextStyl**.

TextStyl

Step 4 –   Pick **TextSize**.

TextSize

Step 5 –   In Appendix B, turn to the **DataCAD Scales & Sizes** chart. You will find the ''text size notes'' should be set to: **5** feet. Type in and enter:

5

Step 6 –   Pick the **Weight** option, to adjust the line weight of your text.

Weight

Step 7 –   Make sure the weight is set to **1**.

1

Step 8 –   Make the **Above** and **Auto** options active.

*Above
*Auto

Step 9 –   Press mouse button **3** once, then pick the **DimStyl**.

DimStyl

Step 10 – Pick **Offset**, to adjust the gap that will be drawn in the extension line of the dimension, as shown in Fig. 14-1.

Offset

Fig. 14-1

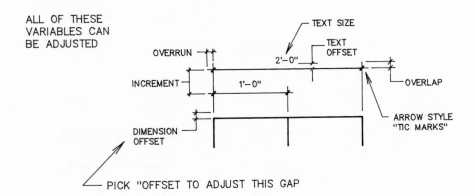

Step 11 – Change the offset to **5** feet, which will be plotted at an ⅛-inch gap.

5

Step 12 – Pick the **Overlap** option. This option adjusts the amount the extension line will overlap the dimension line. (Fig. 14-2)

Overlap

Fig. 14-2

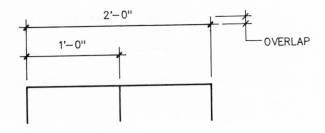

Step 13 – Change the overlap size to **5** feet.

5

Step 14 – Pick the **Incrment** option, which adjusts the space between stacked dimensions, as shown in Fig. 14-3.

Incrment

Fig. 14-3

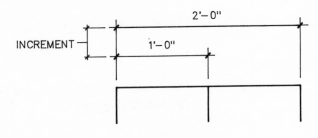

Step 15 – Change the increment spacing to **20** feet, which will be plotted at ½″.

20

Step 16 – Pick the **OverRun** option. This describes the distance the dimension line will over-run the extension line, as in Fig. 14-4.

OverRun

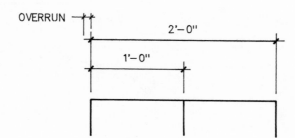

Fig. 14-4

Step 17 – Set the overrun to **5** feet, to plot at ⅛ inch.

5

Step 18 – Press mouse button **3** once, then pick the **ArroStyl** option.

ArroStyl

Step 17 – Make the **TicMrks** option active.

*TicMrks

Step 18 – Pick the **Size** option, to adjust the size of the tic marks.

Size

Step 19 – Change the size of the tic marks to **.75**. This size is in a relative percentage to the text size. Setting it to .75 will create a tic mark ¾ the size of the text.

.75

Step 20 – Pick the **Weight** option.

Weight

Step 21 – Change the weight to **1**.

1

Step 22 – Press mouse button **3** once to quit back to the variables options, and pick the **AutoStyl** option.

AutoStyl

Step 23 – Make sure the following options are active:

> *Strngli
> *PtsOnly
> *LyrSrch

SETTING UP THE TEXT FOR NOTES

Step 1 – Pick the **Text** option from the EDIT menu.

> **Text**

Step 2 – Pick the **Size** option.

> **Size**

Step 3 – Change the size of your text to **5** feet, to be plotted at ⅛ inch.

> **5**

Step 4 – Pick the **Arrows** option.

> **Arrows**

Step 5 – Change the Size of the arrows to **.5**. This will produce an arrow with the **width** adjusted to ½ the set size for text. (Fig. 14-5.)

> **.5**

Fig. 14-5

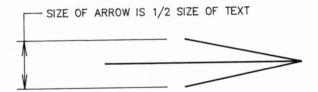
SIZE OF ARROW IS 1/2 SIZE OF TEXT

Step 6 – Pick **Aspect**. This option allows you to adjust the relative length and width of the arrow.

> **Aspect**

Step 7 – You can change the Aspect to **1**. This will result in an arrow head having **45** degree lines, as illustrated in Fig. 14-6. To have a more pointed arrow, you can increase the aspect.

> **1**

Fig. 14-6

ASPECT RATIO
CAN BE SET TO
1– 1, AS SHOWN
HERE

SAME

SAME

CHANGING THE LINE TYPE SPACING

The measurement in repeated patterns of a line type, such as centerline, is adjustable for your own standard at your office. You can find the suggested formulas for this spacing in Appendix B - the *DataCAD Reference Guide*, in the **DataCAD Linetypes** chart.

Step 1 -   Press **F** to enter the Line Type menu, Spacing option.

F

Step 2 -   Referring to the spacing formula for the Propline (Property Line), change the spacing value to **80**. This will give you a 1 inch spacing in the final plotted drawing.

80

Step 3 -   Use the mouse button **3** to quit.

CREATING THE DRAWING BOUNDARY

Referencing Appendix B - the *DataCAD Reference Guide*, you will find the correct drawing boundary size in the section called **Available Drawing Sheet Areas**.

Step 1 -   From the EDIT menu, select the **Polygon** option.

Polygon

Step 2 -   Pick the **Rectangl** option.

Rectangl

Step 3 -   Use the **[Tab]** key to make the **Border** layer active.

[Tab]   (to the Border layer)

Step 4 -   Press **[Insert]** to set the **relative cartesian coordinates** input mode.

[Insert]   (to relative cartesian)

Step 5 -   Pick the start point for your rectangle.

Step 6 -   Referring to the **Available Drawing Sheet Areas** chart, type in the coordinates for the available drawing area of a 36″ × 24″ sheet, plotted at a 1:40 scale.

X = 1280
Y = 920

Step 7 -   Use the / key to **Recalc** your viewing window.

PRE-SETTING THE PLOT SPECIFICATIONS

Step 1 -   Pick the **Plotter** option from the UTILITY menu.

Plotter

Step 2 – Pick the **Scale** option.

Scale

Step 3 – Pick the **1:40** option.

1:40

Step 4 – Pick the **PaperSiz** option.

PaperSiz

Step 5 – Pick **Custom.**

Custom

Step 6 – Type in **23** for 23 inches in the height.

23

Step 7 – Now type in **32** for the width.

32

Step 8 – Press the mouse button **3** to return to the Plotter menu.

Step 9 – Pick the **Layout** option.

Layout

Step 10 – Drag the layout box over to your rectangle, and **object snap** to the rectangle centerpoint.

Step 11 – Now pick the **Set Pens** option, to define which pens will be used with which colors.

Set Pens

Step 12 – Pick **Lt Gray.**

Lt Gray

Step 13 – Enter the appropriate number for your pen: **1.**

1

Step 14 – Continue defining pens with the colors you are using, as described below:

Brown = **1**
Lt Grn = **2**
Lt Cyan = **3**
Lt Mgta = **4**

These pen numbers will later be associated with appropriate pens in the plotter. The recommended pen widths that could be used with this type of numbering are (in point size for wet ink pens):

$$1 = .25$$
$$2 = .35$$
$$3 = .50$$
$$4 = .75$$

Step 14 – Once the numbers are defined, press button **3** to quit back the Plotter menu.

Step 15 – Check to make sure the following options are active:

  *ClrPlot
  *PenSort

Step 16 – Press mouse button **3** to quit.

SETTING MISCELLANEOUS OPTIONS

It is a good idea to go into other menus and set defaults that are the most commonly used. This adds convenience to using the default drawing. As you use the system, you will become aware of many options you use frequently, that could be pre-set. Later, you can go back into the default drawing and make changes.

Step 1 – Press **[Tab]** until the PROPLINE layer is active.

  [Tab] (to Proplin)

Step 2 – Press the **Q** key to quickly change to the property linetype.

  Q (to propline linetype)

Step 3 – Set the **Z-base** and **Z-height** to 0. (If this drawing were a PLAN default drawing, you would want to set the walls to the correct Z-Base and Height.)

  Z

  Z-base   = **0**
  Z-height = **0**

Step 4 – Check that the **W** in SWOTHLUD is small, indicating that you are NOT drawing walls. If it is capitalized, press the = key until the W appears in lower case (SwOTHLUD).

SAVING YOUR DEFAULT DRAWING

Step 1 – Pick the **File I/O** option, found in the UTILITY menu.

  File I/O

Step 2 – Pick **New Dwg.**

  New Dwg

Step 3 - Pick **Yes** to save your default drawing.

Yes

USER REMINDER - *Do* NOT *pick* ABORT, *or you will trash the settings you just created!*

Step 4 - The Default Drawing list is displayed. Notice that your default drawing is added to this list.

GETTING BACK THE DRAWING FILE LIST

Once your default drawings are filed (using the **File I/O, New Dwg, Yes** options), you are ready to begin drawing. To do so, you will want to bring back the original drawing list. This is done by changing the *pathname* again.

Remember, the pathname is a way to describe to the system ''what drawer to look in'', or what *directory*, for your drawings. Currently, you set your pathname to the DEFAULT directory, which exists in the MTEC drawer. This means that only the default drawings are displayed.

Step 5 - Pick the New Path option, to change the drawing file path back to the original setting.

New Path

Step 6 - Type in the name of your desired drawing file path. For example, to return to the DWG path, you would type in **DWG**.

dwg

CHECKLIST FOR DEFAULT DRAWINGS

Make sure the following is set in your default drawing:

____ Layers – Named and color defined

____ Architect – Walls – Height/Base/Width/Centers/Sides//Windows-Doors/same

____ Settings – Scale Type/Angle Type
Miss Dist/Small Grid/Scroll Dist/Distances readout
Delay/Save Delay
Beeps/Negative Distance/Show Z depth

____ Grids – Grid Size – Set Snap on layers/Display of small
Grid 1/Large Grid 2
Grid Color – Set Display of small Grid 1/Large
Grid 2/Mark Size

____ Dimension variables – Text style – Size/Weight
Dim Style – Offset/Overlap/Increment/Over Run
Arrow Style – Size/Weight
Auto Style – Strngline/Pts Only/Layer Search

____ Text variables – Size/Weight/Arrows/Arrow Size

____ Display Settings – ShowTxt/ShowDim/ShwHtch/ShowWgt/UserLin/ShowIns

____ Object Snap defaults – Mid Point/End Point/Quick/Layer Snap

____ Plot specifications – Scale/Paper Size/Color Plot/Pen sort/Set Pens

Formula for common scales: (Can be used for Text and Dimension line sizes)

Plotted at	Created at	Resulting size	Plotted at	Created at	Resulting size
⅛ scale	1 foot	⅛ inch	1:20 scale	2.5 feet	⅛ inch
	2 feet	¼ inch		5 feet	¼ inch
	4 feet	½ inch		10 feet	½ inch
	8 feet	1 inch		20 feet	1 inch
¼ scale	6 inches	⅛ inch	1:40 scale	5 feet	⅛ inch
	1 foot	¼ inch		10 feet	¼ inch
	2 feet	½ inch		20 feet	½ inch
	4 feet	1 inch		40 feet	1 inch

DataCAD Exercise 14

Please complete the following exercise by reading each question carefully, then circling the letter that corresponds to the correct answer.

1. You should create:

   a. 5 default drawings. This is as many as anyone would ever need.
   b. At least 1 for every different scale you will need, and for different layer naming schemes.
   c. 10 default drawings. This is the maximum you can create.

2. To change into another directory in order to access other drawing files (such as the DEFAULT directory), you use the:

   a. Directory menu, New Dir option.
   b. New Dir option, found in the Drawing list menu.
   c. New Path option, found in the Drawing List menu.

3. Default drawings are created in order to:

   a. Save many steps, increase productivity, help eliminate errors, and establish consistency in all of your CADD drawings.
   b. Save many steps, increase productivity, and help eliminate errors. However, it is impossible to establish consistency in your CADD drawings.
   c. Increase the time consuming steps in every drawing. Using Default drawings is not recommended.

4. Your default drawings should reside in the:

   a. MTEC\DEFAULT directory.
   b. MTEC\DWG directory.
   c. MTEC\SYM directory.

5. To create additional layers in your drawing, you use the Layers menus, then the:

   a. AddLayer option.
   b. NewLayer option.
   c. On/Off option.

6. Once you have added layers to your drawing, you should:

   a. Use the Snap option found in the Layers menu to define a snap setting for each layer.
   b. Name your layers.
   c. Leave the Layers menu. The layers will be automatically named.

7. To define Architectural or Decimal units for your drawing, you use the:

   a. Settings menu, then pick the ScaleTyp option.
   b. Settings menu, then pick the Units option.
   c. Units menu, then pick the ScaleTyp option.

8. The MissDist option defines the:

   a. Distance the viewing window changes when you press the arrow keys.
   b. Gap that is created between lines when you object snap to another line.
   c. Distance you can miss an object by, and still be able to pick it or object snap to it.

9. The ScrlDist option defines the:

   a. Distance the viewing window changes when you press the arrow keys.
   b. Gap that is created between lines when you scroll to another line.
   c. Distance you can miss an object by, and still be able to pick it.

10. The NegDist option:

    a. Allows you to move the cursor in a negative distance.
    b. Allows you to input negative (–) coordinates and angles.
    c. Makes the coordinate readout display a minus sign (–) when you are moving the cursor in the negative direction.

11. The SaveDlay option sets the:

    a. Delay time of the coordinate readout display.
    b. Minutes between automatic saves.
    c. Delay time of the File I/O, Save option.

12. The ScaleTyp, AngleTyp, MissDist, ScrlDist, SaveDlay and NegDist options are all found in the:

    a. Settings menu.
    b. Units menu.
    c. Definitions menu.

13. The "snap spacing" refers to:

    a. How you have set the spacing in the Object Snap menu.
    b. The increments your cursor jumps to when the "Snap" mode is on (e.g., 1', 4', 6", etc.).
    c. The spacing between the grids.

14. To define the snap spacing, you use the:

    a. Snap Spc option, found in the Grid menu.
    b. Set Grid Snap option, found in the Object Snap menu.
    c. GridSize, Set Snap options, found in the Grid menu.

15. Snap spacing can:

    a. Be different for each layer.
    b. Not be different for each layer.
    c. Not be changed once you set it.

16. The actual scale of the drawing:

    a. Is determined once you define a plot scale in your default drawing. All walls and lines are drawn full scale as you create them, then are plotted at the appropriate scale. Only descriptive items are scaled as you draw them.
    b. Effects the way you create walls and other lines. These types of entities must be scaled as you draw them.
    c. Is defined in the Settings menu.

17. To define the pens your plotter will use as the drawing is plotted, you use the:

    a. Layer menu, Color and Set Pens options.
    b. Plotter menu, Set Pens option.
    c. Plotter menu, Color option.

18. Different pens are associated with different entities in your drawing by defining:

    a. Line Types.
    b. Color.
    c. Line Widths.

19. When setting your Dimension variables, you:

    a. Have to define variables for all the different types of dimensions.
    b. Only have to define the variables for Linear and Angular dimensions.
    c. Only have to define the variables for Linear dimensions. These variables will then be set for all of the dimension types.

20. The Text Size that you define in your default drawing is set at:

    a. The appropriate size in relation to the plotting scale. (E.g., If the drawing is to be plotted at ¼″, text created 6 inches high will be plotted at ⅛″ high.)
    b. The size you want it plotted. It will always turn out the correct size, regardless of the plotted scale.

21. The text size must be adjusted in:

    a. The Text menu only.
    b. Both the Text and Dimensions menu.
    c. The Text, Dimension, and Plotter menus.

22. The most important thing to know about your drawings BEFORE you create your default drawings, is the:

    a. Text size.
    b. Paper size.
    c. Plot scale.

DataCAD
Exercise 15 - Final

THE following questions were compiled from the numerous calls received by the author from over 200 DataCAD users. Read each question and possible answers carefully, then circle the letter that you feel corresponds to the correct answer.

1. You are dimensioning your project, and try to use object snap to lock onto corners of the walls. You get a message "No Entity found within Object Snap distance", and the dimension could not be drawn. You should:

   a. Call someone for help.
   b. Check that LyrSnap is active in the Object Snap menu.
   c. Make LyrSrch active in the Dimensions menu.

2. The project you were working on is too big for the present layout you have defined in the Plotter menu. Your next step is to:

   a. Use the Enlarge menu, to reduce the size of your project.
   b. Start the drawing all over again, since you created it at the wrong scale.
   c. Try the next smaller scale in the Plotter menu, Scale option, then place your layout again to see if it fits.

3. If you want to change the size of existing text in your drawing, you use the:

   a. Text menu, Modify option, then use Area to pick all of the text at once to change.
   b. Change, Text, Size options, type in a new size, then use Area to pick all of the text at once to change.
   c. Erase menu, erase all of the existing text, then create your text all over again.

4. You just started DataCAD, and none of the drawings you created appear in the drawing list. To get the drawing list that contains your drawings back, you:

   a. Pick the New Path option, and type in the correct directory path for your drawings.
   b. Press the [Esc] key, and start DataCAD over again.
   c. Just start a new drawing. Your previous drawings have obviously been deleted, and all of your work is ruined.

5. A corner of two walls overlap each other, when they should be trimmed to one another. To fix this, you use the:

   a. CleanUp menu, and the L Intsct option.
   b. CleanUp menu, and the Corner option.
   c. Geometry menu, and the L Intsct option.

6. When you are inserting doors in walls, and you get the message "No walls found to cut", you must:

   a. Make sure LyrSnap is active in the Object Snap menu.
   b. Pick the LyrSrch option found in the DoorSwng menu, and pick the correct layer for the walls.
   c. Try again. You just didn't pick close enough.

7. Your linetype is currently set to "Proplin". To change the current setting to "Solid", you:

   a. Press the Q key until Solid is displayed.
   b. Use the Change menu, and pick the LineType option, then select Solid.
   c. Press the K key until Solid is displayed.

8. You want to pull up a Template you created, but it is not displayed in the Template list. You should:

   a. Pick New Path, then type in the correct directory pathname for your template.
   b. Use File I/O, and get another drawing that had the Template displayed in it before.
   c. Pick New Path, and type in the name of your Template. DataCAD will find the template for you.

9. To set the current input mode, you use the:

   a. [Insert] key.
   b. [Space bar].
   c. [Tab] key.

10. To use coordinate input, you press the:

    a. [Insert] key.
    b. [Space bar].
    c. [Tab] key.

11. You are dimensioning a wall, and although the wall is drawn correctly, the dimension is off by a few inches. Most likely, you:

    a. Forgot to change to the correct dimension layer.
    b. Do not have your increment snap set correctly.
    c. Are not using Object Snap.

12. You are drawing an insulation line. However, it is the wrong size and looks more like a straight line. To change the current size, you use the:

    a. LineType menu, Size option.
    b. LineType menu, Spacing option.
    c. Change menu, Size option.

13. The 3-D perspective you created does not appear in your drawing. All of your layers are on, and you have recalculated the view window. You may have forgotten to:

    a. Pick the SaveImag option when you created the 3-D view.
    b. Use LyrSrch when you created the image.
    c. Pick the CopyImag option in 3-D Views.

14. To save the image when you use Hide to remove the hidden lines in your 3-D view, you must pick:

    a. SavImag option AFTER completing the hidden line removal process, but BEFORE leaving the menu.
    b. SavImag option BEFORE beginning the hidden line removal process.
    c. Save Lyr, and name a new layer for your view.

15. You started a new drawing. You notice that your drawing has the wrong layer names for the type of drawing you will be creating. What probably happened, is:

    a. You named your drawing wrong.
    b. The wrong Default drawing is set.
    c. The wrong pathname was set for the drawing list.

16. To set your snap increments, you press:

    a. S.
    b. [Shift] S.
    c. [Shift] X.

17. The dimension you just created has the wrong text size and the dimension extension lines are adjusted improperly. You should:

    a. Check the wall you are dimensioning. It may be drawn wrong.
    b. Set the dimension variables in Dim Styl and TextStyl before creating additional dimensions.
    c. Change the text size, using the Text menu, Size option.

18. You just displayed the drawing you worked on for two weeks, and all of the dimensions are gone! A good idea would be to:

    a. Check that the dimension layer is displayed, and that in the Display menu, the ShowDim option is active.
    b. Create all of the dimensions again.
    c. Delete the drawing, and start over again.

19. You are inserting a window in a wall, and although the window was created correctly, the wall was not cut. To fix this, you:

  a. Set the LyrSrch option to the correct layer.
  b. Pick the CutOut option until it is active.
  c. Press the [Tab] key until the correct layer is active.

20. To reduce the size of your detail, but NOT change the associated dimensions, you should use the:

  a. Enlarge menu, and make the DimSet option active BEFORE reducing the size of your detail.
  b. Enlarge menu, Explode option, to explode the associated dimensions BEFORE reducing the size of your detail.
  c. Dimension menu, Linear, Explode options, to explode the associated dimensions by Area, BEFORE reducing the size of your detail.

21. As you create your dimensions, you are not allowed to pick the distance the dimension appears from the object you are dimensioning. To allow this, you:

  a. Turn off the Snap.
  b. Use the Pick Dist option.
  c. Pick the Dim Styl option, and set the FixdDis to OFF.

22. All of the symbols you are placing are coming in at the wrong angle. What probably happened?

  a. There is an angle set in the DymnRot option.
  b. The DymnRot option is active (*).
  c. Your drawing must have been rotated accidentally.

23. To set the angle degrees that are locked onto when drawing lines or walls in the Ortho Mode, you use the:

  a. Object Snap menu, Angle option.
  b. Settings menu, OrthAngl option.
  c. Grid menu, Snap Ang option.

24. Even though you have defined your pens in the Plotter menu, your multi-pen plotter plots your entire drawing with pen number one. You should check that:

  a. SetPens is active.
  b. ClrPlot is active.
  c. UsePens is active.

25. Yesterday, you displayed a drawing that contained a lot of text. Today, however, most of the text is gone. You have even checked that the text layer is displayed. Next, you should:

  a. Call someone for help.
  b. Display the other layers too, since you could have had the wrong layer active when you created most of the text. Then check that ShowTxT (in Settings) is active.
  c. Create the text over again. Obviously, the text is gone, since you couldn't have made a mistake in setting your active layer.

26. Your hatch pattern came in all wrong. In fact, it looks like a line-box-line is drawn instead of a solid line in the pattern. The first thing to do is:

    a. See what the current linestyle is set to. It probably is set to Box, and it should be set to Solid.
    b. Reset the pattern in the Hatch menu.
    c. Check the LineType option in the Hatch menu.

27. What is a quick way to draw lines that are parallel to other lines, but at different distances? Use the:

    a. Geometry menu, Parallel option.
    b. Geometry menu, Offset option, turn Dynamic off, then use the PerpDist option to enter specific values.
    c. Copy menu, RectArray option for each line.

28. Every 5 minutes, an "automatic save occurs". To change this to every 20 minutes, you use the:

    a. Settings menu, SaveDlay option.
    b. Settings menu, AutoSav option.
    c. File I/O menu, AutoSav option.

29. You just deleted the wrong group, and 316 entities were erased by mistake. Before doing anything else, you should:

    a. Press the [>] key, or the UnDo option if you were in the Erase menu.
    b. Press the [Shift] [<] keys.
    c. Pick the UnErase option.

30. When creating a Site plan, in your default drawing you would set:

    a. Bearing angle type, and Engineering scale type.
    b. Normal angle type, and Architect scale type.
    c. Bearing angle type, and Decimal scale type.

Appendices

Appendix A:
The DataCAD
Operations Guide

TABLE OF CONTENTS

The DataCAD Operations Guide

This operations guide is a step-by-step "cookbook" designed to help you in your daily use of DataCAD. This guide is revised to DataCAD release 3.6a.

STARTING INFORMATION

If you want to do this:	Follow these steps:

STARTING YOUR COMPUTER:

Starting your Computer

1. Open diskette drive door.
   (Disk drive door should always be left open when not in use.)
2. Turn processor on.
3. Turn display screen on.

STARTING DATACAD:

Starting DataCAD

1. Type in:
   cd \ mtec
2. Type in:
   dcad
3. Press **[Return]** key after reading copyright screen.
4. Pick a drawing from the drawing list, or key in a new drawing name.

CHANGING DRAWING LISTS

Changing to another drawing list (directory)

1. Start DataCAD, until the drawing list is displayed.
2. Pick **New Path**.
3. Type in the path name for your directory.
   Example: **dwg**
   Notice: If your drawing directory is NOT in the MTEC directory, put a \ before the name.
4. Press **[Enter]**.
5. If it is a new directory, pick **Yes**.

DATACAD MENUS:

Switching EDIT and UTILITY menus

1. Press mouse button **3** to toggle between menus.

Picking a menu option

1. Move the mouse (cursor) to highlight option.
2. Press mouse button **1**.

EXITING DATACAD:

Exiting DataCAD and saving your drawing

1. Pick the **Quit** option, found in the UTILITY menu.
2. Pick **Yes**, or type **Y**.

Exiting DataCAD and **NOT** saving any drawing changes

1. Pick the **Quit** option, found in the UTILITY menu.
2. Pick **Abort**.
3. Pick **Yes**, or type **Y**.

RETRIEVING THE AUTOMATIC SAVE FILE:

To access the "automatic save" file of your drawing

1. Start DataCAD.
2. Pick the name of the drawing you were last working on from the drawing list.

If you want to do this:	Follow these steps:
	3. If there is an automatic save file for this drawing, you will be prompted: **WARNING: An autosave file (.ASV) for this drawing is present. Are you sure you want to continue?** 4. Pick **Yes**. 5. Pick **Yes** again to "rename your file". 6. Type in a new name for your .ASV file. It should not match the original file name. Do NOT add the DC3 extension, as the system does this for you. Example: Original file - **SITE001** rename .ASV file to - **SITE0012** 7. Press **[Enter]**. 8. The drawing list is a displayed, and the new drawing name you designated is added to the list.

DataCAD Drawing Operations

(Listed alphabetically)

If you want to do this:	Follow these steps:

CHANGING EXISTING ITEMS

Changing the color of an existing item

1. Pick **Change** from the EDIT menu.
2. Make sure ***Entity** is active (* = active).
3. Pick **Color**.
4. Pick desired new color from menu.
5. Pick entities to change to new color.

Changing the color of a group of items (many items created at one time)

1. Pick **Change** from the EDIT menu.
2. Make sure ***Group** is active (* = active).
3. Pick **Color**.
4. Pick desired new color from menu.
5. Pick one entity indicating the group to change to new color.

Changing the color of many items in an area

1. Pick **Change** from the EDIT menu.
2. Make sure ***Area** or ***Fence** is active (* = active).
3. Pick **Color**.
4. Pick desired new color from menu.
5. Pick two points indicating an area around the items you wish to change, or multiple points for your fence.
6. If using Fence, press mouse button **3** to close it.

Changing other attributes of existing items (LineType, LineWgt, Color, Spacing, OverSht, Z-Base, Z-Height, Text)

1. Pick **Change** from the EDIT menu.
2. Make sure ***Entity, *Group, *Area,** or ***Fence** is active, as applicable.
3. Pick and set the options that apply to the type of change. (You can set as many as desired.)
4. Pick items or area to change.
5. If using Fence, press mouse button **3** to close it.

Changing the content of text

See TEXT, Edit existing text

COLORS:

Switching colors (Quick toggle)

1. Press **K** to scroll forward.
2. Press **[Shift] K** to scroll backward.

Assigning a color to a layer

See LAYERS.

Changing the color of an item

See CHANGING EXISTING ITEMS.

COORDINATE INPUT:

Definition of Cartesian coordinates (X,Y,Z)

1. **Relative -**
   FROM a start point.
   X = across the screen, horizontal.
   Y = up and down, vertical.
   Z = depth (Height of walls).
2. **Absolute -**
   From the 0,0 origin.
   Same X,Y,Z as above.

If you want to do this:	Follow these steps:
Definition of Polar angles	1. **Normal -** Counterclockwise movement. 0 horizontal at 3:00 position, 90 at 12:00, 180 at 9:00, 270 at 6:00. 2. **Bearing -** North, East, South, and West positions 3. **Compass -** Clockwise movement. 0 at 12:00, 90 at 3:00, 180 at 6:00, 270 at 9:00.
Setting Normal or Compass Angle Type	1. Pick **Settings** from UTILITY menu. 2. Pick **AngleTyp**. 3. Pick **Normal** or **Compass** as applicable. 4. Press mouse button **3** to quit.
Setting Bearing Angle Type	1. Pick **Settings** from UTILITY menu. 2. Pick **AngleTyp**. 3. Pick **Bearing**. 4. Press mouse button **3** to quit back to Settings menu. 5. Pick **ScaleTyp**. 6. Pick **Decimal** and **Units** until they are active (*).
Typing in Cartesian relative coordinates	1. ALWAYS pick starting point. 2. Press **[Ins]** key until **Current input mode is relative cartesian (X,Y).** is displayed. 3. Press the **[Space bar]**. 4. Type in X (horizontal) distance, and **[Enter]**. 5. Type in Y (vertical) distance, and **[Enter]**. 6. Your new line/wall is drawn. 7. Press the **[Space bar]** again to input next X,Y distance. 8. This input mode will remain set until you change it.
Typing in polar angles (Normal or Compass Polar)	1. ALWAYS pick starting point. 2. Press **[Ins]** key until **Current input mode is relative polar (distance, angle).** is displayed. 3. Press the **[Space bar]**. 4. Type in distance, and **[Enter]**. 5. Type in angle, and **[Enter]**. 6. Your new line/wall is drawn. 7. Press the **[Space bar]** again to input next distance and angle. 8. This input mode will remain set until you change it.
Typing in angles (Bearings polar)	1. Pick starting point. 2. Press **[Ins]** key until **Current input mode is relative polar (distance, angle).** is displayed. 3. Press the **[Space bar]**. 4. Type in distance, and **[Enter]**. 5. Type in angle (ex. **N90E** would draw a horizontal line towards the right), and **[Enter]**. 6. Your new line/wall is drawn. 7. Press the **[Space bar]** again to input next distance and angle.
Using a reference point for coordinate input	1. Press **[~]** key. 2. Pick point or corner to measure from (use OBJECT SNAP!). 3. If necessary, use **[Ins]** key to set input mode. 4. Press the **[Space bar]**.

If you want to do this:	Follow these steps:
	5. Type in and **[Enter]** coordinates for the FIRST point of wall (or other item you are creating).
	6. Continue using the **[Space bar]** to type in your coordinates as needed.

COPYING:

Creating a single copy of an item or group of items	1. Press **C** key (EDIT/Copy menus).
	2. Pick two points indicating distance to move the new copy to.
	3. Pick **Entity** or **Group** until it is active (*), whichever is applicable.
	4. Pick item to copy.
Creating a copy of many items at once	1. Press **C** key (EDIT/Copy menus).
	2. Pick two points indicating distance to move the new copy to.
	3. Pick **Area** or **Fence** until it is active (*).
	4. Pick two diagonal points indicating a rectangle around items to be copied, or multiple points if using Fence.
	5. If using Fence, press mouse button **3** to close.
Creating multiple copies in one or two directions	1. Press **C** key (EDIT/Copy menus).
	2. Pick **RectArray**.
	3. Pick two points indicating the distance to move the new copies horizontally and vertically.
	4. Type in the TOTAL number of copies you want in the X direction (minimum = 1).
	5. Type in the TOTAL number of copies you want in the Y direction (minimum = 1).
	6. Pick **Entity, Group, Area** or **Fence** until the desired option is active (*).
	7. Pick item(s) to copy.
Making copies by dragging to position	1. Press **M** (EDIT/Move menus)
	2. Pick **Drag**.
	3. Pick **AndCopy** until it is active (*).
	4. Pick **Entity, Group, Area,** or **Fence** until the desired option is active (*).
	5. Pick item(s) to copy.
	6. Drag copies to position, and pick or object snap to place.
Copying items from one layer to another	1. Press **L**.
	2. Pick **To Layer**.
	3. Pick the layer you want to copy ''to''.
	4. Pick items to copy by **Entity, Group, Area,** or **Fence**.
	5. Press mouse button **3** to quit.

DEFAULT DRAWINGS:

Creating the default drawing file	1. Start DataCAD, or start a new drawing so that the drawing list is displayed.
	2. Pick **Default**.
	3. Press **[Space bar]** once to clear any current default and press **[Enter]**. **-or-** pick a default you wish to copy for your new default drawing (If necessary, pick **New Path**, and type in the default pathname to retrieve list: **default**.
	4. When you are returned to your original drawing list, pick **New Path**.
	5. Type in and **[Enter]** the name for the drawing default directory: **default**

If you want to do this:	Follow these steps:
	6. If this is a new directory, pick **Yes**.
	7. Start a new drawing, giving it a descriptive name that defines the final plot scale and type. Example: **1-4PLAN** for a ¼″ plan type of drawing.
	8. Define all necessary settings and defaults, create and name layers, plot scale and paper size, and other default drawing characteristics.
	9. Pick **File I/O**.
	10. Pick **New Dwg**.
	11. Pick **Yes** to save.
	12. Pick **New Path** to return to your original drawing list.
	13. Type in and **[Enter]** the name of your drawing directory.
Using the default drawing	1. Start DataCAD, or start a new drawing.
	2. Pick **Default** from opening screen.
	3. If necessary, pick **New Path**, and type in the default pathname: **default**
	4. Pick the desired default drawing.

DIMENSIONING:

If you want to do this:	Follow these steps:
Creating a single horizontal or vertical dimension	1. Press **D** key (UTILITY/Dimension menu).
	2. Press **[Tab]** key until dimension layer is active.
	3. If LyrSrch is not already active, Press **[Shift] X**, and pick **LyrSrch** until it is active (*), then quit this menu.
	4. Pick **Linear**.
	5. Pick **Horiznt** or **Verticl** until it is active (*Horiznt).
	6. Object snap to the first corner of wall or item to dimension from.
	7. Object snap to next item to dimension to.
	8. Pick location of dimension line.
	9. Pick text position, if Auto Text is not used.
Creating a string line dimension (horizontal or vertical)	1. Press **D** key (UTILITY/Dimension menu).
	2. Press **[Tab]** key until dimension layer is active.
	3. If LyrSrch is not already active, Press **[Shift] X**, and pick **LyrSrch** until it is active (*).
	4. Pick **Linear**.
	5. Pick **Horiznt** or **Verticl** until it is active (*Horiznt).
	6. Object snap to the first corner of wall or item to dimension from.
	7. Object snap to next item to dimension to.
	8. Pick location of dimension line.
	9. Pick text position, if Auto Text is not used.
	10. Pick **Strnglin**.
	11. Object snap to next item to dimension.
	12. Continue object snapping to items until all items are dimensioned.
Creating a stringline dimension with an overall dimension	1. Follow steps 1 through 11 above.
	2. Press mouse button **3** to quit back to the Linear Dimensions menu. (DO NOT LEAVE MENU.)
	3. Pick the **OverAll** option.
Setting dimension variable	1. Press **D** key (UTILITY/Dimension menu).
	2. Pick **Linear**.
	3. Pick **TextStyl**.
	4. Adjust values in applicable options.

If you want to do this:	Follow these steps:
	5. Press mouse button **3** once to quit. 6. Pick **DimStyl.** 7. Adjust values in applicable options. 8. Press mouse button **3** once to quit. 9. Pick **ArroStyl.** 10. Adjust values in applicable options. 11. Press mouse button **3** once to quit. 12. Pick **AutoStyl.** 13. Pick **Strngli, PtsOnly,** and **LyrSrch** until they are active (*). 14. Press mouse button **3** to quit.

DOORS AND WINDOWS:

Adding doors	1. Press **A** key (EDIT/Architct menus). 2. Pick **DoorSwng.** 3. Pick **LyrSrch.** 4. Pick the layer that the appropriate walls are on. This layer will remain set until you change it. 5. Pick hinge side on wall. 6. Pick strike side on wall. 7. Pick swing direction. 8. Pick outside of wall.
Setting head height of doors	1. Press **A.** 2. Pick **DoorSwng.** 3. Pick **Head Hgt.** 4. Pick or type in head height of door. 5. Press **[Enter].**
Adding windows	1. Press **A.** 2. Pick **Windows.** 3. Pick one jamb side on wall. 4. Pick second jamb side on wall. 5. Pick outside of wall.
Adding doors and windows on multiple story buildings	1. Press **Z.** 2. Change the Z-Base and Z-Height to correct values for the walls on the story you will be adding doors and windows to. 3. Doors and windows will be inserted into the walls at that level.

DXF FORMATTED FILES

Notice-If you are transferring files to AutoCAD, make sure there are NO special characters in the names of your layers (! @ # $ % & * - __ + = ?), as these are reserved for special uses in AutoCAD.

Creating a DXF File from a DataCAD drawing	1. Have the drawing you wish to transfer displayed on your screen. 2. Press **L** (UTILITY/Layers menus). 3. Pick **On/Off.** 4. Check that your layer names do not have special characters in them. 5. Press mouse button **3** once. 6. Pick **All On.** 7. Pick **Yes.** 8. Press mouse button **3** to quit. 9. Pick **File I/O.** 10. Pick **WriteDXF.** 11. Pick **New Path.** 12. Type in the correct path for your DXF files: **dxf**

If you want to do this:	Follow these steps:
	13. If it is a new directory, pick **Yes** to create it.
	14. Press **[Enter]** to accept present drawing name, or type in new name. Do NOT add the .dxf extension to the drawing name.
	15. The DXF file is created (filename.dxf).
Retrieving a DXF file into DataCAD	1. Load DXF file into \MTEC\DXF directory.
	2. Start DataCAD.
	3. Start a new drawing.
	4. Pick **File I/O.**
	5. Pick Read DXF.
	6. Make sure ***Intract** is active for user prompts, or that ***Auto** is active for no user prompts.
	7. Pick **Begin.**
	8. Pick **New Path.**
	9. Type in and **[Enter]** the correct path for your DXF files: **dxf**
	10. Pick the drawing you wish to convert to DataCAD.
	11. If ***Intract**, follow the prompts to define the linetypes. If ***Auto**, best guesses will be made for linetypes.
	12. The drawing will be loaded into the present drawing file.

ERASING:

Erasing entire areas	1. Press **E** (EDIT/Erase menus).
	2. Pick **Area** or **Fence** until it is active (***Area**).
	3. Pick two points indicating a rectangle around the items you wish to erase, or multiple points if using Fence.
	4. If using Fence, press mouse button **3** to close it.
Erasing picked items or groups	1. Press **E** (EDIT/Erase menus).
	2. Make sure ***Entity** or ***Group** is active, as applicable. (* = active.)
	3. Pick the items or group to erase.
Erasing the last line created	1. If necessary, press mouse button **3** to quit drawing lines.
	2. Press the **[,]** (comma) key.
Erasing the last group created	1. Press the **[Shift]** and **[<]** keys simultaneously.
	2. If the last items drawn were created as a group, they will be erased.
Restoring the last entity or group erased	1. Press the **[.]** (period) key.
	2. If the last item erased was a entity, it will be restored.
	3. If the last item erased was a group, it will be restored.

GRIDS:

To define grids	1. Press **G.** (UTILITY/Grids means)
	2. Pick **GridSize.**
	3. Pick **SetDispl** for small grids.
	4. Pick **Custom.**
	5. Type in or pick from menu desired spacing for X grid. Example: **4**
	6. Press **[Enter].**

If you want to do this:	Follow these steps:
	7. Type in or pick from menu desired spacing for Y grid. Example: **4**
	8. Press **[Enter]**.
	9. Pick **SetDisp2** for large grids.
	10. Pick **Custom**.
	11. Type in or pick from menu desired spacing for X grid. Example: **16**
	12. Press **[Enter]**.
	13. Type in or pick from menu desired spacing for Y grid. Example: **16**
	14. Press **[Enter]**.
	15. Press mouse button **3**.
	16. Pick **GridColr**.
	17. Pick **SetDisp1** for small grids.
	18. Pick desired color from menu. Example: **Lt Red**
	19. Pick **SetDisp2** for large grids.
	20. Pick **MarkSize**.
	21. Pick desired display size of large grid. Example: **2**
	22. Press **[Enter]**.
	23. Pick desired color from menu. Example: **Lt Blue**
	24. Press mouse button **3**.
	25. Pick **Disp1On** until active (*Disp1On).
	26. Pick **Disp2On** until active (*Disp2On).
	27. Press mouse button **3** to quit.
Setting Grid Snap	See SNAP

HATCHING

Defining the boundary	1. Press **[Tab]** until correct layer that will hold hatching pattern is active.
	2. Draw outline for pattern, using **object snap** when applicable to match existing geometry.
	3. Make sure to **object snap** to close boundary.
Creating the hatch	1. Press **H**.
	2. Pick **Pattern**.
	3. Pick the desired hatch pattern.
	4. If necessary, pick **Scale**, and enter the desired scale of your pattern. Example: **80**.
	5. Pick **Group** until it is active **(*Group)**.
	6. Pick the boundary. It will become gray and dashed.
	7. Pick by entity if necessary to add to your boundary.
	8. When boundary is correct, pick **Begin**.
	9. Press mouse button **3** to quit.
Deleting the hatch	1. Press **E** (EDIT/Erase).
	2. Make sure ***Group** is active.
	3. Pick Hatch to erase.
	4. Press mouse button **3** to quit.
Deleting the hatch if it was the last item created	1. Press the **[Shift]** <. 2. The last group will be erased.

INCREMENT SNAP:

See SNAP

If you want to do this:	Follow these steps:

LAYERS:

Defining Layers	1. Press **L** key.
	2. Pick **NewLayer**.
	3. Key in the number of new layers needed (ex. 5): **5**
	4. Pick **Name**.
	5. Pick layer to "name".
	6. Key in new name for layer, and **[Enter]**.
	7. Continue until all layers are named.
	8. Press mouse button **3** to quit.
Changing active layers (Quick toggle)	1. Press **[Tab]** key to scroll forward.
	2. Press **[Shift] [Tab]** to scroll backward.
Assigning a color to a layer, using Layer menu	1. Press **L** key.
	2. Press **[Tab]** until correct layer is active.
	3. Pick **Color**.
	4. Pick the desired color from menu.
	5. Press mouse button **3** to quit.
Assigning a color to a layer, using Quick keys	1. Press **[Tab]** until correct layer is active.
	2. Press **K** key to scroll to correct color.
	3. Press **[Tab]** until next layer is active.
	4. Press **K** key to scroll to correct color.
	5. Continue until all layers have colors defined.
Turning on and off layers for viewing	1. Press **L** key.
	2. Pick **On/Off**.
	3. Pick layers to turn on or off for viewing. (* = Displayed, $ = Active.)
	4. Press mouse button **3** to quit.
Turning on all layers for viewing	1. Press **L**.
	2. Pick **All On**.
	3. Pick **Yes**.
	4. Press mouse button **3** to quit.
Turning off all layers but one	1. Press **L**.
	2. Pick **ActvOnly**.
	3. Pick the layer you wish displayed.
	4. Press mouse button **3** to quit.
	5. This layer becomes your active layer.
Saving a layer to a layer file	1. Display the drawing that contains the layer you wish to save.
	2. Press **L** key.
	3. Pick **SaveLayr**.
	4. Pick layer to save.
	5. Key in name for your layer file.
	6. A copy of your layer will be saved to file.
	7. Press mouse button **3** to quit.
Loading a layer file into a drawing	1. Display the drawing you wish to load the layers in, or create a new drawing.
	2. Press **L**.
	3. If necessary, use **NewLayer** to create the layers to hold the layer files.
	4. Press **[Tab]** until correct layer is active (empty layer that will hold the new layer file).
	5. Pick **Loadlayr**.
	6. Pick **Yes** (this will erase the original layer and layer name).

If you want to do this:	Follow these steps:

7. Pick the name of the layer file you wish to load.
8. The layer is added to your drawing.
9. Continue adding all necessary layers.
10. Press mouse button **3** to quit.

Moving items to another layer

See MOVE, Moving items to another layer

Copying items from one layer to another

See COPY

Erasing all items on a layer

1. Press **L**.
2. Pick **ErseLyr**.
3. Pick the layer that contains the items you wish to erase.
   CAUTION - All items on the layer will be erased!
4. Pick **Yes**.
5. Press mouse button **3** to quit.

Deleting a layer from the layer list

1. Press **L**.
2. Pick **DelLayer**.
3. Pick the layer you wish to remove from the list.
   CAUTION - All items on the layer will be erased also!
4. Pick **Yes**.
5. Press mouse button **3** once.
6. Pick the **On/Off** option.
7. Notice the layer is gone from the list.
8. Press mouse button **3** to quit.

NOTICE - The following layer viewing techniques allow you to temporarily view layers. These layers may not be active, or even exist in the current drawing file. Do NOT attempt, to draw *until you have pressed the [Esc] key to refresh the screen!* This will return you to the true screen conditions.

Temporarily viewing one layer, with automatic window extends

1. Press **L**.
2. Pick **ViewLayr**.
3. Pick **Extends** and **LyrRfsh** until active (*).
4. Pick **Select**.
5. Pick the layer you wish to view. It will appear, and be automatically windowed to it's extends.
6. Do NOT attempt to draw.
7. After viewing the layer, press the **[Esc]** key to return to the real screen conditions.

Temporarily viewing a saved layer file with

1. Press **L**.
2. Pick **ViewFile**.
3. Pick **LyrRfsh** until active (*).
4. Pick **Select**.
5. Pick **New Path**.
6. Type in and **[Enter]** the pathname for your layer. files:
   lyr
7. Pick the layer file you wish to view. It will be displayed on your screen.
8. Do NOT attempt to draw.
9. After viewing the file, press the **[Esc]** key to return to the real screen conditions.

LINESTYLES:

Changing linestyles

1. Press **Q** key.
2. Linestyle will toggle forward through available types, and be displayed at the lower left hand corner of the DataCAD menu.

If you want to do this:	Follow these steps:

3. New items you create will be in active linestyle.
4. Press **[Shift] Q** to toggle backwards.

MOVE:

Moving a single item or Group of items

1. Press **M** (EDIT/Move menus).
2. Pick two points indicating distance and direction to move (arrow will be displayed).
3. Make correct layer active (press **[Tab]**), or pick ***LyrSrch** until it is active.
4. Pick **Entity** or **Group** until it is active (*Entity).
5. Pick desired items or group to move.

Moving an area of items

1. Press **M** (EDIT/Move menus).
2. Pick two points indicating distance and direction to move.
3. Make correct layer active (press **[Tab]**), or pick ***LyrSrch** until it is active.
4. Pick **Area** from menu.
5. Pick two points indicating a rectangle around the items you wish to move.

Moving and copying items at the same time

1. Press **M**.
2. Pick two points indicating the distance and direction of the move.
3. Pick ***AndCopy** until it is active.
4. Make correct layer active (press **[Tab]**), or pick ***LyrSrch** until it is active.
5. Pick **Entity**, **Area**, or **Group** as applicable.
6. Pick items or area to move and copy.

*NOTICE - The ***AndCopy** option will remain active until you change it. (Unless you are moving to a layer, at which time AndCopy is not applicable.)

Moving items in one layer

1. Press **M**.
2. Pick two points indicating distance and direction to move.
3. Press **[Tab]** until layer with items is active.
4. Pick **LyrSrch** until it is **INACTIVE** (LyrSrch).
5. Pick **Entity**, **Group** or **Area** from menu.
6. Pick desired items or area to move.

Moving items to another layer

1. Press **M**.
2. Pick **To Layer**.
3. Pick the layer you want the items moved to.
4. Press **[Tab]** until the layer with the items is active, or pick **LyrSrch** until it is active.
5. Pick **Entity**, **Group**, or **Area** from menu.
6. Pick items or area to move.

Moving an item by dragging it

1. Press **M**.
2. Pick **Drag**.
3. Pick **Entity**, **Group**, or **Area** from menu.
4. If copy is desired, pick ***AndCopy**.
5. Pick item(s) or area to move.
6. Drag the items using the cursor to the new location.

OBJECT SNAP:

Setting the Object Snap modes

1. Press **[Shift] X**.
   (Utility/Object Snap menus)
2. Pick the desired settings for your Object snap, until they are active (*End Pnt).

If you want to do this:	Follow these steps:
	3. Commonly used settings are: ***End Pnt** ***Mid Pnt** ***Center** ***Intsect** 4. Press mouse button **3** to quit.
Picking the center of a circle or arc	1. Press **[Shift] X**. 2. Pick **None**. 3. Pick **Center** until it is active (*Center). 4. Press mouse button **3** to quit. 5. Move cursor to arc or circle. 6. Press mouse button **2** to object snap to the center.
Turning on Layer Snap (to grab items on different layers when Object snapping)	1. Press **[Shift] X** keys. (Object Snap menu) 2. Pick **LyrSnap** until it is active (*LyrSnap). 3. Press mouse button **3** to quit.

ROTATING:

Rotating items	1. Press **R** (EDIT/Rotate menus). 2. Pick the point indicating the centerpoint that items will be rotated about. 3. If necessary, pick **NewAngle**, to indicate a new angle other than previously set. 4. Type in desired angle, or pick from menu. 5. Pick **Entity, Group,** or **Area** until active (*), as applicable. 6. Pick item(s) or area to be rotated.
Undoing the last rotation	1. While still in the Rotation menu, pick **Undo**.

SYMBOLS   See TEMPLATES AND SYMBOLS

SNAP

Defining Increment Snap (Grid Snap)	1. Press **S** (UTILITY/Grids/GridSize/Set Snap menus). 2. Type in the desired X value, then **[Enter]**. 3. Type in the desired Y value, then **[Enter]**.
Turning on the Snap Mode	1. Press **X** until **Snap On** is displayed.

TEMPLATES & SYMBOLS:

Adding symbols to your drawing	1. Press **T**. (UTILITY/Template menus.) 2. If the wrong template is active, pick **NewFile**. 3. Pick the correct template name from menu. 4. The template is displayed with the symbols. 5. Press **[Tab]** until correct layer is active. 6. Pick the appropriate symbol from the template. 7. Pick the position for your symbol on your drawing and your symbol will be placed. 8. Press button **3** on the mouse to quit placing the symbol.
Getting other template lists (Changing template directories)	1. Press **T**. 2. If a template is displayed, pick **New File**. 3. Pick **New Path** from the template list.

If you want to do this:	Follow these steps:
	4. Type in the pathname for the directory that contains the desired template list. Example: **tpl** 5. The templates that are connected to the directory pathname will be listed.

Retrieving the templates and symbols that came with DataCAD	1. Press **T**.
	2. If a template is displayed, pick **New File**.
	3. Pick **New Path** from the template list.
	4. Type in *one* of the MTEC template path names, and press **[Enter]**. The proper names for these paths are:
	    tpl \ furn
	    tpl \ plumb
	    tpl \ elec
	    tpl \ mech
	    tpl \ struct
	    tpl \ dwg
	5. The templates that are connected to the directory pathname will be listed.

Creating new templates	1. Press **T**. 2. If another is already displayed, pick **NewFile**. 3. Type in new template name and [enter]. 4. Pick **Yes**. 5. Type in additional field information, if applicable. 6. Press mouse button **3** to quit. 7. Your new (empty) template is displayed.
Creating new symbols	1. Display drawing that has items for the new symbols. 2. Press **T**. 3. If the wrong template is displayed, pick **New File**. 4. Pick the correct template for your new symbols. 5. Pick **SaveSymb**. 6. Pick **Auto Path** to save the symbols to the current template. 7. If this is the first symbol for your template, pick **Yes**. 8. Type in the file name for your new symbol (8 characters limit). Example: **ftg1** 9. Pick **LyrSrch** until (*). 10. Pick the items to be saved as a symbol by **Entity, Group, Area,** or **Fence**. 11. When all symbol components are gray and dashed, pick **Continue**. 12. Pick a reference point for later placing your symbol on your drawing. 13. For ''Item name'', type in the name you wish to appear when you put your cursor over the template box for that symbol. Example: **1 Story Footing** 14. Fill in any applicable field names. 15. Press mouse button **3** to quit.
Changing the symbol name that appears when you place the cursor in the template box	1. Press **T**. 2. If wrong template is displayed, pick **New File**. 3. Pick **EditFlds.** 4. Pick the symbol that will have the name changed. 5. Pick **Item nam.** 6. Type in and **[Enter]** new name. 7. Press mouse button **3** twice to quit to Template menu. 8. Pick **New File**.

If you want to do this:	Follow these steps:

| | 9. Pick the same template. |
| | 10. Now move the cursor into the symbol box, and the new name will be displayed. |

Changing symbols in a template (Redefine)	1. Display drawing with items for new symbol.
	2. Press **T**.
	3. If wrong template is displayed, pick **New File**.
	4. Pick the correct template to display.
	5. Pick **Redefine**.
	6. Pick symbol in template box to change.
	7. Pick the items to be saved as your new symbol by **Entity, Group,** or **Area**. (Symbols cannot be used!)
	8. Pick **Continue**.
	9. Pick reference point for new symbol.
	10. The original symbol will be replaced with your new symbol. Any existing symbols that matched the original symbol on your drawing will be replaced also.

Deleting a symbol from a template	1. Press **T** and display the template with the symbol you wish to delete (see "Displaying a template").
	2. Pick **Del Symb**.
	3. Pick symbol you want deleted from template.
	4. Pick **Yes**.
	5. Pick **Yes**.
	6. Press mouse button **3** to quit.

Replacing symbols in your drawing (Updating)	1. Press **T** and display the template containing the new symbol (see "Displaying a template").
	2. Pick **Replace**.
	3. Pick the symbol on your drawing to indicate the type of symbol you will be replacing.
	4. Pick the new symbol from the template.
	5. Pick the symbols on your drawing that you want to replace by **Entity, Group, Area,** or **Fence**. -Or- pick **All** to replace all of the symbols on the drawing that match the type of symbol you want to replace.
	6. Press mouse button **3** to quit.

Rotating symbols as you add them	1. Press **T** and display the desired template.
	2. Pick **Rotate**.
	3. Pick the appropriate angle of rotation from the menu, or type it in and press **[Enter]**.
	4. Press **[Tab]** until correct layer is active.
	5. Pick the symbol from the template.
	6. Place the symbol (it is rotated automatically).
	7. If you are through adding rotated symbols, pick **Rotate** and change the value back to **0'-0**.
	8. Press mouse button **3** to quit placing your symbol.

NOTICE - The rotation value will stay until you change it. Remember to pick 0-0' to take out rotation angle.

| Turning off templates - Quick toggle | 1. Press **[Alt]** and **B** keys simultaneously. |

| Turning off templates from "Template" menu | 1. Press **T**. |
| | 2. Pick **TemplOff**. |

NOTICE - The following section explains the beginning set-up for piping symbols. This is an advanced technique in DataCAD. It involves setting up the template correctly, then editing the actual text file of the template. Editing of the file is NOT performed in DataCAD, but by using EDLIN or other text editor. You should only attempt to pipe symbols if you are well versed in using EDLIN (the DOS text editor) or have the SNAP MENU text editor. You should also be very comfortable in your ability to complete the assignment.

If you want to do this:	Follow these steps:
Preparing symbols for piping	1. Create the symbol. This will be referred to as the "**actual symbol**".
	2. Create the description you will use for piping. This could be text describing the actual symbol. This will be referred to as the "**descriptive symbol**".
	3. Create the template that you will use, or display an existing one you will be adding to.
	4. Use **SaveSymb** to save the **descriptive symbol** first.
	5. Use **SaveSymb** to save the **actual symbol** second. It is important that the **descriptive symbol** is immediately followed by the **actual symbol** in your template. (It will save a lot of typing for you.)
	6. Once you have completed saving your descriptive and actual symbols, continue to the section in SYSTEM OPERATIONS called "PIPING SYMBOLS".

TEXT:

Creating text	1. Press **[Alt] T** (Edit/Text menus).
	2. Press **[Tab]** until correct layer is active.
	3. Pick the start point.
	4. Type in text.
	5. Press **[Enter]** to add second line of text, if applicable.
	6. Press mouse button **3** to quit.
Creating text with arrows	1. Follow "Creating text" to add text to your drawing.
	2. Pick **Arrows**.
	3. Pick start of leader line close to text.
	4. Pick elbow points, if desired.
	5. Pick where arrow will be pointing.
	6. Press mouse button **3** to quit.
	7. Arrow will appear at last pick position.
To edit existing	1. Pick **Change** from the EDIT menu.
	2. Pick **Text** from menu.
	3. Pick **Content**.
	4. Pick the text you wish to edit, at the LOWER LEFT CORNER point!
	5. Type in new content.
	6. Press **[Return]** or mouse button **3** to quit.
Fitting text in an area	1. Press **[Alt] T**
	2. Pick **Fit Text**
	3. Press **[Tab]** until correct layer is active.
	4. Pick starting point of text
	5. Pick end point of area
	6. Pick point for height of area
	7. Type in text
	8. Press mouse button **3** to quit
Changing text settings to match existing text (Size, aspect, etc.)	1. Pick Identify from EDIT menu.
	2. Pick the text you want to match, at the LOWER LEFT CORNER point! Text will change to gray.
	3. Pick all items on the menu.
	4. Press **[Alt] T** to return to text menu.
	5. Continue creating new text.
3-D VIEWS	See VIEWS-3D

If you want to do this:	Follow these steps:

VIEWS (GO TO VIEW):

Saving the current view (and layer settings, view scale)

1. Press **V** (UTILITY/GotoView).
2. Pick **SaveView**.
3. Pick one of the **View #** options from the menu.
4. Type in the name of your view.
5. The current view will be saved.
6. Press mouse button **3** to quit.

Saving a windowed view

1. Press **V**.
2. Pick **WindowIn**.
3. Pick two points to indicate a rectangle around the area you wish to zoom into.
4. Press mouse button **3** to quit back to GotoView menu.
5. Pick **SaveView**.
6. Pick one of the **View #** options from the menu.
7. Type in the name of your view.
8. The zoomed in view will be saved.
9. Press mouse button **3** to quit.

Recalling a view with layer settings reset to match original saved view conditions

1. Press **V**.
2. Pick **LyrSet** until it is ACTIVE (*LyrSet).
3. Pick the **Viewname** you wish to see from the menu.
4. Your view will be displayed, and your settings (active layer, layers set on and off) will be reset to the conditions when the view was saved.
5. Press mouse button **3** to quit.

Recalling a view without changing the current layer settings

1. Press **V**.
2. Pick **LyrSet** until it is TURNED OFF (LyrSet).
3. Pick the **Viewname** you wish to see from the menu.
4. Your view will be displayed, and your settings will not be changed.
5. Press mouse button **3** to quit.

Renaming a view

1. Press **V**.
2. Pick **NameView**.
3. Pick the **Viewname** you wish to rename from the menu.
4. Type in the new name for your view.
5. Press mouse button **3** to quit.

Recalling last window view

1. Press **P**.

VIEWS - 3D:

NOTICE -**BEFORE** creating your 3D view, **turn off** the layers you do not wish to view in 3D.

Creating a 3D perspective view at eye level

1. Press **[Pg Up]** until drawing is reduced to approximately one third the screen size.
2. Press **[Arrow left]** and **[Arrow down]** until drawing is displayed over to the upper right hand corner.
3. Press **Y** (EDIT/DCAD 3D/3D Views menus)
4. Pick **Prspect** from menu.
5. Check that **EyePnt Z** and **CentPntZ** are set to **5'-0"**.
6. Pick the eye point for the cone of vision, in lower left hand corner of screen.
7. Pick **FixdCone** to turn it OFF, if applicable (NO *).
8. Object snap to lower left corner of building or pick a point for picture plane placement.
9. Your perspective will be displayed.

If you want to do this:	Follow these steps:
Creating a birds-eye perspective view	1. Press **[Pg Up]** until drawing is reduced to approximately one third the screen size. 2. Press **[Arrow left]** and **[Arrow down]** until drawing is displayed over to the upper right hand corner. 3. Press **Y** (EDIT/DCAD 3D/3D Views menus). 4. Pick **Prspect** from menu. 5. Pick **EyePnt Z**. 6. Change the eye-point to a new height, and **[Enter]**. Example: **30'-0"** 7. Pick **CentPntZ**. 8. Type in and **[Enter]: 5.0** 10. Pick the eye point for the cone of vision, in lower left hand corner of screen. 11. Pick **FixdCone** to turn it OFF, if applicable (NO *) 12. Object snap to lower left corner of building or pick a point for picture plane placement. 13. Your bird's eye view will be displayed. 14. The bird's eye settings (eye point and center point) will remain set until you change it.
Returning to PLAN view of drawing	1. Before leaving **3D View**. pick **Ortho**.
Quick Key for ortho view (plan)	1. Press **[Alt] 0** (zero).
Saving a 3D view	1. Press **Y**. 2. Create desired view. 3. Pick **SaveImag**. 4. Pick **NewLayer**. 5. Type in the name of the new layer that will hold the 3D image. Example: **Persp1** 6. Pick **Yes** to display this layer or **No** to turn new layer off. 7. If necessary, move 3D view to better location (see MOVE: ''Moving items in one layer'' -or- Moving a group of items).
WALLS:	
Drawing walls (Quick key)	1. Press **[=]** key (''Wall'' key) until ''Wall width'' prompt is displayed. 2. Pick or type in wall width. 3. Press **[Enter]**. 4. Press **[Tab]** until correct wall layer is active. 5. Use cursor to pick placement, or use coordinate input (see COORDINATE INPUT).
Cleaning ''T'' wall intersections as they are created	1. Press the **[\]** key until a prompt is displayed: **Wall ''T'' intersection will be cleaned.** (This sets the *Clean in the Architect menu.)
Cleaning up wall intersection after they are created	1. Press **[Alt] U**. (EDIT/Cleanup menus) 2. Pick **L intersection** or **T intersection**. 3. Press **[Tab]** until correct wall layer is active. 4. Pick two points to indicate a rectangle around intersection. 5. If ''T intersection'', pick one line of wall to trim ''to''.

If you want to do this:	Follow these steps:
Defining wall height	1. Press **Z** key. 2. Type in and **[Enter]** new "Z" base (bottom) and "Z" height (top). Example: Z-Base = **0.0** Z-Height = **8.0**
Picking wall placement	1. Move cursor with mouse. 2. Watch coordinate readout. 3. Press mouse button **1** for each end point of wall. 4. Press mouse button **3** to quit or disconnect.
Placing walls dimensioned at the center (Commercial interior walls)	1. Press **A**. 2. Pick the **Centers** option until it is active (*). 3. Press **[Tab]** until correct wall layer is active. 4. Pick the start and end points of your wall. (The single line that is originally drawn represents the center-line of your wall.)
Placing walls dimensioned to a side (Exterior walls)	1. Press **A**. 2. Pick **Sides** until it is active (*). 3. Press **[Tab]** until correct wall layer is active. 4. Pick the start and endpoints of your wall. (The single line that is drawn represents one side of your wall.) 5. Pick to establish the other side of your wall. The wall will be fattened to the side you indicate with your pick. Example: Pick to the inside of the building if you are drawing exterior walls, which are dimensioned to the outside.

WINDOWING

Zooming in (Windowing in)	1. Press the **/** key (has a **?** on it). 2. Pick two diagonal point to indicate a rectangle around the items you wish to "window-in" to. 3. Press mouse button **3** to quit.
Getting a full view of your drawing	1. Press the **/** key. 2. Pick **Extends**. 3. If full view is not displayed, pick **Recalc**. 4. Press mouse button **3** to quit.
Moving the viewing window to the right	1. Press the **[right arrow]** key.
Moving the viewing window to the left	1. Press the **[left arrow]** key.
Making the drawing smaller	1. Press the **[Page Up]** key.
Making the drawing larger	1. Press the **[Page Down]** key.
Returning to the previous window	1. Press the **P** key.

System Operations

(Listed alphabetically)

If you want to do this:	Follow these steps:

DOS - DRAWING FILES MANAGEMENT

BACKUPS:

NOTICE - Backups of all drawings on your hard disk should be made on a weekly basis. (Example: Every Friday at 4:30 p.m.) This is a safeguard against possible hard disk error.

Diskette backups of individual drawings should be made as "COPIES" (See COPYING DRAWINGS TO FLOPPY DISKETTES). However, if the drawing does not fit on 1 diskette, and therefore must be backed-up on several diskettes, use Backup. "Backup" is the only command that allows you to split a drawing onto multiple diskettes.

Backing up all
drawing files

1. Exit DataCAD and use DOS.
2. *IMPORTANT* - Make sure you are in the Dos root directory by typing in:
   **cd **
3. Press **[Enter]**.
4. Now type in:
   backup c:\ *.dc3 a:/s
5. Check that you typed in everything correctly, then press **[Enter]**.
6. Insert a formatted diskette into drive A, following the prompt, and press return.
7. Continue following the prompts until all of your drawings are backed up.
8. Label, date, and number all diskettes sequentially.

Restoring your
backups

1. Exit DataCAD and use DOS.
2. Make sure you are in the root directory by typing in:
   **cd **
3. Press **[Enter]**.
4. Now type in:
   restore a: c:\ *.* /s
5. Check that the command is typed correctly, then press **[Enter]**.
6. Insert the #1 backup disk into drive A. If the diskette is NOT #1, you will be prompted to reinsert #1.
7. Continue following the prompts until the restoration is completed.

COPYING DRAWING TO FLOPPY DISKETTE:

NOTICE - A copy to diskette of the current drawing you are working on should be made daily. (Example: At the end of the day's work on the drawing, copy it to diskette.) This is to safeguard possible errors, accidental changes, or deletion of the file on hard disk.

If the drawing does NOT fit on a single diskette, use Backup (See BACKUPS).

Copying one drawing
to a diskette in
drive A:

1. Exit DataCAD and use DOS.
2. Type in **cd** (change directory) and the project directory pathname that holds your drawings. Be sure to use the \ key to separate the directory names.
   Example: **cd \mtec\proj01**

If you want to do this:	Follow these steps:

	3. Press **[Enter]**.
	4. Insert a formatted diskette in drive A.
	5. Type in **copy**, the name of your drawing, and end the command with **a:** for drive specification. Separate each field with a space. Example: **copy drawing1.dc3 a:** Press **[Enter]**.
Copying all the drawings in a directory to a diskette in drive A:	1. Exit DataCAD and use DOS. 2. Type in **cd** (change directory) and the project directory pathname that holds your drawings. Be sure to use the \ key to separate the directory names. Example: **cd \ mtec \ proj01** 3. Press **[Enter]**. 4. Insert a formatted diskette in drive A. 5. Type in: **copy *.dc3 a:** 6. Press **[Enter]**.

COPYING DRAWINGS FROM FLOPPY DISKETTE:

Copying one drawing FROM a diskette in drive A:	1. Exit DataCAD and use DOS. 2. Type in **cd** (change directory) and the project directory pathname that you want to copy your drawing to. Be sure to use the \ key to separate the directory names. Example: **cd \ mtec \ proj01** 3. Press **[Enter]**. 4. Insert the diskette that contains the drawing you wish to copy to the hard disk, in drive A. 5. Type in **copy a:** and the name of your drawing. The drawing will be copied to the current directory. Separate the fields with a space. Example: **copy a:drawing1.dc3** **6. Press [Enter]**.
Copying all the drawings from a diskette in drive A: to the hard disk	1. Exit DataCAD and use DOS. 2. Type in **cd** (change directory) and the project directory pathname that you want to copy your drawings to. Use the \ key to separate the directory names. Example: **cd \ mtec \ proj01** 3. Press **[Enter]**. 4. Insert the diskette that holds your drawings in drive A. 5. Type in: **copy a:*.dc3** 6. Press **[Enter]**.

PIPING TEMPLATE SYMBOLS:

NOTICE - Prepare your symbols for piping using DataCAD (see TEMPLATES & SYMBOLS).

Template piping is designed to make a template easier to use and display faster. When a piped template is displayed, only text or other simple description for each symbol is shown in the symbol boxes. Once you place the symbol, the *actual symbol* appears.

The directions below assume that you are using, and have experience with, a text editor or EDLIN to change your template file.

Using a text editor to pipe your template symbols	1. Make a copy of the template file you will be editing, giving it an extension of .BAK. This file can be used if a mistake occurs to the original file.

If you want to do this:	Follow these steps:
	2. Using your text editor, enter the template file you wish to pipe. (Contains both descriptive and actual symbols.)
	3. Notice that the **descriptive symbol** should be followed by the **actual symbol** on the next line! (Otherwise you will have to retype everything in.) An example of this file is below:
(title)	**DataCAD template file. version 01.10.**
(one blank line)	
(number of columns)	**2**
(number of rows)	**8**
	*
(separater)	
(symbol pathnames)	**sym \ furn \ tabltext**
	sym \ furn \ table
	sym \ furn \ sinktext
	sym \ furn \ sink
	sym \ furn \ lamptext
	sym \ furn \ lamp
	3. Edit the file, so the *descriptive symbol* is **first**, on the same line as the *actual symbol*, separated by a vertical bar "¦" as shown below. This bar is called a "piping symbol." There should be NO spaces in the line (Note - *tabltext* is the descriptive symbol, and *table* is the actual symbol.)
	sym \ furn \ tabltext ¦ sym \ furn \ table
	4. Make sure you do not add an extra line or spaces in the template file. There should be *only one blank line*, and that is the one right after the title.
	5. When you have condensed your file, you may want to edit the number of columns and rows to match.
	6. Exit the editor when you are through, saving the changes you made to the template file.
	8. Start DataCAD, and test your template.

Appendix B:
The DataCAD
Reference Guide

DataCAD

Mouse Input Device

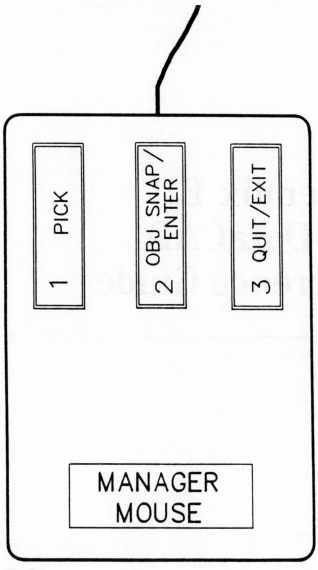

Fig. B-1

DataCAD
Menu Organization
Edit Menu

F1 Move
F1 Entity
F2*Group
F3 Area
F4 Fence
F5Sel Set
F6 LyrSrch
F7
F8New Dist
F9Invert
F0
S1To Layer
S2 AndCopy
S3 Move Z
S4
S5Drag
S6
S7
S8
S9
S0Exit

F2 Copy
F1 Entity
F2*Group
F3 Area
F4 Fence
F5Sel Set
F6 LyrSrch
F7
F8New Dist
F9Invert
F0
S1To Layer
S2
S3
S4RectArry
S5CircArry
S6
S7
S8
S9
S0Exit

F3 Rotate
F1 Entity
F2*Group
F3 Area
F4 Fence
F5Sel Set
F6 LyrSrch
F7
F8NewAngle
F9Invert
F0NewCentr
S1
S2 AndCopy
S3
S4
S5
S6
S7
S8
S9
S0Exit

F4 Mirror
F1 Entity
F2*Group
F3 Area
F4 Fence
F5Sel Set
F6 LyrSrch
F7
F8New Line
F9*FixText
F0
S1
S2 AndCopy
S3
S4
S5
S6
S7
S8
S9
S0Exit

F5 Stretch
F1 Point
F2*Box
F3
F4
F5
F6 LyrSrch
F7
F8New Dist
F9Invert
F0
S1
S2
S3
S4
S5
S6
S7
S8
S9
S0Exit

F6 Enlarge
F1 Entity
F2*Group
F3 Area
F4 Fence
F5Sel Set
F6 LyrSrch
F7
F8Enlrgmnt
F9Invert
F0Center
S1
S2 AndCopy
S3 Enlrg Z
S4
S5
S6
S7
S8
S9
S0Exit

F7 Erase
F1 Entity
F2*Group
F3 Area
F4 Fence
F5Sel Set
F6 LyrSrch
F7
F8Undo
F9Partial
F0
S1Clr Undo
S2
S3
S4
S5
S6
S7
S8
S9
S0Exit

F8 LinkEnts
F1 Entity
F2*Group
F3 Area
F4 Fence
F5Sel Set
F6 LyrSrch
F7
F8
F9
F0 Un-Link
S1
S2
S3
S4
S5
S6
S7
S8
S9
S0Exit

F9 Cleanup
F1Fillets
F2Chamfer
F3
F41Ln Trim
F52Ln Trim
F6
F7WeldLine
F8
F9T Intsct
F0L Intsct
S1
S2
S3
S4
S5
S6
S7
S8
S9
S0Exit

F0 Change
F1 Entity
F2*Group
F3 Area
F4 Fence
F5Sel Set
F6 LyrSrch
F7
F8 LineTyp
F9 LineWgt
F0 Color
S1 Spacing
S2 OverSht
S3 Z-Base
S4 Z-Heigh
S5
S6Text
S7
S8
S9
S0Exit

Fig. B-2

DataCAD
Menu Organization
Edit Menu

S1 Identify	S2 EditSets	S3 Architct	S4 Polygons	S5 Curves
F1EntType	F1Show	F1*Walls	F1No.Sides	F12 Pt Arc
F2Layer	F2Add To	F2*Sides	F2	F23 Pt Arc
F3Color	F3Del From	F3 Centers	F3*Dynamic	F3CentAngl
F4LineType	F4Clear	F4*Clean	F4*CntrPnt	F4Cent Arc
F5Spacing	F5Name Set	F5 Cap	F5*Vertex	F5CentChrd
F6LineWgt	F6	F6 Hilite	F6*Diametr	F6EndPtRad
F7OverSht	F7	F7Width	F7*Inscrib	F7EndPtAng
F8Z–Base	F8	F8	F8	F8StartDir
F9Z–Height	F9 Append	F9DoorSwng	F9	F9Tangent
F0	F0SetActiv	F0Windows	F0 Rectngl	F0
S1	S1	S1Cut Wall	S1	S1Rad Circ
S2	S2	S2	S2	S2Dia Circ
S3	S3	S3	S3	S33Pt Circ
S4	S4	S4	S4	S4
S5	S5	S5	S5	S5Ellipse
S6	S6	S6	S6	S6Polyline
S7Angle	S7	S7	S7	S7Bezier
S8Length	S8	S8	S8	S8B–Spline
S93D Views	S9	S9	S9	S9CurvData
S0Exit	S0Exit	S0Exit	S0Exit	S0Exit

S6 Text	S7 LineType	S8 DCAD 3D	S9 Macros	S0 Utility
F1Size	F1Solid	F13D Views	DCAD_AEC	F1To Scale
F2Angle	F2Dotted	F2Hide	F2	F2GotoView
F3Weight	F3Dashed	F33D Line	F3	F3Layers
F4Slant	F4Dot–Dash	3D Arc	F4	F4Template
F5Aspect	F5ElecLine	Settings	F5	F5Hatch
F6	F6Tel Line	F6	F6	F6Geometry
F7Arrows	F7Box	F7	F7	F7Measures
F8TextFile	F8PropLine	F8	F8	F8Dmension
F9	F9Insul	F9	F9	F9Freehand
F0Justify	F03/4Plywd	F0	F0	F0Settings
S1	S1	S1	S1	S1Grids
S2*Left	S2ScrlFwrd	S2	S2	S2Display
S3 Center	S3	S3	S3	S3Obj Snap
S4 Right	S4	S4	S4	S4
S5	S5*Factor	S5	S5	S5Plotter
S6Fit Text	S6LineWgt	S6	S6	S6File I/O
S7	S7Color	S7	S7	S7Directry
S8Factor	S8Spacing	S8	S8	S8WindowIn
S9FontName	S9OverSht	S9	S9	S9Quit
S0Exit	S0Exit	S0Exit	S0Exit	S0Exit

Fig. B-3

DataCAD
Menu Organization
Utility

F1 To Scale	F2 GotoView	F3 Layers	F4 Template	F5 Hatch
F112"	F1View 1	F1On/Off	F1New FIle	F1*Entity
F26"	F2View 2	F2All On	F2TemplOff	F2 Group
F33"	F3View 3	F3SetActiv	F3Dvisions	F3 Area
F42"	F4View 4	F4ActvOnly	F4	F4 Fence
F51-1/2"	F5View 5	F5	F5SaveSymb	F5Sel Set
F61"	F6View 6	F6Name	F6Del Symb	F6 LyrSrch
F73/4"	F7View 7	F7Color	F7SymName	F7
F81/2"	F8View 8	F8	F8Replace	F8HtchType
F93/8"	F9View 9	F9NewLayer	F9Redefine	F9Pattern
F01/4"	F0View 10	F0ErseLayr	F0PurgeSym	F0Scale
S13/16"	S1	S1DelLayer	S1Re-Load	S1Angle
S21/8"	S2SaveView	S2	S2	S2Origin
S33/32"	S3NameView	S3SaveLayr	S3Rotate	S3
S41/16"	S4To Scale	S4LoadLayr	S4Enlarge	S4
S51:20	S5WindowIn	S5	S5Z Offset	S5
S61:40	S6*LayrSet	S6ViewLayr	S6 Explode	S6
S71:100	S7	S7ViewFile	S7EditFlds	S7
S81:1000	S8	S8	S8Reports	S8Begin
S9	S9	S9*LyrRfsh	S9	S9
S0NoChange	S0Exit	S0Exit	S0Exit	S0Exit

F6 Geometry	F7 Measures	F8 Dmension	F9 FreeHand	F0 Settings
F1Divide	F1Ref Pnt	F1*Horizntl	F1	F1Password
F2Intrsect	F2Snap Pnt	F2 Vertcal	F2	F2ScaleTyp
F3Offset	F3Line	F3 Aligned	F3	F3AngleTyp
F4Tangents	F4PntToPnt	F4 Rotated	F4	F4EditDefs
F5	F5Diameter	F5*Assoc	F5	F5MissDist
F6	F6Radius	F6Entity	F6	F6SmalGrid
F7	F7Chord	F7AutoDim	F7	F7ScrlDist
F8	F8ArcLnth	F8	F8	F8DistDlay
F9	F9Crcmfrnc	F9	F9	F9SaveDlay
F0	F0	F0	F0	F0
S1	S1InclAngl	S1	S1	S1 DrwMrks
S2	S2ExclAngl	S2	S2	S2*Beeps
S3	S3LineAngl	S3TextStyl	S3	S3 BigCurs
S4	S4	S4Dim Styl	S4	S4 NegDist
S5	S5Area/Per	S5ArroStyl	S5	S5*Show Z
S6	S6Takeoffs	S6AutoStyl	S6	S6 FixdRef
S7	S7	S7Explode	S7	S7 DisSync
S8	S8	S8Change	S8	S8
S9	S9	S9	S9	S9
S0Exit	S0Exit	S0Exit	S0Exit	S0Exit

Fig. B-4

DataCAD
Menu Organization
Utility

S1 Grids	S2 Display	S3 Obj Snap	S4	S5 Plotter
F1*Snap On	F1*ShowTxt	F1 Nearest		F1Plot
F2*Disp1On	F2*ShowDim	F2*End Pnt		F2Backgrnd
F3*Disp2On	F3*ShwHtch	F3*Mid Pnt		F3To File
F4	F4*ShowWgt	F4 N Pnts		F4Scale
F5GridSize	F5*UserLin	F5*Center		F5PaperSiz
F6	F6 Ovrsht	F6 Quadrnt		F6PenSpeed
F7GridColr	F7*ShowIns	F7*Intsect		F7PenWidth
F8	F8*ShowAtrs	F8 Perpend		F8Partial
F9	F9	F9 Tangent		F9Layout
F0Snap Ang	F0SmallTxt	F0		F0Lyout Sz
S1Angle	S1BoxColor	S1 None		S1LyoutDiv
S2Grid Org	S2SmallSym	S2*FastSym		S2 Rotate
S3	S3ArcFactr	S3*Fast 3D		S3*ColrPlot
S4	S4	S4MissDist		S4Set Pens
S5	S5	S5*LyrSnap		S5*PenSort
S6	S6	S6*SrchHch		S6
S7	S7	S7 Quick		S7
S8	S8	S8 Sel Set		S8
S9	S9	S9 Apertur		S93D Views
S0Exit	S0Exit	S0Exit		S0Exit

S6 File I/O	S7 Directry	S8 WindowIn	S9 Quit	S0 Edit
F1New Dwg	F1Project	F1Extents	F1Abort	F1Move
F2SaveDwg	F2Employee	F2Re—Calc	F2	F2Copy
F3Copy Dwg	F3Rate	F3	F3	F3Rotate
F4	F4Deprtmnt	F4	F4	F4Mirror
F5Read DXF	F5Phase	F5	F5 Yes	F5Stretch
F6WriteDXF	F6Service	F6	F6 No	F6Enlarge
F7	F7	F7	F7	F7Erase
F8Copy	F8To File	F8	F8	F8LinkEnts
F9Delete	F9	F9	F9	F9Cleanup
F0Rename	F0ScrlFwrd	F0	F0	F0Change
S1 .BAK	S1	S1	S1	S1Identify
S2*.DC3	S2SymFiles	S2	S2	S2EditSets
S3 .FRM	S3	S3	S3	S3Architct
S4 .LYR	S4	S4	S4	S4Polygons
S5 .PLT	S5	S5	S5	S5Curves
S6 .SM3	S6	S6	S6	S6Text
S7 .TPL	S7Pause	S7	S7	S7LineType
S8 .TXT	S8Total	S8	S8	S8DCAD 3D
S9	S9	S9	S9	S9Macros
S0Exit	S0Exit	S0Exit	S0Exit	S0Utility

Fig. B-5

DataCAD Hatch Patterns

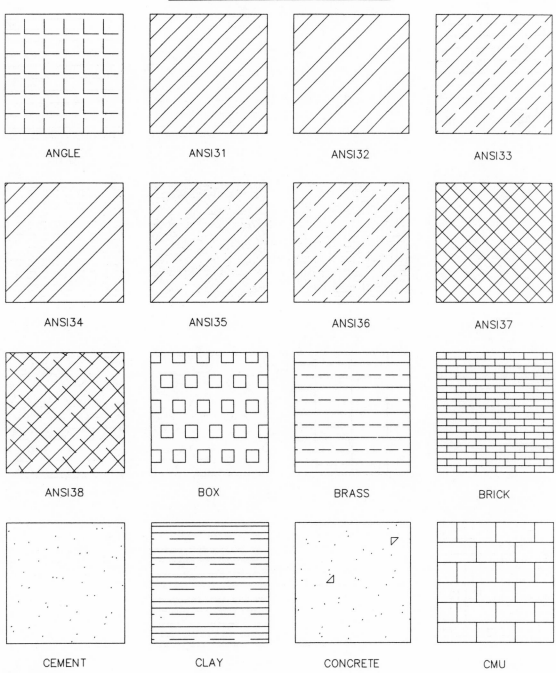

Fig. B-6

DataCAD Hatch Patterns

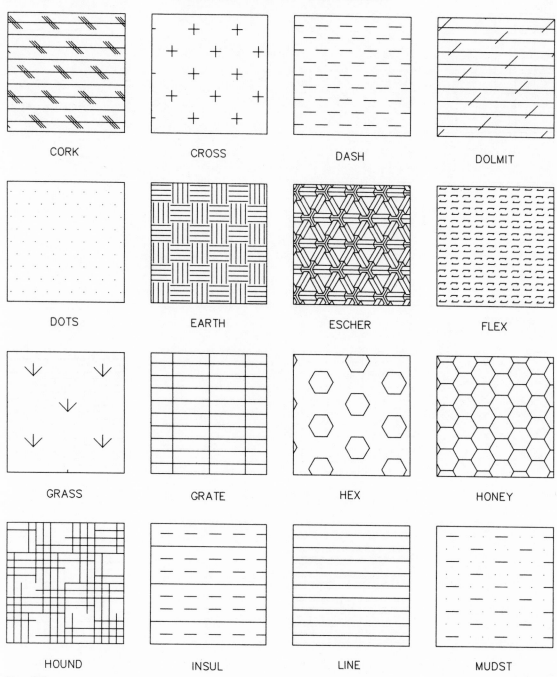

CORK	CROSS	DASH	DOLMIT
DOTS	EARTH	ESCHER	FLEX
GRASS	GRATE	HEX	HONEY
HOUND	INSUL	LINE	MUDST

Fig. B-7

DataCAD Hatch Patterns

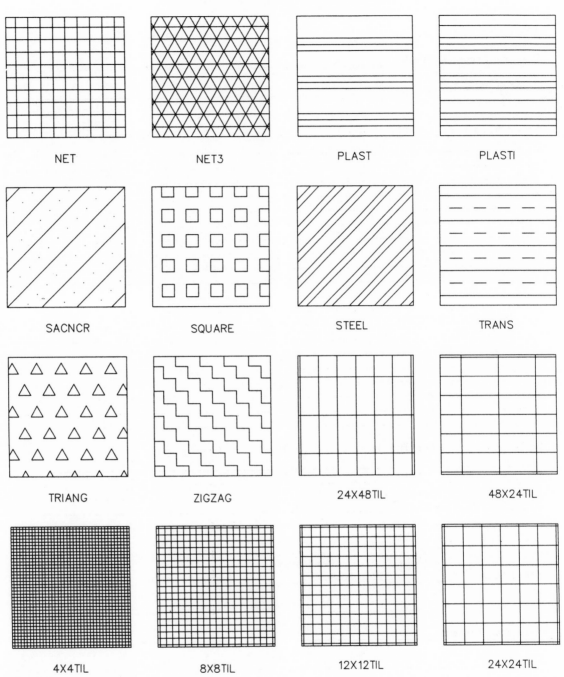

Fig. B-8

DataCAD Drawing Outline

Job Name: _____ Job No: _____

Drawing Name (w/ path): _____

Drawing Description: _____

Layer Name:	Description:	Layer Name:	Description:
_____	_____	_____	_____
_____	_____	_____	_____
_____	_____	_____	_____
_____	_____	_____	_____
_____	_____	_____	_____
_____	_____	_____	_____
_____	_____	_____	_____
_____	_____	_____	_____
_____	_____	_____	_____
_____	_____	_____	_____
_____	_____	_____	_____
_____	_____	_____	_____
_____	_____	_____	_____
_____	_____	_____	_____
_____	_____	_____	_____
_____	_____	_____	_____
_____	_____	_____	_____
_____	_____	_____	_____
_____	_____	_____	_____
_____	_____	_____	_____
_____	_____	_____	_____
_____	_____	_____	_____

Go To View:	Description:	Go To View:	Description:
_____	_____	_____	_____
_____	_____	_____	_____
_____	_____	_____	_____
_____	_____	_____	_____

Descriptive

Sheet Size: _____ Plot Scale: _____ Symbols Scale: _____

Text Size (notes): _____ (titles): _____

Text Font (notes): _____ (titles): _____

Notes: _____
_____
_____
_____

Fig. B-9

DataCAD Template Outline

Template Name (w/ path):

_____

Template Description:

_____

Symbols:

Symbol Name (w/ path):   Description:

_____   _____
_____   _____
_____   _____
_____   _____
_____   _____
_____   _____
_____   _____
_____   _____
_____   _____
_____   _____
_____   _____
_____   _____
_____   _____
_____   _____
_____   _____
_____   _____
_____   _____
_____   _____
_____   _____
_____   _____
_____   _____
_____   _____
_____   _____
_____   _____
_____   _____
_____   _____
_____   _____
_____   _____
_____   _____

Notes:

_____
_____
_____
_____
_____
_____
_____

Fig. B-10

DataCAD
Available Drawing Areas

Final Plot Scale	36" x 24" Actual Drawing Area	42" x 30" Actual Drawing Area	Typical Detail Box
12"	2'-8" x 1'-11"	3'-2" x 2'-5"	6 1/4" x 5 3/4"
6"	5'-4" x 3'-10"	6'-4" x 4'-10"	1'-1/2" x 11 1/2"
3"	10'-8" x 7'-8"	12'-8" x 9'-8"	2'-1" x 1'-11"
1.1/2"	21'-4" x 15'-4"	25'-4" x 19'-4"	4'-2" x 3'-10"
1"	32' x 23'	38' x 29'	6'-3" x 5'-9"
3/4"	42'-8" x 30'-8"	50'-8" x 38'-8"	8'-4" x 7'-8"
1/2"	64' x 46'	76' x 58'	12'-6" x 11'-6"
3/8"	85'-4" x 61'-4"	101'-4" x 77'-4"	16'-8" x 15'-4"
1/4"	128' x 92'	152' x 116'	25'-0" x 23'-0"
3/16"	170'-8" x 122'-8"	202'-8" x 154'-8"	33'-4" x 30'-8"
1/8"	256' x 184'	304' x 232'	50'-0" x 46'-0"
3/32"	341'-4" x 245'-4"	405'-4" x 309'-4"	66'-8" x 61'-4"
1/16"	512' x 368'	608' x 464'	100'-0" x 92'-0"
1:20	640' x 460'	760' x 580'	125' x 115'
1:40	1280' x 920'	1520' x 1160'	250' x 230'
1:100	3200' x 2300'	3800' x 2900'	625' x 575'

Formula:
X limit in feet = (Available width in inches)/Plot Scale
Y limit in feet = (Available height in inches)/Plot Scale

* When entering Custom Sheet Size in the Plotter menu use 32 & 23 for 24x36 sheets and use 38 & 29 for 30x42 sheets (inside border limits).
Fig. B-11

DataCAD
Suggested Colors/Pens Assignments

Color Number	Color Name	Pen Position In Plotter	Wet Ink Pen Size			
F1	White	0	1#	.50mm	.020"	(medium)
F2	Red	2	00#	.30mm	.012"	
F3	Green	3	0#	.35mm	.014"	(fine)
F4	Blue	4		.40mm	.016"	
F5	Cyan	5	1#	.50mm	.020"	(medium)
F6	Magenta	7	2.5#	.70mm	.028"	(bold)
F7	Brown	6	2#	.60mm	.024"	
F8	Lt Gray	1	000#	.25mm	.010"	(extra fine)
F9	Dk Gray	1	000#	.25mm	.010"	(extra fine)
F0	Lt Red	2	-- empty --			
S1	Lt Grn	3	0#	.35mm	.014"	(fine)
S2	Lt Blue	4		.40mm	.016"	
S3	Lt Cyan	5	1#	.50mm	.020"	(medium)
S4	Lt Mgta	7	2.5#	.70mm	.028"	(bold)
S5	Yellow	6	2#	.60mm	.024"	

Fig. B-12

DataCAD EditDefs Scales

Architectural

The following settings can be used to modify the scale settings in Datacad software for architectural drawings:

Scale:	Setting:
1/32" = 1'-0"	0.00260416
1/16" = 1'-0"	0.00520833
3/32" = 1'-0"	0.00781250
1/8" = 1'-0"	0.01041666
3/16" = 1'-0"	0.01562500
1/4" = 1'-0"	0.02083333
3/8" = 1'-0"	0.03125000
1/2" = 1'-0"	0.04166666
3/4" = 1'-0"	0.06250000
1" = 1'-0"	0.08333333
1 1/2" = 1'-0"	0.12500000
2" = 1'-0"	0.16666666
3" = 1'-0"	0.25000000
6" = 1'-0"	0.50000000
12" = 1'-0"	1.00000000
24" = 1'-0"	2.00000000

Formula:

To calculate the scaling value for additional architectural scales, express the fraction in decimal form, and divide by 12 to convert the feet to inches. For example, 1/4" = 1'-0" would be 0.25" = 1'-0", or 0.02083333" = 1".

Fig. B-13

DataCAD Editdefs Scales

Engineering

The following settings can be used to modify the scale settings in Datacad software for engineering drawings:

Scale:	Setting:
1:10	0.00833333
1:20	0.00416666
1:33 1/3	0.00250000
1:40	0.00208333
1:50	0.00166666
1:80	0.00104166
1:100	0.00083333
1:200	0.00041666
1:400	0.00020833
1:600	0.00013888
1:1000	0.00008333

Formula:

To calculate the scaling value for additional engineering scales, express the ratio in decimal form and divide by twelve to convert the feet to inches. For example, 1:10 would be 0.1/12 or 0.00833333.

Fig. B-14

DataCAD
Scales & Sizes

Final Plot Scale	Text Size "Notes"	Text Size "Titles"	*Descriptive* Symbol Enlargement	Detail Enlargement Factor
12"	1/8"	1/4"	1	1
6"	1/4"	1/2"	2	.5
3"	1/2"	1"	4	.25
1.1/2"	1"	2"	8	.125
1"	1.1/2"	3"	12	.0833
3/4"	2"	4"	16	.0625
1/2"	3"	6"	24	.0417
3/8"	4"	8"	32	.0313
1/4"	6"	1'-0"	48	.0208
3/16"	8"	1'-4"	64	.0156
1/8"	1'-0"	2'-0"	96	.0104
3/32"	1'-4"	2'-8"	128	.0078
1/16"	2'-0"	4'-0"	192	.0052
1:20	2'-6"	5'-0"	240	.0042
1:40	5'-0"	10'-0"	480	.0021
1:100	12'-6"	25'-0"	1200	.0008

Formulas:

Text in inches = ((12/(drawing scale)) x (desired text height))
Titles in inches = ((12/(drawing scale)) x (desired title height))
Descriptive Symbol Enlargement Factor = (12/(drawing scale))
Detail Enlargement Factor = ((drawing scale)/12)

* NOTE – Roman text will plot at 3/32" high based on the above chart.
   – Roman titles will plot at 3/16" high based on the above chart.
   – Symbol enlargement size is designed only for *descriptive symbols* created at actual size (not building component symbols).

Fig. B-15

DataCAD Linetypes

Samples	Linetype	Spacing Formula
————————	Solid	Any scale.
····················	Dotted	(.125/plot scale) = spacing (feet)
— — — — — — — — — ·	Dashed	(.125/plot scale) x 2 = spacing (feet)
——— · —	Dot-dash	(.125/plot scale) x 16 = spacing (feet)
——·——·—	Elecline	(.125/plot scale) x 8 = spacing (feet)
——'——'—	Tel Line	(.125/plot scale) x 8 = spacing (feet)
—◇——◇—	Box	(.125/plot scale) x 8 = spacing (feet)
——————— - - —	Propline	(.125/plot scale) x 16 = spacing (feet)
⨷⨷⨷⨷⨷⨷⨷⨷	Insul	wall width/2 = spacing
▬▬▬▬▬▬▬▬	3/4 Plywd	3/4"
————————	1/2 Plywd	3/4"
ᴡᴡᴡᴡᴡᴡᴡᴡ	Hedge	height x 2 = spacing
——————— - —	Centrlin	(.125/plot scale) x 16 = spacing (feet)
———⌇———	Section	(.125/plot scale) x 8 = spacing (feet)
⟋⟋⟋	Shingles	exposed length x 2 = spacing
⟋⟋⟋⟋	LapSidng	exposed length = spacing
——⌐——	Shiplap	length of 1 board = spacing
⊟⊟⊟⊟⊟⊟⊟	Brick	8"
▭ ▭ ▭	4" Block	8"
▭ ▭	8" Block	8"
▭ ▭	12"Block	8"
▬▬▬▬▬▬▬▬	Rigid	Ins thickness = spacing
▬▬▬▬▬▬▬▬	Grass	height x 2 = spacing
———————·———	Groundlin	(.125/plot scale) x 8 = spacing (feet)

Fig. B-16

DataCAD 3.6   CR*CADD
Quick keys:

					Esc Refresh / Tab Active Lyr	Ins Scroll Coord / Del Stop Refresh	Home Center Dwg / End Stop Lyr Refresh	PgUp Zoom Out / PgDn Zoom In	Space Bar Begin Coord / Arrow Keys Pan
A	Append SS	Gg	Grids	Mm	Move	s	Snap Spc	Y	3d Hide	+	Big Cursor	/	Window In
a	Architct	Hh	Hatch	Nn	Obj Snap	Tt	Template	y	3d Views	=	Walls On/Off	?	Coord. I.D.
Bb	Tangents	Ii	Digitizer	Oo	Ortho On/Off	v	GotoView	Zz	Z Base/Hgt	[	Grid 1 On/Off	.	Erase Entity
Cc	Copy	J	3d Line	Pp	Prev View	V	3d Views	~	Snap Pnt	]	Grid 2 On/Off	<	Erase Group
Dd	Dmension	j	3d Edit	Qq	LineType	Ww	Line Wgt	.	Ref Pnt	:	Utility Menu	,	Restore Last Entity/Group
Ee	Erase	Kk	Color	Rr	Rotate	X	Obj Snap Menu	–	Set OvrSht	::	Edit Menu	.	Wall Cap On/Off
Ff	Spacing	Ll	Layers	S	Sel Set	x	Snap On/Off	_	Disp OvrSht	:	LyrSrch On/Off	\	Wall T Clean On/Off

Fig. B-17

Appendix C:
Answers to Exercises

Exercise 1 - Beginning DataCAD

1. a	6. b	11. a
2. b	7. c	12. b
3. c	8. a	13. c
4. a	9. b	14. a
5. b	10. c	

Exercise 2 - Drawing Set-Up

1. b	6. b	11. a
2. c	7. a	12. b
3. a	8. b	13. c
4. a	9. b	
5. b	10. c	

Excercise 3 - Basic Drafting

1. a	7. b	13. a
2. b	8. c	14. b
3. c	9. c	15. b
4. a	10. a	16. a
5. c	11. a	
6. a	12. b	

Exercise 4 - Windowing

1. b	7. b
2. a	8. b
3. b	9. c
4. c	10. a
5. b	11. b
6. a	

Exercise 5 - Adding Symbols

1. a	7. c
2. c	8. b
3. b	9. c
4. b	10. a
5. b	11. c
6. a	12. a.

Exercise 6 - Dimensions and Text

1. a	6. c
2. a	7. a
3. c	8. b
4. b	9. c
5. b	10. a

Exercise 7 - Viewing in 3D

1. b	7. b
2. a	8. a
3. c	9. a
4. b	10. c
5. a	11. a
6. c	

Exercise 8 - Plotting your Drawing

1. c	7. b	13. a
2. b	8. a	14. c
3. c	9. c	15. b
4. a	10. b	16. a
5. a	11. a	17. c
6. c	12. b	18. a

Excercise 9 - Initial Site Plans

1. b	7. c	13. b
2. b	8. a	14. c
3. b	9. c	15. c
4. c	10. a	16. b
5. b	11. a	17. a
6. b	12. b	18. b

Exercise 10 - Dimensional Lines

1. b	6. a	11. a
2. a	7. c	12. c
3. a	8. b	13. b
4. c	9. a	14. a
5. b	10. b	

Exercise 11 - Copying Techniques

1. a	8. a	15. a
2. b	9. b	16. c
3. b	10. c	17. b
4. c	11. c	18. c
5. a	12. b	19. b
6. b	13. c	20. a
7. c	14. a	

Exercise 12 - Details

1. c	6. a
2. b	7. b
3. a	8. b
4. b	9. a
5. c	10. b

Exercise 13 - Templates and Symbols

1. a	7. a	13. c
2. b	8. b	14. b
3. b	9. a	15. c
4. c	10. a	16. c
5. b	11. b	
6. a	12. b	

Exercise 14 - Default Drawings

1. b	9. a	17. b
2. c	10. c	18. b
3. a	11. b	19. c
4. a	12. a	20. a
5. b	13. b	21. b
6. b	14. c	22. c
7. a	15. a	
8. c	16. a	

Exercise 15 - Final

1. b	11. c	21. c
2. c	12. b	22. a
3. b	13. a	23. c
4. a	14. b	24. b
5. a	15. b	25. b
6. b	16. a	26. a
7. a	17. b	27. b
8. a	18. a	28. a
9. a	19. b	29. a
10. b	20. c	30. c

Index

Index

Other Bestsellers of Related Interest

ADVANCED MS-DOS® BATCH FILE PROGRAMMING
—Dan Gookin

Batch file programming is a way of communicating with your computer . . . a way of transforming DOS into a system that works the way you want it to. In this book, Dan Gookin explains unique methods of using batch files to create a work environment that will improve your efficiency, productivity, and overall relationship with your computer. All the necessary tools, batch file structures, commands, and helpful techniques can be found here. 400 pages, 733 illustrations. Book No. 3197, $24.95 paperback, $34.95 hardcover

VersaCAD® TUTORIAL: A Practical Approach
—Carol Buehrens

Includes all versions of VersaCAD, including the recently released 5.0! This book presents an introduction to VersaCAD and basic drafting principles before leading you step-by-step through the more advanced and creative options available. Among the features: Geometric configurations—Properties of linestyles, pen, and levels—Plotting—Tablet overlays—Dimensions, textures, sizing—Modifying, copying, grouping. 312 pages, 439 illustrations. Book No. 3003, $19.95 paperback, $28.95 hardcover

SUPERCHARGED GRAPHICS: A Programmer's Source Code Toolbox
—Lee Adams

This advanced graphics learning resource provides programs from which you can create your own graphics. Complete source code and user documentation are given for four major programs: drafting, paintbrush, 3D CAD, and animation. Covering hardware, software, and graphic management aspects, this computer-graphics tutorial demonstrates keyboard control techniques, mouse control techniques and more! 496 pages, 180 illustrations. Book No. 2959, $19.95 paperback, $29.95 hardcover

HARD DISK MANAGEMENT WITH MS-DOS® AND PC-DOS®
—Dan Gookin and Andy Townsend

Whether you're a novice struggling with your hard disk system, an intermediate user in need of advice, or an old hand looking for some expert tips . . . this sourcebook can give you a big boost in understanding hard disks and using them to their fullest advantage. And if you're trying to decide whether or not to purchase a hard disk system, this is an ideal book to buy before you invest! 320 pages, 42 illustrations. Book No. 2987, $16.95 paperback only

THE C⁴ HANDBOOK; CAD, CAM, CAE, CIM
—Carl Machover

Increase your productivity and diversity with this collection of articles by the international industry experts, detailing what you can expect from the latest advances in technology. Machover has created an invaluable guide to identifying equipment requirements, justifying investments, defining and selecting appropriate systems, and training staff to use the systems effectively. 449 pages, 166 illustrations. Book No. 3098, $44.50 hardcover only

MS-DOS® BEYOND 640K: Working With Extended and Expanded Memory
—James Forney

Find out how some relatively inexpensive hardware and software enhancements can give your 8088, 80286, or 80386-based computer the ability to run larger applications, create multiple simultaneous work environments, maintain larger files, and provide all the memory you need. This book provides a clear picture of all the alternatives and options available, even up-to-the-minute tips and techniques for using Lotus 1-2-3® , Release 3.0, in extended memory! 248 pages, Illustrated. Book No. 3239, $19.95 paperback, $29.95 hardcover

Other Bestsellers of Related Interest

80386: A Programming and Design Handbook—2nd Edition
—Penn Brumm and Don Brumm

"This book has all the information you require to design, build, and program your own 80386-based system."—**Computing Magazine**

Now, with the guidance of system applications experts Penn and Don Brumm, you can exploit this advanced processor. Revised and expanded, this book explains and demonstrates such advanced features as: 32-bit instruction enhancements, memory paging functions, debugging applications, and Virtual 8036 Mode. 480 pages, 108 illustrations. Book No. 3237, $24.95 paperback, $34.95 hardcover

HIGH-PERFORMANCE CAD GRAPHICS IN C
—Lee Adams

Imagine creating accurate 3D images of real objects. By changine a few lines of program code you can rotate, move your viewpoint, and display the image as either transparent wireframe or solid models. Adams not only shows you how, but also gives you the CAD graphics programs! You can explore new techniques for creating and illustrating technical plans, drawings, and more using the most popular C compilers, graphics adapters, and monitors. 560 pages, 195 illustrations. Book No. 3059, $24.95 paperback, $34.95 hardcover

Look for These and Other TAB books at Your Local Bookstore

To order call toll free 1-800-822-8158
(in PA and AK call 717-794-2191)
or mail coupon to TAB BOOKS Inc., Blue Ridge Summit, PA 17294-0840.

Title	Product No.	Quantity	Price

□ Check or money order enclosed made payable to TAB BOOKS Inc.

Charge my ☐ VISA ☐ MasterCard ☐ American Express

Acct. No. _____ Exp. _____

Signature: _____

Name: _____

Address: _____

City: _____

State: _____ Zip: _____

	Subtotal	$ _____
Postage and Handling ($3.00 in U.S., $5.00 outside U.S)		$ _____
In PA, NY, & ME add applicable sales tax		$ _____
	TOTAL	$ _____

TAB catalog free with purchase; otherwise send $1.00 in check or money order payable to TAB BOOKS Inc. and receive $1.00 credit on your next purchase.

Orders outside U.S. must pay with international money order in U.S. dollars.

TAB Guarantee: If for any reason you are not satisfied with the book(s) you order, simply return it (them) within 15 days and receive a full refund.

BC